BUSINESS ANALYTICS

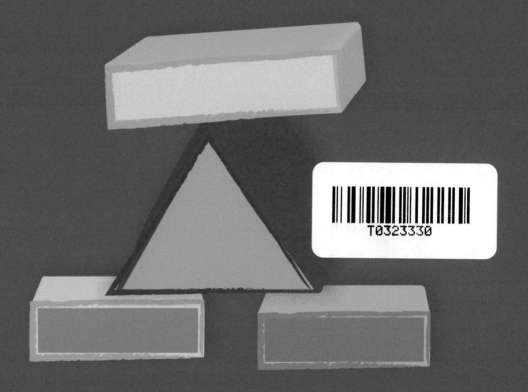

BUSINESS ANALYTICS

COMBINING DATA, ANALYSIS & JUDGEMENT TO INFORM DECISIONS

MARY ELLEN GORDON

§ Sage

1 Oliver's Yard
55 City Road
London EC1Y 1SP

2455 Teller Road
Thousand Oaks, California 91320

B 1/I 1 Mohan Cooperative Industrial Area
Mathura Road
New Delhi 110 044

3 Church Street
#10-04 Samsung Hub
Singapore 049483

Editor: Ruth Stitt
Editorial assistant: Charlotte Hegley
Production editor: Sarah Cooke
Copyeditor: Christine Bitten
Proofreader: Brian McDowell
Indexer: Silvia Benvenuto
Marketing manager: Lucia Sweet
Cover design: Naomi Robinson
Typeset by: C&M Digitals (P) Ltd, Chennai, India
Printed in the UK

Library of Congress Control Number: 2022949130

British Library Cataloguing in Publication data

A catalogue record for this book is available from the British Library.

ISBN 978-1-5297-9612-4
ISBN 978-1-5297-9611-7 (pbk)

At SAGE we take sustainability seriously. Most of our products are printed in the UK using responsibly sourced papers and boards. When we print overseas we ensure sustainable papers are used as measured by the Paper Chain Project grading system. We undertake an annual audit to monitor our sustainability.

CONTENTS

ACKNOWLEDGEMENTS

I'm grateful to the professors at Babson College and the University of Massachusetts who first sparked my own interest in analytics, and to all of the colleagues and clients who helped me continue to learn as the discipline has evolved.

I appreciate the help of the analytics professionals who were interviewed for this book and appear in the Analytics in Practice sections: Nicholas Agar, Varun Chaudhary, Scott Christian, Chris Knox, Kate Kolich, Ngapera Riley, Joe Salz, Andrew Siffert, Takeshi Tawarada, and Rock Zhu. The experiences and perspectives that they shared were extremely helpful in illustrating the breadth of applications of business analytics and the types of issues that arise in their implementation.

Students in several courses I teach unknowingly pilot tested a lot of the material in this book. Seeing what did and didn't work for them made this a better book. Several current and former students also contributed more directly. Ngoc Bui, Elizabeth Ingham, and Andrei Stoian did an independent study that helped generate some of the data for the 4tE case. David Gaffney's research helped form my thinking about the disconnection between decision-makers and analytics professionals. Naruebet Thanuwohan helped create the instructor resources and also carefully checked formatting and other details before the manuscript was submitted, and Victoria University of Wellington provided funding for that.

Thank you to Ruth Stitt, Jessica Moran, and Charlotte Hegley for shepherding this book through the publishing process, and for providing helpful feedback and advice along the way.

ABOUT THE AUTHOR

Mary Ellen Gordon teaches business analytics and a variety of other related degree and executive education courses at Victoria University of Wellington, in Wellington New Zealand. She also has extensive professional experience in business analytics in various roles in the United States and in New Zealand, including:

- Founding and leading the team that implements Apple-branded surveys to support marketing of Apple products worldwide.
- Heading research at Flurry, where she mined insights from app analytics data collected from more than a billion smartphones and tablets each month.
- Analysing data coming from a variety of third-party data sources for Apple's iAd group.
- Founding and leading a market research consulting firm (Market Truths) that specialised in web surveys and research in and about virtual worlds.

Mary Ellen's Bachelor's and Master's degrees are from Babson College, in Wellesley Massachusetts, and her PhD is from the University of Massachusetts at Amherst. She has published academic research in a variety of marketing and information systems journals and conference proceedings. She has also previously taught at and for the University of Canterbury, the University of Massachusetts, Waikato University, Cardean University, and EducAsia.

PREFACE

I want to start this business analytics textbook by telling you a few of business analytics' dirty little secrets. The first is that there isn't general consensus on what that combination of words even means. People who teach business analytics as a subject or have it in their job title come to it from different disciplinary backgrounds, and therefore we bring different knowledge, skills, and baggage with us. Some people think of business analytics as statistics rebranded for business or business school students. But for me, it's more literal than that. I think of it as all of the analytical techniques used by businesses – and other types of organisations – to aid decision-making. That includes the use of statistics, but is not limited to that. It also includes non-statistical analytical methods and, very importantly, a lot more attention to the context in which the analytical methods are being applied and the decisions they are being used to inform than is the case in most statistics courses.

The second dirty little secret about business analytics is the irony that there has been surprisingly little analysis of the effectiveness of businesses' use of analytics. The third is that the evidence that does exist is not particularly encouraging. The digital revolution has resulted in the generation of vast troves of data, and with it a belief that mining that data would produce transformational insights for organisations. There certainly are examples where that has happened, but there is also evidence that often businesses' experiences with analytics fall short of their expectations.

From 2012–2017 *Sloan Management Review* published research reports based on data collected from a survey of a large number of executives from around the world (see Ransbotham and Kiron, 2018). Year after year, around three quarters of respondents reported a 'somewhat or significant increase in access to useful data over the past year'. But year after year only around half described their organisations as: 'somewhat or very effective at using insights [from data] to guide future strategy.'

Around that same time period, data science programmes were proliferating, as was enthusiasm for things such as machine learning and artificial intelligence. And yet, none of that closed that gap between the growing availability of data and the ability of organisations to derive insights from it. If anything, the gap appeared to be growing. Things such as deep knowledge of the theoretical underpinnings of statistics and familiarity with the latest and greatest algorithms have value, but in my view are not the answer to closing that gap. Based on my own experience and many of those shared by post-experience students in graduate and executive education courses I teach, I believe that stubborn gap reflects disconnection between people who want to use results derived from analytics to make business decisions and those charged with collecting, storing, and analysing the data required to generate those results.

Often analytical skills are not widely distributed within businesses and other organisations, but instead are concentrated within dedicated analytical teams. The downside of that is that the analytical teams may lack a deep understanding of the challenges and opportunities facing the business and its decision-makers, and the contextual factors that surround those. It also means that people working in other parts of the business may lack a deep understanding of data and analytics and therefore how analytics could be used to help address the challenges and opportunities they face. This book is grounded in my belief that integrating analytical capabilities with subject matter expertise can help businesses use analytics effectively to guide strategic, tactical, and operational decisions.

I hope the book provides students who plan to focus on analytics or a related discipline with a foundation in basic analytical techniques upon which you can build as you continue your studies, but also an understanding of how analytics are applied within organisations. I also want to make sure that you start your career in analytics with an appreciation of the legal, ethical, and cultural responsibilities that are an inherent part of working with data that relates to people. Previous generations of people working in analytics have not always understood those responsibilities, and their lack of understanding created problems for their organisations, themselves, and sometimes others as a consequence.

For students who want to use results from analytics to make decisions within businesses, or are already doing that, I hope the book helps provide you with a sense of what analytics can – and can't – do, and how it can complement judgement derived from your subject matter expertise. I hope it equips you with the confidence to implement basic analytical techniques yourself. While the newest, fanciest, tools and techniques tend to get the most attention, a surprising amount of insight can be gained using analytical methods that require little more than basic arithmetic combined with good judgement about what questions to investigate and what data to use to do it. Even if you never execute highly sophisticated analytical techniques yourself, many of them are grounded in more basic techniques. That means that the more you learn, the better able you will be to identify the most useful forms of analysis, to ask good questions of colleagues presenting analytical results, and to evaluate the validity, reliability, and utility of analytical results for yourself.

Regardless of the career that you are currently in or aspire to, in a world of growing mis- and disinformation, I hope that having grounding in the fundamentals of analytics will enable you to be a more informed consumer of data and analytical results presented to you by others in any context, including in your role as a citizen.

ONLINE RESOURCES

Business Analytics is accompanied by a range of online resources designed to support teaching.

Instructors can visit **https://study.sagepub.com/gordon1** to access:

- **PowerPoint slides** that can be downloaded and adapted to suit individual teaching needs.
- **Testbank** provide multiple-choice questions that can be used in class, for exams, and that can be used in a virtual learning environment.
- **Datasets** that can be downloaded and used alongside the textbook and questions in the testbank.
- A **Resource Pack** that can be downloaded into university learning platforms and be customized as required.

1
HOW DATA AND ANALYTICS CAN ENHANCE HUMAN DECISION-MAKING IN ORGANISATIONS

WHAT WILL YOU LEARN FROM THIS CHAPTER?

- What business analytics are, what types of questions they can be used to answer, and what problems they can be used to address.
- What populations and samples are, and why that distinction is important when analysing data and interpreting results of data analysis.
- Why data and judgement are complementary as opposed to being alternative ways of making decisions.
- Some tips for increasing the chances that analytics projects will be successful.

WHAT ARE BUSINESS ANALYTICS?

Business analytics can be thought of as the analysis, synthesis, and use of data for organisational decision-making. The organisations making decisions can be anything from one person's side hustle to a Fortune 500 company, to a government department, to a non-profit organisation.

The types of decisions organisations make with analytics can be just as varied. They include large strategic decisions, such as entering or exiting a market, as well as small operational decisions, such as when to re-order specific supplies or repair a particular piece of equipment.

The term analytics is often used interchangeably with terms such as data science, data analysis, and statistics. There are a lot of overlaps among those and no generally accepted definitions of exactly where the boundaries are between them. For the purposes of this book, think of business analytics as being more specific to the use of data and analysis for organisational decision-making than data science, which encompasses data of any type used for any purpose. Business analytics definitely involves the analysis of data, but again, data of a specific type and for the purposes of helping organisations run more efficiently or effectively. It also involves thinking about where the data that will be analysed comes from, and if necessary, setting up systems to collect it, but is not as focussed on managing extremely large **datasets** as data science often is. Statistics are often used as part of business analytics, and throughout this textbook 'Statistics Explainer' boxes will be used to describe the statistical concepts that are most fundamental to business analytics. The first one explains the difference between **populations** and **samples** and the implications of this difference for doing and interpreting analytics.

STATISTICS EXPLAINER

Populations and samples

Populations and **samples** are two important statistical terms. The meaning of population in statistics differs from how it is used in everyday language. In statistics it refers to every instance (also sometimes called elements, units, **cases**, or observations) of the particular thing being studied. When that thing is people who live in a particular place, it is like the everyday use of the term – for example, the population of Canada. But the thing being studied could be a group of people defined by something other than or in addition to geographic borders – for example, all employees of a particular organisation or all of their customers. The thing being studied could also be something other than people. For example, all dogs or Mini Coopers registered in London.

A sample is a sub-set of a population – for example, 1000 Canadians, every 10th employee of an organisation, or 500 owners of Mini Coopers registered in London. In many situations, it's not feasible to collect information about each element of the population so we collect data from a sample. For example, it would be much easier to get information from 1000 Canadians than from all of them, and that's what happens in many opinion polls. As long as we are careful about how we select the sample, we can make inferences (i.e., projections or estimates) about the whole population we're interested in based on the data we collect from the sample.

Statisticians are very focussed on exactly how best to select samples and to use them to make inferences about populations, and a lot of statistical theory has been developed for making inferences or generalisations from observed samples to populations that are difficult or impossible to observe in their entirety. That's often true for people, but also things such as food or manufactured products. In some instances those things need to be measured in a way that destroys them. By sampling a subset of fruit you can make infer-ences about the quality of the entire crop without destroying all of it, or by measuring a subset of manufactured products you can make inferences about the expected lifespan of all products produced in the same facility without destroying all of them.

While statistics has traditionally focussed more on samples than on populations, busi-ness analytics often focusses on data from populations rather than samples. Particularly now that so much information has been digitised, many organisations have access to infor-mation about all of their customers, employees, equipment, website visits, etc. That makes some statistical tests irrelevant because we are just counting items in a population rather than counting items in a sample and using what we learn from that to make an estimate for a population. Statistics are still relevant in business analytics in some situations though, and those will be discussed throughout the book in subsequent Statistics Explainers.

WHAT ABOUT JUDGEMENT?

You may be thinking that many organisations are full of people with a lot of experience in their particular domain, and wondering: why not just leave them to make judgement-calls based on all of that experience instead of bothering with analysing a lot of data?

Judgement has always been important in organisations, and remains so, but there are several problems with relying on judgement alone. Research across a number of disci-plines, from psychology to economics, to neuroscience, has shown that judgement can be clouded by a number of different unconscious biases. These include things such as paying more attention to things that have happened recently, are more familiar, or are more repre-sentative of a category. Another common bias is overconfidence, which tends to be greater among those with the most expertise in a particular domain (Mahajan, 1992).

In part because of these biases – which we all have in one form or another – even different experts can come to different judgements about the same situation. There are limits to what even experts are able to experience and perceive on their own, and there need to be ways to discuss and resolve differences among experts and to communicate insights to non-experts, and that's where business analytics comes in.

HOW DATA, ANALYTICS, AND JUDGEMENT CAN COMBINE TO ENHANCE HUMAN DECISION-MAKING IN ORGANISATIONS

To be clear, business analytics are not a replacement for judgement, but rather a complement to it. As shown in Figure 1.1, judgement is great for determining organisational priorities and the decisions that need to be made in service of those priorities. But often specific information, including answers to particular questions, may be very useful in helping to make those decisions. By providing those answers, business analytics can inform current and future judgements. To implement those analytics, judgement needs to be applied to determine exactly what questions to seek answers to, what analytical processes to apply, and to what data.

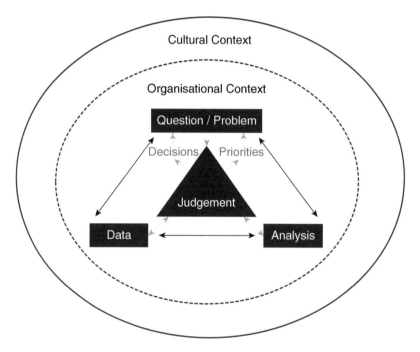

Figure 1.1 Business analytics ecosystem

That's also an iterative process, so once data has been analysed, judgement can be used to identify questionable results that require further investigation to ensure they are not due to some sort of problem such as a data entry error or a flawed analytical process. Working with data is complicated, so problems such as these do happen. Subject matter experts can often quickly spot results that are unlikely or unexpected. The further investigation that follows in a situation like that may result in improvements to the way data are collected, processed, or analysed. These improvements are very useful, as is discovering that the unexpected result appears to be valid even after carefully checking how it was generated. Unexpected results can give organisations important insights about how to mitigate a threat, take advantage of an opportunity, or be more efficient or effective.

Judgement can also be used to identify additional questions that arise as a result of the answer to a given question. And, very importantly, answers to questions derived from careful application of analytics should inform future judgements. As indicated previously, even experts have decision biases, but exposure to data and evidence can help mitigate biases. For example, a business owner who believes that all of her customers are very satisfied because her friends keep telling her how great her products are should reconsider her beliefs if faced with results from a carefully conducted survey of 1200 customers showing that 55% are actually dissatisfied or very dissatisfied, and only 10% are very satisfied.

It's important to note that business analytics are not applied in a vacuum. They take place within a broader organisational context. That means that the types of questions and problems organisations address with analytics, and how they address those questions, may vary. That may be due to the nature of each organisations' activities or priorities, or to what data it has access to. In general though, many types of analytics used by a wide range of organisations fall within four broad categories, corresponding to different functional areas present in most organisations: marketing/communications, HR, operations, and finance. A chapter of this book is devoted to each of those categories of analytics so you'll be able to see many examples of how analytics can help organisations make decisions within those functional areas.

Organisations themselves also exist within a broader context. They have operations situated in different countries, those countries have different cultures, and those cultural differences give rise to differences in laws, regulations, and norms about how business analytics can and should be used. Those laws, regulations, and norms are also subject to change over time, making it very important that anyone who is involved with business analytics thinks about not just if analysing particular data a given way will produce the information they are seeking to answer a question or address a problem, but also that it will do so in a way that is legal, ethical, and culturally acceptable. The next chapter of the book will talk more about that.

Business analytics can be used to answer questions about many things, including:

- How many of something there are (e.g., app users, season ticket holders, shoes of a given style in a given size, etc.), and if/how that's changing over time.
- What proportion of things fall into different categories (e.g., new versus repeat customers, home owners versus renters in a given area, etc.).
- What's 'typical' in a given situation (e.g., amount of money spent per customer, hours spent per person per month watching streaming movies, posts per user per day on a social media platform, etc.), and if/how that's changing over time.
- How much variation there is across people in the types of things just described.
- Whether knowing one piece of information can help you predict another (e.g., Do people who are extroverts tend to get paid more? Do employees who graduated from one university tend to perform better than those who graduated from another? Do people who go grocery shopping in the evening tend to spend more than those who go during the day?)

This type of information can be very helpful in informing decisions; however, decisions often come in the form of 'should' type questions and business analytics alone cannot answer those. Examples of 'should' type questions include things such as:

- Should we expand our business into Australia?
- Should we change the way we hire engineers?
- Should we buy a new piece of equipment?
- Should we pay our lowest paid employees more?

The reason that business analytics alone can't answer these questions and others like them is that the questions don't have definitive answers, but instead require consideration of often competing values. For example, expanding into a new market comes with the potential for both risk and reward, and so the extent to which the organisation values each of those needs to be taken into account. Similarly, decisions about hiring engineers may require trade-offs between valuing the reliability associated with following proven practices and the potential benefits of developing a more diverse, and potentially even more highly skilled workforce. Buying a new piece of equipment requires trading off the cost of the new equipment against things such as greater efficiency or reduced chances of down-time. Paying the lowest paid employees more may require making trade-offs between an organisations' perceived obligations to its shareholders and those to its employees and broader community.

There are other similar types of questions that don't start with 'should'. For example, questions related to things such as fairness and justice also typically require consideration of competing values. Answering all of those 'should' questions and others like them can only be done using judgement to weigh competing values, but that judgement can often be informed by analytics. For example, while analytics can't tell you if something is fair, it can tell you what proportion of a given group of people believe it is fair.

PLANNING ANALYTICS PROJECTS

Most organisations use at least some business analytics, but very few can afford the time and cost that would be involved in using analytics in every situation where they could be applied. Therefore, one of the first things that organisations need to consider is which forms of analytics would be most valuable to them. Those are generally situations in which different results from the analytics would result in different actions. For example, many organisations use analytics to determine the probability of things such as whether a given e-mail is spam or a given transaction is fraudulent. Millions of decisions in a day about whether to let an e-mail or transaction go through may be made based on those types of analytics. In contrast, there are other types of analytics that might influence far fewer, but individually more important decisions, such as whether to make a major investment. Both of those examples are different from situations where data is collected and analysed, but for purely informational purposes and with no action taken regardless of the results or with actions taken completely independently of the results that emerge from the data. For example, many organisations do regular customer, stakeholder, or employee satisfaction surveys, but those are only useful if the organisation makes changes to improve the satisfaction of those who are dissatisfied or to attract more customers, employees, or stakeholders who are similar to the survey respondents who are already highly satisfied with them. If no action is going to be taken based on a particular form of analytics, regardless of what the results show, it may not be worth implementing that form of analytics.

As part of determining whether it's likely that action will be taken based on results from analytics, it's important to get input from those who would be taking action or are experts in the area of interest. This is because someone solely focussed on analytics may think something is important that actually isn't or not realise that something is important when it is. For example, services such as Google Analytics are widely used to get information about how visitors are using websites. They provide data on **metrics** such as the number of visitors to a site and the average time spent on the site. Because those metrics are readily available, those who are new to analytics can easily get caught up with them without really considering if those answer important questions for their organisation or if different results from them will produce different actions. For some organisations, such as social networking sites, those may indeed be important metrics since they generate their revenue by selling ads and the more visitors who come to the site and the longer they stay the more opportunities there are to show ads. However, for other types of organisations, such as those selling offline products or services, metrics related to the number or duration of visits to their website are only useful to know if they are related to the value of products or services that are sold or something else that leads to sales of products or services, and that is not always the case. In fact, the websites of some organisations that sell offline products or services may primarily be used for customers just to get a quick piece of information, such as the address of a physical location or trouble-shooting information. In situations like that, spending more time on a website might be a bad thing rather than a good thing because it may indicate that visitors are not finding what they're looking for easily.

Even small differences in exactly what data is collected, processed and analysed may make a big difference in how useful it is to decision-makers and others working in the area of interest. Going back to the previous example, that may mean not just assuming that more visitors to a website or more time on a website is a good thing, but first checking to see if there is any relationship between those things and what an organisation is ultimately trying to do, such as sell more of something. Or suppose an organisation wanted to use analytics to help reduce its greenhouse gas emissions. That's a fairly technical area, and in some cases requires conforming to particular reporting requirements, so without consulting those within the organisation who operate facilities and equipment that emit greenhouse gases, and those involved with sustainability, it would be easy to omit important information from the data collection or reporting processes or to analyse results in a way that is less helpful to them than it could be.

For those reasons, as shown in Figure 1.2, it's often easiest to start by thinking about what decisions need to be made within an organisation and what types of analytics would be helpful in informing those decisions. The value of analytics in those situations can be tested by questioning what results from analytics would produce different outcomes. For instance, in the climate change example, whether emissions from a certain process exceeding a certain value would lead to a change in the way that process is executed or stopping it completely. Those initial conversations can also produce other important information about the context surrounding the decision, such as there being only one opportunity per year to change or stop a process (e.g., for operational or contractual reasons), so if results from analytics are going to be used to influence the decision, they need to be available by a certain date.

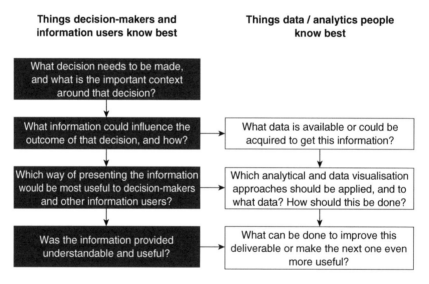

Figure 1.2 Planning analytics projects

As shown in Figure 1.2, once they know what information is needed by decision-makers and other information users, people working directly in data and analytics can then consider which data sources to use to get that information. Just as decision-makers and other subject matter experts have deep knowledge of how the information will be used, people who work directly with data often have deeper knowledge of all of the potentially applicable data sources and their pros and cons. Decision-makers and data users may be aware of some, but not all, of these and often are not familiar enough with the details of how data are stored and collected to know what's possible and what is not.

Sometimes the data required to provide the information needed doesn't exist or would be expensive or time-consuming to acquire. It's very important for the people involved with analytics to discuss this with the people who want to use the information. That way there can be a conversation about trade-offs between things such as the accuracy and specificity of the data and the cost and timeliness. Getting that balance wrong can result in frustration for both the people working in analytics and the recipients of their work, so it's best to avoid that by identifying challenges and coming to a mutual agreement about how to resolve them from the outset.

It's also important to consider how those using results from analytics want to receive them for them to be most useful. For example, some types of information are only valuable if they are available quickly and other types of information are only valuable if they are presented at a specific level of **granularity** (e.g., for a particular geographic region as opposed to a whole country or for an individual product as opposed to a whole product line or all products an organisation sells). The exact format in which the information is presented may also be important. For example, very specific real-time information available via an app or text message may be much more useful to a technician working in the field than a long written report including a lot of additional information. The best way to find out what would be most useful is to talk to the individuals who will need to use the information. That can include working together to develop a mock-up of the way they would like to receive the information. A variety of options and tips for packaging analytics into the format that will be the most useful for the target audience are discussed in Chapter 5 on communicating analytical results.

Once it's clear what information users need, why they need it, and how they would find it most useful to get it, it's possible to work backwards to determine what data needs to be collected and how it needs to be analysed and processed. Then that work can be executed. While that has its own challenges, as will be discussed throughout the rest of the book, starting out with a very clear idea of the desired outcome is critical.

Once analytical results are available, it's important to ensure they meet users' needs, to modify the way data is being analysed or presented if necessary, and, based on that and other feedback from users of the information, to get ideas for making the next deliverable even more useful. Just as answering one question using analytics often gives rise to other questions, executing one analytics project often gives rise to ideas of how to make the next one even more impactful.

SUMMARY

Business analytics involve applying analytical techniques to data to inform organisational decision-making, whether that's at the operational, tactical, or strategic level. Analytics are not a replacement for human judgement, but rather a complement to it. Human judgement informs things such as what data to collect and what questions to use data to try to answer. It is also useful for identifying and further querying data or results that are suspicious. Analytical results that survive that scrutiny can then be used by decision-makers to inform decisions and possibly to modify their future judgements.

Business analytics can provide the answers to factual questions that can be used to inform decision-making, but, in and of themselves, they can't make decisions or answer 'should' type questions because those often involve trade-offs among competing values.

While an understanding of data, statistics, and other quantitative methods are an important part of business analytics, on their own they are not sufficient. Because the problems business analytics addresses are set in an organisational context and in a broader societal context, knowledge of those is necessary to ensure the most relevant questions are being asked and that data is being collected in an appropriate way.

ANALYTICS IN PRACTICE

Using data to make decisions in a pandemic

There is probably no better example of a situation in which analytics and judgement needed to be combined to inform decision-making than in the response to the Covid-19 pandemic. Governments and health officials around the world had to make decisions about things such as whether to restrict travel, prohibit certain types of organisations from opening, or require people to stay home, wear masks, or be vaccinated. Even in the very early days of the pandemic there was some data available about things such as the rate of transmission of other infectious diseases. Over the course of the pandemic, much more data became available, including confirmed cases, hospitalisations, and deaths by location, and later vaccination rates by location and demographic factors including age, gender, and ethnicity.

Much of that data became public fairly quickly, and yet decision-makers around the world and even within the same country, often reached different decisions about what to do in the face of that data. These differences stem from the different judgements they were applying to the analytics they were seeing. For example, decision-makers around the world could see the rate at which cases grew in early hotspots such as China and Italy, but had to make judgements about the likelihood of cases spreading into their jurisdictions and whether the rate of transmission in their locations would be faster or slower than what had been observed in some of those early hotspots. At that point, analytics could not answer those questions definitively. Health officials needed to give advice and make decisions based on things such as their experience with other infectious diseases and population and lifestyle differences that might influence the rate of transmission.

Chris Knox watched this process play out in New Zealand. He started the pandemic as Head of Data for the *New Zealand Herald*, one of New Zealand's largest newspapers, watching as Covid-related data accumulated around the world. He then went to work for the Ministry of Health in New Zealand as the Delta and Omicron waves of the pandemic passed through New Zealand. New Zealand followed an elimination strategy through the early stages of the pandemic, and Chris noted that by 1 January 2022, New Zealand had recorded a total of only 51 deaths and 12,000 Covid cases. But the arrival of Omicron meant that soon there were twice the number of cases each day as there had been in the entire pandemic up to that point. Fortunately from a decision-making standpoint, New Zealand had a clear example to follow in modelling the likely course of the outbreak:

> We were lucky in the sense that Australia was almost running itself as a model for us ... a few months, and then a few weeks ahead both for the Delta and Omicron outbreaks.

As more data came in, health officials and others around the world began to use their judgement to question the quality of some of the data. For example, as many people tested positive for Covid-19 without ever displaying any symptoms, it became clear that case numbers might be fairly accurate in places with very high rates of testing, but be less accurate in places where testing was very limited. That, in turn, could affect calculation of things such as the percentage of cases that resulted in hospitalisations or deaths. To try to get a sense of the prevalence of Covid in the community, Chris Knox and his colleagues analysed data coming from hospitals, where everyone being admitted was being tested for infection control purposes:

> There was a lot of effort put in to try and understand what the actual prevalence might be, so one of the things that was done to try and get an estimate of that was to look at everyone entered the hospital was supposed to get a RAT, so you can use your hospital-going population as kind of a sample.

Similarly, there were questions about whether the death rate was being under-stated as a result of deaths being attributed to other factors even though they may have been accelerated or precipitated by Covid. In situations such as this, judgement and past experience enabled people to scrutinise things such as models predicting future cases or deaths or cross-country comparisons to assess whether data quality issues may limit the usefulness of the results being produced. That's particularly true for international comparisons since different countries may have been following different procedures to decide whether or not to attribute a particular death to Covid.

Judgement was also applied to decisions about how to communicate data about the pandemic, including what data to communicate. For example, while New Zealand had been doing wastewater testing from fairly early in the pandemic, results from that were only widely released publicly once the Omicron wave had hit and New Zealand had widespread community transmission of Covid. Chris Knox, explained why the wastewater results were not more widely disseminated sooner:

(Continued)

> It [wastewater testing] was used pretty heavily early on, but it was a real false positives game, and that's partly why it didn't float up to the public much because it would have just been alarming.

Even armed with high quality data and relatively similar populations and lifestyles, different decision-makers made radically different decisions about how to respond to the pandemic. This highlights the limits of analytics as part of the decision-making process in that they can be used to predict things such as cases, hospitalisations and deaths, but those predictions need to be weighed against other human costs such as limiting access to education and childcare and the economic costs associated with restricting business activities. No single 'correct' answer about exactly what measures should be put in place to mitigate the spread of Covid-19 could be derived using analytics. Instead, decision-makers needed to balance competing individual and societal values with the analytics informing the consequences expected to occur as a result of making different possible decisions.

You can hear more thoughts from Chris Knox about New Zealand's experiences using data to inform Covid-related decisions here: https://vimeo.com/760913731/32348d121a

RUNNING CASE STUDY: 4TE, PART 1[1]

Sitting in her office in January 2023, Emily Ryan felt like it was the first time she had been able to stop and take a breath in years. She and her husband Matt had started their company, 4tE – short for 'For the Earth' – in early November 2019. They knew that starting a new business would be a lot of hard work, but at the time they had no idea how much harder the pandemic would make that, and life in general, over the next few years.

The idea for 4tE came over the 2018-2019 holiday period as Emily and Matt were chatting with their families about their concerns about the environment. There was mounting evidence of climate change and its potential consequences, such as the recent wildfires in California. Nonetheless, Matt and Emily felt that people – including themselves -- were just not doing enough to change the trajectory. They tried to buy food that was in season and produced locally as much as possible. They also tried to reduce waste by buying things in as little packaging as possible and storing them in reusable containers. Guests visiting over the holidays had commented on how stylish all of the reusable containers Emily had curated over the years made their pantry look. That gave them the idea of starting a business to help other people make their day-to-day lives more sustainable while also making their pantries a bit more stylish.

---

[1]The 4tE case is fictitious.

They worked on their business plan through the early part of 2019 and settled on the idea of selling pantry staples in attractive packaging that could be reused by consumers at home, but also returned to the store for commercial cleaning and refilling. They reasoned that would appeal to people who wanted to reduce waste and to those who wanted to create the same type of tidy pantry Matt and Emily's guests had admired in their home. That type of thing had become quite a trend as a result of popular books and TV shows. In keeping with their own values and lifestyles, Emily and Matt also wanted to focus on products that were relatively healthy, plant-based, and produced locally to the extent possible. They thought that would appeal to the growing number of vegans and vegetarians in their area and generation.

By the spring of 2019 they had come up with the name 4tE, and they spent the next few months working through operational details. That culminated in leasing space in the middle of Portland, Oregon walking distance from where Emily and Matt lived. Matt quit his position in supply chain management and Emily quit her marketing role in time to open before Thanksgiving 2019. Emily and Matt both used analytics in their corporate jobs; however, since time and money were both limited as they were setting up 4tE, they based most of their initial decisions on a combination of instinct and their own observations and preferences without much actual data or analysis. They had intended to develop more robust analytics practices once they were up and running, but then came that first whirlwind holiday season, followed by Covid and the need to get online sales up and running much faster than they originally planned.

It was only now that Emily was really able to step back and consider how the data that they had accumulated over the intervening years might help them to make decisions about 4tE's future. Those decisions included:

- Whether to open another physical store.
- Whether to expand the area where they offer deliveries.
- Whether to expand the number or type of products they offer.

EXERCISES

1   Read part 1 of the Running Case Study that will be used throughout this book, in the previous section. Identify one decision in addition to those listed that 4tE may face that could be informed using analytics.

   a   What is the decision?

   b   What specific questions might they need answers to that could help them make that decision?

   c   What data could be used to answer one of those questions?

d You'll learn more about analysis later in the text, but knowing what you know now, think about how they might aggregate, analyse, or synthesise the data you identified to answer the question you identified.

e How would judgement inform the question, the data, or the analysis in the situation you have identified?

f In what ways would values come into the final decision?

2 Open an app or website that you use regularly. Identify one decision the people who operate that app or website may be facing that could be informed using analytics.

a What is the decision?

b What specific questions might they need answers to that could help them make that decision?

c What data could be used to answer one of those questions?

d You'll learn more about analysis later in the text, but knowing what you know now, think about how they might aggregate, analyse, or synthesise the data you identified to answer the question you identified.

e How would judgement inform the question, the data, or the analysis in the situation you have identified?

f In what ways would values come into the final decision?

3 Consider the educational institution from which you are taking this course. Identify one decision it may be facing that could be informed using analytics.

a What is the decision?

b What specific questions might they need answers to that could help them make that decision?

c What data could be used to answer one of those questions?

d You'll learn more about analysis later in the text, but knowing what you know now, think about how they might aggregate, analyse, or synthesise the data you identified to answer the question you identified.

e How would judgement inform the question, the data, or the analysis in the situation you have identified?

f In what ways would values come into the final decision?

2
WHY ORGANISATIONAL, LEGAL, CULTURAL, AND ETHICAL CONSIDERATIONS SHAPE WHAT CAN AND SHOULD BE DONE WITH DATA AND ANALYTICS

WHAT WILL YOU LEARN FROM THIS CHAPTER?

- That organisational considerations influence what's feasible and useful to do with data for and about them.
- That legal considerations restrict what you *can do* with data.
- That it's important to take cultural and ethical considerations into account when deciding what you *should do* with data.
- That making sure data use is legal, ethical, and culturally appropriate is everyone's job.

ORGANISATIONAL CONSIDERATIONS

While business analytics sound like a single thing, their application varies greatly among organisations and even among functional areas within a given organisation. That's because the questions organisations and teams within organisations are trying to answer with data, the data they have available to them, and the analytical tools and techniques they use vary.

To understand why, it's useful to think about the analytics process as a cycle, as shown in Figure 2.1.

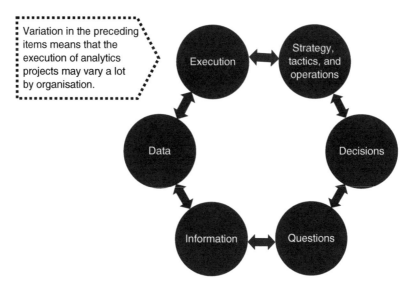

Variation in the preceding items means that the execution of analytics projects may vary a lot by organisation.

Execution

Strategy, tactics, and operations

Data

Decisions

Information

Questions

Figure 2.1   The analytics cycle

Strategy, Tactics, and Operations

At any given time every organisation, and every part of an organisation, is trying to do certain things. Some of those are big strategic things that affect the overall direction of the organisation or group. Some of them are tactical things intended to help achieve broader strategic objectives, and some of them are day-to-day operational things. But, while all organisations and parts of organisations are trying to achieve certain things at all of those three levels most of the time, the details vary greatly depending on the organisation.

For example, a strategy for Netflix might be to expand into a new content area whereas a strategy for a healthcare organisation, such as a Ministry of Health in countries that have those or a non-profit such as Kaiser Permanente in the United States, might be to shift more services toward front-line providers such as general practitioners and away from specialists and hospitals. Tactically, to help to execute its strategy of expanding into a new content area, Netflix might contract with some high-profile creators of the new type of content whereas, to execute a strategy of shifting care toward front-line providers, a healthcare organisation may contract for training opportunities for the front-line providers. An operational activity for Netflix would be making sure the new content is delivered on your device without lags or glitches, whereas an example of an operational activity for a healthcare organisation would be your GP delivering a specific healthcare service to you that previously would have required a hospital or specialist visit.

Decisions

To execute their strategies, tactics, and operations, organisations need to make a variety of decisions. Continuing with the previous example, Netflix would have had to make decisions about whether to expand into additional content areas at all, which content area(s) to expand into, and how to expand into those areas. A healthcare organisation would need to make decisions about which services may be and must be offered by different types of providers, and how to implement a transition if and when some services that were previously delivered by one type of provider are shifted to another.

One way to think about those decisions is as a collection of possible options. For example, Netflix could have considered whether to expand into sports, gaming, podcasts, books, none of those, or some combination of those. Or the healthcare organisation could have considered shifting certain specific procedures from hospitals or specialists to GPs, with options for hospital/specialist only, GP only, or both for each procedure considered. Historically, and sometimes even now, such decisions may have just been made based on the best judgement of the decision-maker, perhaps informed by the opinions of some others, but as discussed in Chapter 1, data can complement judgement. Using data to inform judgement about a decision is likely to make the decision more sound, less risky, and easier to explain and justify to others.

Questions

Often it's not just one data point that's needed to inform a decision, but a series of them. To identify all of the data needed to inform a decision, it's useful to first consider the specific questions that need to be answered to inform the decision. In the Netflix example, that might be things such as:

- How many current subscribers are interested in content related to sports, gaming, podcasts, and books?
- How many people who are not current subscribers are interested in content related to sports, gaming, podcasts, and books?
- Does interest in content related to sports, gaming, podcasts, and books vary by country, gender, age or other factors? If so, how?
- Would existing customers be willing to pay more for their subscriptions if sports, gaming, podcasts, or book content was added?
- Would existing customers be more likely to continue their subscriptions if sports, gaming, podcasts, or book content was added?
- Would people who are not currently subscribers be more likely to subscribe if sports, gaming, podcasts, or book content was added?

Or in the healthcare organisation example, questions that might help inform their decisions could include:

- What percentage of GPs have enough training to perform procedure X?
- What percentage of GP offices have staff who have enough training to allow the GP to perform procedure X?
- What percentage of GP offices have the equipment required to perform procedure X?
- If procedure X is performed in GP offices rather than hospitals or the offices of specialists, is the success rate likely to be lower?
- If procedure X is performed in GP offices rather than hospitals or the offices of specialists, is the rate of adverse outcomes likely to be greater?
- If procedure X is performed in GP offices rather than hospitals or the offices of specialists, is the overall cost to the health system likely to be lower?
- If procedure X is performed in GP offices rather than hospitals or the offices of specialists, are waiting times for the procedure likely to reduce?
- If procedure X is performed in GP offices rather than hospitals or the offices of specialists, will that enable more people with other conditions to be treated in hospitals or by specialists?

Information

Breaking down the questions that need to be answered to inform a particular decision makes it easier to identify the specific pieces of information that are needed. For example, taking the first question in the Netflix example, we know we need a count of current subscribers who are interested in content related to sports, gaming, podcasts, and books. Taking the first question in the healthcare example, we know we need to find out what training is required to perform procedure X and what percentage of GPs have it.

While it may seem obvious that the types of information just described would be useful, people in many organisations now have so much information available to them they can find it challenging to know which information to focus on. Identifying the specific questions that need to be answered to make specific decisions and the specific information that's needed to answer those questions makes it easier not to be overwhelmed by all of the information that may be available. It also helps identify gaps in information. Paradoxically, even though people in many organisations are overwhelmed by the amount of information they have, those same people can find that they still don't have the specific information that they need to answer their most important questions and to make their most important decisions.

Data

As data and analytics have become more prominent, many organisations have had difficulty gaining all of the benefits from data that they expected. One common reason for that is that the people tasked with getting insights from the data don't have a full understanding of their organisation's strategic, tactical, and operational activities, the decisions that the organisation is trying to make in support of those activities, the questions that need to be answered to make those decisions, and the information needed to answer those questions. In contrast, the people who understand those things well often don't have a good understanding of the details of the data the organisation has, has access to, or could feasibly acquire.

Many people who want to use data to inform a decision assume that getting the necessary data is a straightforward and unambiguous task, but that is rarely the case. As noted previously, many organisations have an almost overwhelming amount of data and that can mean that something that sounds like one thing to a decision-maker is, or could be, measured in multiple ways, even with data the organisation already has. Similarly, probably at least in part as a result of that large volume of available data, many decision-makers assume that the organisation will already have the data needed to make a decision, yet that is often not the case.

Let's go back to the Netflix example used earlier in this section, and specifically the first bullet point under questions to see why. That question was: 'How many current subscribers are interested in content related to sports, gaming, podcasts, and books?'. That seems straightforward enough, right? But when we say current subscribers, do we really mean subscribers from a particular country or all subscribers worldwide? And do we mean people who pay for subscriptions? Everyone who lives in a household where someone is paying for a subscription? Or all people who use a Netflix account of a paying subscriber? And when we say 'current subscribers', does that include people who signed up for a free trial yesterday? Does it include people who get Netflix as part of a bundle from their Internet service provider or another company, or only people who subscribe directly through Netflix? The answer to the question 'How many current subscribers are interested in content related to sports, gaming, podcasts, and books?' depends on the answer to all of those other questions and others. So if, for example, we get the data for everyone who watches Netflix via a paid account and yet the decision we are trying to make is really focussed on the people who pay for Netflix subscriptions, then the answer we provide may be misleading.

We might think that answering the question will be easy once we have clearly and carefully defined what we mean by 'current subscribers', but even then it's not clear that Netflix would already have the data we need. Netflix does have data about what people watch on Netflix, so it could, for example, count the number of pieces of sports-related content subscribers have viewed or the number of minutes they have spent viewing it, but does that truly reflect their interest in content related to sports? Possibly not. Maybe some subscribers are not aware of the sports content Netflix has or they are interested in content related to sports, but not in the particular sports-related content that Netflix does have. And Netflix is even less likely to have data that is a reflection of subscribers' interest in content related to gaming, podcasts, and books because those are not types of content Netflix has traditionally offered. So answering that question may require going out and gathering new data. Even though Netflix already has a mind-boggling amount of data available to it, it may not have the particular data needed to answer that particular question.

Similar challenges apply to the first question for the healthcare example. That was: 'What percentage of GPs have enough training to perform procedure X?'. To answer this question, we would need to know what training is required to perform each procedure. We may be lucky and find that there is some certification given to those who have demonstrated an ability to perform a particular procedure, but that is unlikely to be the case for many procedures, so then we would need to figure out how we would establish whether or not a given GP had enough training to do a procedure. We could just ask them. Or we could invite or require them to take some sort of test. Again, the answer to our main question will depend on the answer to those other questions, and either way we are likely to have to collect some new data even though many healthcare organisations also hold vast amounts of data.

Execution

Having worked through the process of determining exactly what data is required to provide the information needed to answer questions that can help inform a decision in the service of a larger strategy, tactic, or operational activity, we typically need to do some sort of analysis or aggregation of the data. For instance, in our two examples, that would involve counting the number of subscribers or calculating a percentage of GPs. Chapter 4 will discuss a variety of ways that data can be analysed, aggregated, and synthesised to answer questions. As discussed in that, the exact form this will take will vary based on a combination of the question and the data because different questions require different types of analysis and different forms of analysis require different data. Using an inappropriate analytical technique for either the question or the data, or implementing it incorrectly, could create inaccurate or misleading results.

Organisational Context

Because the parts of the analytics cycle vary among organisations and among different parts of a particular organisation, specific implementations of analytics tend to be unique even though they draw on a common body of data types and analytical techniques, many of which will be discussed in Chapters 3 and 4. Another thing that makes each implementation of analytics unique is that the broader organisational context, introduced in Chapter 1, also varies. Even organisations of the same type or in the same industry can have very different histories, values, cultures, resources, positioning, and priorities. Those things mean that their strategies, tactics and operations vary, which in turn means that the decisions they need to make vary, the questions they need answered to make those decisions vary, the information and data they need to answer those questions vary, and the analytical approaches they use to get answers to their questions from that data vary.

For example, as we will see in Chapter 6, nearly all organisations want to understand their customers or other stakeholders, but the data they have available to do that varies. Some organisations, such as banks, credit card companies, and retailers, have data on what customers spend money on. Others, as with online platforms like Alphabet (Google) and Meta (Facebook), have data on how users spend their time online. Many organisations collect data on how satisfied customers or stakeholders are. Those differences mean that even if multiple organisations had precisely the same question about customers or stakeholders, they might answer it using different data and, by extension, different analytical techniques. Or, at the very least, some organisations might find it easier to answer than others because they would already have the specific type of data collected whereas others would not.

LEGAL CONSIDERATIONS

Having identified the specific data needed to provide the information required to answer organisations' questions and inform their decisions, it's tempting to want to jump in and get started working with that data to get those answers. But those involved with analytics need to pause to consider whether what they want to do with that data is legal. This may seem surprising. Someone working as a data analyst or data scientist may believe that it's someone else's job to make sure their organisation's data use is legal. Many organisations do employ or contract with lawyers, and some even have employees with titles such as 'Chief Data Officer'. While people in roles like that are certainly concerned with ensuring their organisations are using data legally, any organisation large enough to have people in those roles is likely to have too much data for them to be able to monitor all use of all data at all times. And smaller organisations may not have anyone in a role with a major focus on the legal use of data, even though they have and use a lot of data.

Laws and regulations governing the use of data have grown over time and that trend is accelerating. Something that may seem fine to do with data – and maybe even was fine previously, or is fine somewhere else – may actually be a violation of current local privacy regulations or other laws. For example, previously it was common to take data collected for one purpose and use it for another. This practice was so common it had a name – data exhaust. It seems like an ingenious and efficient use of data since it creates value from data that already exists. A data scientist or analyst with access to the data could easily use the data for something other than its original purpose without their manager or their organisations' legal team knowing about it, yet this practice is no longer permitted in many jurisdictions and could get the organisation that collected and used the data into legal trouble.

The growth in data-related legislation, and the rate at which it's evolving, means it's important for anyone working with data in any organisation to be aware of what is and isn't legal to do with data – or at least to know when to seek expert guidance. It's a complex area because what is and isn't legal to do with data varies by location and has been changing over time. The next sub-sections discuss some of the key features of major pieces of privacy legislation affecting people in English-speaking countries as they are at the time of writing, but because laws and regulations affecting privacy vary by location and change over time it is important to check the data-related laws and regulations that affect the locations you are working in on a regular basis.

EU - GDPR

GDPR is perhaps the best-known and most impactful set of data-related regulations. GDPR is an initialism for General Data Protection Regulation (GDPR). It applies to data from and about residents of the European Union, regardless of where data about them is collected or used, so in that sense its impact has been felt all around the world since at least some organisations in most countries hold or collect data about Europeans.

The actual text of the GDPR legislation is fairly long and very detailed; however because it applies to so many organisations around the world, guidelines and checklists for ensuring compliance are widely available. Table 2.1 summarises some key features regarding collection, accuracy, use, and deletion of data under GDPR and compares it to privacy legislation enacted in other locations.

As can be seen from Table 2.1, it requires that organisations identify their reasons and legal basis for collecting data. It also requires that the parties providing data explicitly consent to its use for clearly specified purposes. Organisations collecting data also need to provide contact details for themselves and for the relevant Data Protection Officer if one is in place. Organisations must also ensure that the data is as accurate as possible and have procedures for correcting or deleting inaccurate data. Organisations must reveal if data will be provided to third parties, and if so, why. They must also get permission for each new use of data, so exploiting 'data exhaust' without permission is not allowed. Organisations are required to keep data secure, so holding data that is hacked or breached could also result in legal trouble for an organisation. One of the things that makes GDPR unique is that it also requires data portability, or the ability to export data from one platform, such as a bank or social media company, so that it can be uploaded to another. It also requires people to be able to request to have their data deleted or to withdraw their consent for its use, and that organisations indicate whether data will automatically be deleted in particular circumstances, such as after a given period of time or inactivity.

Many major organisations incurred large fines for violating GDPR during the first three years of its existence (BBC, 2021). Alphabet (Google) incurred fines of more than 50 million Euros for not being sufficiently transparent about the data it was collecting and processing to serve ads, and not getting explicit consent for doing that. H&M was fined more than 35 million Euros for recording meetings with employees without their consent.

Table 2.1 Examples of data-related laws and regulations

Location	Collection	Accuracy	Use	Deletion
EU GDPR (applies to data about European residents regardless of where the data is collected or used). See: https://gdpr.eu	• Must identify the reasons and legal basis for collecting data. • Generally requires explicit, free, consent. • Must provide contact details for the party controlling the data and any data protection officer.	• Data must be accurate to the extent possible. • Action must be taken to rectify or erase inaccurate data.	• Must indicate whether the data will be provided to a third party, and if so, why. • Must get new permission for new use of data. • Must keep data secure. • Must allow for data portability.	• Must indicate if the data will automatically be deleted after a certain period of time. • Must allow the party providing the data to request its deletion or withdraw consent for use.
China (applies to data about Chinese residents regardless of where the data is collected or used). See: https://digichina. stanford.edu/work/knowledge-base-personal-information-protection-law/	• Must be collected for a lawful purpose, and only the data necessary for that purpose can be collected. • There must be transparency about what data is being collected and how it will be handled. • Must identify who is collecting the information.	• Must avoid adverse effects from inaccurate or incomplete information.	• The information must be secure, including generally keeping it in China. • Cannot harm national security or the public interest. • Use of information in automated processes must be transparent and non-discriminatory.	• Individuals may withdraw consent for the use of their information or request that it be deleted.
United Kingdom See: https://ico.org.uk	• Same as GDPR.	• Same as GDPR.	• Same as GDPR.	• Same as GDPR.
New Zealand See: www.privacy.org.nz	• Information must be collected for a necessary purpose related to what the organisation does. • Should generally be collected from the person it is about, and that person should be aware it is being collected. • The process must be fair, lawful, and not too intrusive.	• Data must be reasonably accurate, current, complete, and not misleading. • People may request changes or to attach a correction.	• Must take reasonable steps to protect against loss, misuse, disclosure, etc. • Can only be used for the original purpose or something related to it; new permission must be granted for any other use. • Unique identifiers must be necessary and not shared.	• Required to destroy information after it is no longer needed.

British Airways was fined £20 million for failing to secure customer data, which was intercepted by hackers. Marriott International was also fined – more than £18 million – in relation to a hack of customer information relating to residents of the EU.

More information about GDPR can be found at: https://gdpr.eu.

China - Personal Information Protection Law

In November 2021, the Chinese Personal Information Protection Law came into effect. Given the size of the Chinese market, the law has the potential to have as much influence as GDPR. The reason it's relevant to people working with data in even English-speaking countries is that it also applies to all data about Chinese residents, regardless of where it is stored or processed. One implication of the law may be that more of that data will be stored and processed in China than was previously the case because the law requires that data about Chinese people be stored and processed within China unless an organisation goes through a government process to get permission for those things to be done elsewhere. Perhaps the most far-reaching aspect of the Chinese law, and the greatest difference from GDPR, is a requirement that the data cannot harm national security nor the public interest. Concerns about how provisions such as that may be interpreted – particularly since it's the Chinese government itself that makes the interpretation – caused some US-based online platforms, including LinkedIn and Yahoo, to withdraw from the Chinese market just before the law went into effect (Burgess, 2021).

For more information, see: https://digichina.stanford.edu/work/translation-personal-information-protection-law-of-the-peoples-republic-of-china-effective-nov-1-2021/

UK - UK GDPR

The UK was part of the EU when GDPR came into force, and when it left the EU it amended the detail of its privacy legislation to reflect the change, but largely left the substance of GDPR in place as UK legislation. Like GDPR, UK GDPR applies to organisations outside of the UK if they are collecting, storing, or processing information about residents of the UK.

More information about data privacy in the UK can be found at: https://ico.org.uk

New Zealand - New Zealand Privacy Act 2020

New Zealand has a Privacy Act, which was updated in 2020. It is based on 13 principles. Many of its provisions are similar to those already described for GDPR, but it is more restrictive when it comes to unique identifiers. These are things such as ID numbers which correspond to one, and only one, person, such as a driver's licence or passport number. The New Zealand Privacy Act only allows those to be created when they are necessary and prohibits them from being shared across organisations. For example, the US practice of using a social security number as a unique identifier across multiple organisations and data sources would not be permitted in New Zealand.

Financial penalties for breaching the New Zealand Privacy Act are relatively modest; however there can be public relations ramifications for organisations that breach the Act. For example, the Privacy Office issued a widely publicised compliance notice to the Reserve Bank of New Zealand following a data breach (Office of the Privacy Commissioner, 2021a), and has been outspoken about its belief that Facebook (Meta) is in violation of the Act (Office of the Privacy Commissioner, 2021b).

More information about the New Zealand Privacy Act can be found at: www.privacy.org.nz

USA, Canada, and Australia - Combination of Federal and State/Provincial Laws

The US, Canada, and Australia all have states or provinces with their own legislation related to the use of data, as well as federal legislation in the case of Canada and Australia, so the exact requirements vary by location even within those countries.

The California Consumer Privacy Act has received a lot of attention because it is one of the first attempts at privacy legislation in the US, because California is home to many of the technology companies that currently hold vast amounts of consumer data, and because California is such a large state and therefore its actions are often followed by other states. Nonetheless, that Privacy Act has a narrower scope than those described previously. It only applies to large for-profit organisations and not government organisations or non-profits. Additional information is available at: https://oag.ca.gov/privacy/ccpa. At the time of writing, the only other US states with comprehensive privacy legislation in place were Colorado, Connecticut, Utah and Virginia, but more limited legislation was in place in some other states and additional privacy legislation was under consideration in many other states. For more information, see: www.ncsl.org/research/telecommunications-and-infor-mation-technology/state-laws-related-to-internet-privacy.aspx.

Canada and Australia both have national Privacy Acts, though Canada also has a Personal Information Protection and Electronic Documents Act and additional national and province-level legislation. Its Privacy Commissioner has a website to help individuals and organisations determine which of those applies in their particular situation. That is available at: www.priv.gc.ca/en/report-a-concern/leg_info_201405/

Australia's national Privacy Act is older than New Zealand's, but has many similar principles. Unlike New Zealand's legislation, it only applies to government agencies and private sector organisations that generate at least three million Australian dollars a year in revenue. More information on the Australian Privacy Act is available at: www.oaic.gov.au/privacy/the-privacy-act, and information about privacy in individual Australian states is available at: www.oaic.gov.au/privacy/privacy-in-your-state.

CULTURAL CONSIDERATIONS

As can be seen from the previous section, there are some similarities across countries in the laws governing the use of data, but there are some differences too. Some of those differences are likely due to the ways that different cultures think about data. For example, cultures may vary in how they tend to balance the potential benefits that can be derived from data for society with the privacy of individuals. Differences such as those can go beyond what's strictly legal or not legal to do with data to what different cultures perceive as being acceptable to do with data. There are also practical issues to consider when comparing data derived from different cultures, and cultural differences within countries to be aware of.

Cultural Comparability

In many situations, people want or need to use analytics that compare countries, or cultures within countries, on particular metrics. That type of information can be extremely useful, but when using cross-cultural comparisons, it's important to ensure you are indeed comparing the same things. For example, if you wanted to compare the total or average weight or volume of goods sold across countries, you wouldn't want to use metric units of measures (e.g., grams or litres) for some countries and imperial measures (e.g., pounds or ounces) for others. Similarly, if you wanted to compare the total or average value of goods sold across countries, you would want to do your comparisons all in the same currency rather than mixing, say, dollars, euros and pounds. Even in those situations, what seems like a direct comparison can be complicated. For example, the value of currencies relative to one another fluctuates, so your comparison will vary based on exactly when you convert the value of one currency to another.

Comparison can become even more challenging for other types of data, such as responses to survey questions. There is extensive anecdotal and research evidence demonstrating that people from different countries often use the types of scales that are common in surveys (e.g., strongly disagree to strongly agree or very dissatisfied to very satisfied) differently. People in some cultures tend to use the ends of scales more than people in other cultures where it's more common to tend to stick more toward the middle or to avoid one end of the scale. Those differences can make it hard to know if, for example, a higher average satisfaction rating in one country compared to another is a function of the customers in one country being genuinely more satisfied compared to those in another or a tendency of people in one country to rate everything somewhat more favourably than people in the other country.

Comparative analysis of text-based data, such as product reviews, answers to open-ended survey questions, and comments in social media, can be even more complicated. In many cases, those may need to be translated into the same language, but important aspects of what was said can be lost in translation. For example, it's common to categorise text-based comments about organisations or their products or services based on sentiment (i.e., whether the comment is generally positive, negative, or neutral) and topic (e.g., is someone talking about the quality of a product or the quality of service), and a subtle difference in how something is translated could make a difference in how that particular comment is categorised. And because the way people talk about things varies across cultures, there are situations in which even the categories used to classify things may vary too.

Cultural Differences Within Countries

Analytics-related cultural variations can occur within, as well as between countries. Indigenous data sovereignty movements have emerged in many countries, and are a notable example. Native peoples in countries including Australia, New Zealand, Canada, and the United States have argued that they should control data for and about themselves. While the details and progress of these movements vary by country, they share many common elements, including the views that:

- Working with data inherently involves a variety of subjective choices and those choices have generally been driven by the needs and assumptions of those in power, which have typically not included many indigenous people.
- Data has often been used in ways that have been detrimental to the individual and collective needs, aspirations, and wellbeing of indigenous people. It has also often been used in ways that have promoted negative stereotypes of indigenous people or stigmatised them.
- Even when the intention has been to help, or at least not harm, indigenous people, data about them has often been inaccurate or incomplete because those involved in collecting and analysing the data lacked the cultural knowledge required to collect high-quality data about and from indigenous people or to analyse and interpret it accurately.
- Comparative data that shows worse outcomes for indigenous people are often implicitly or explicitly attributed to the nature or the actions of the people or their culture without adequate examination of the extent to which the outcomes have been shaped by systems and forces in the broader society that have tended to disadvantage indigenous people.
- Data that would be helpful to indigenous people is often not collected at all or is collected in ways that make it not as useful to them as it could be. Often that's because it is not sufficiently granular or **disaggregated** (i.e., broken down into sub-groups) or there are not enough observations in the most granular sub-groups (e.g., indigenous women or people in a specific tribe) to draw meaningful conclusions. That makes it hard for them to get the data they need to achieve their own aspirations and address their own problems as effectively as possible.

People and groups involved in indigenous data sovereignty movements in a variety of countries came together to develop principles for indigenous data governance (Carroll et al., 2020). They are called the CARE principles, and state that those working with indigenous data should:

- Generate **C**ollective benefit for indigenous people.
- Give **A**uthority to control the data to indigenous people.
- Behave **R**esponsibly toward the indigenous people providing the data.
- Use the data **E**thically.

These principles have already been adopted by a variety of organisations, including the Smithsonian (Carroll et al., 2020).

More information about the Māori data sovereignty movement in New Zealand can be found in the Analytics in Practice section of this chapter. For more information on indigenous data sovereignty more generally, see: https://apo.org.au/sites/default/files/resource-files/2020-10/apo-nid310768.pdf.

While perhaps not as well-organised when it comes to data and analytics, other cultural groups within countries may share similar concerns. Groups that have been marginalised by the dominant culture in their country based on things such as gender, ethnicity, sexual orientation, or religion may be mistrustful of anyone trying to collect data from or about them. People who are economically insecure, have vulnerable immigration status, or have political views in opposition to those in power may share that mistrust. The next section provides some tips for using analytics ethically in these and other situations.

ETHICAL CONSIDERATIONS

What are Data Ethics?

Nicholas Agar, a data ethics consultant and Distinguished Visiting Professor at Carnegie Mellon University in Australia, describes data ethics as: *'considered judgements about what's right and wrong'*[1]. He notes this goes beyond what is legal – especially in a rapidly developing area, such as analytics: *'you need the ethics first because you can't trust the law because the written laws generally are just full of gaps'*. The judgement required involves asking questions such as whether the benefits of the use of the data to the people from whom it's being collected will exceed any costs or detrimental aspects.

---

[1]You can hear more of Professor Agar's thoughts on data ethics in this video: https://vimeo.com/650378262/f42631978b, which is where the quotes in this section are from.

Nick notes that making such judgements is not always easy since we all tend to perceive situations from our own perspective, and those may differ greatly from the people whose data we want to use: '*If everyone making the decisions looks like me, we might well be doing our best, but I bet we'll make assumptions that aren't quite right because we'll think that what's right for us is right for everyone*'.

This helps us to see that the discussion in the previous section about indigenous data sovereignty, which is elaborated on in the Analytics in Practice box in this chapter, can be extended to other groups in the sense that we should be thinking about not just whether we think a particular use of data is okay for us, but we should also be thinking about whether the people to whom the data pertains will think it's okay for them and that they will benefit from it. Since their perspective may be different from ours, and they may perceive things about the situation that we don't, we should get their input to make sure we understand their perspective and are not overlooking any potential unintended negative consequence that may arise from the collection, analysis, storage or use of data.

Why is it Important to Consider Data-Related Ethics?

Unfortunately, there have been many examples of major organisations encountering data-related ethical problems. For example, Amazon used data about existing employees to try to predict which applicants would make the best future employees, but found that resulted in discrimination against women (Zaric et al., 2021). That wasn't because anyone intended to discriminate against women, but rather because Amazon's existing employees were disproportionately men, and so the machine learning algorithm 'learned' that good employees participate in activities that are disproportionately participated in by men, and not in activities that are disproportionately participated in by women.

Data-related ethical concerns have also often been raised in relationship to ad targeting. For example, in one field study, researchers (Lambrecht and Tucker, 2019) bought ads on Facebook, Instagram, Google and Twitter promoting careers in STEM (science, technology, engineering, and maths), indicating that the ads were intended for people of all genders. They found that the ads were shown to more men than women on all of the platforms tested. Again, there was no intent to discriminate by any of the platforms. The outcome resulted from the fact that the ad tech systems that determine who sees which ad are optimised for cost-effectiveness and overall advertisers are willing to pay more to show ads to women than men. Therefore, men were more cost-effective to show the STEM ads to than women and so that's who the ads were shown to most often.

Examples like these receive a lot of attention because they involve high-profile companies, but that should not be interpreted to mean that companies like these are disproportionately likely to run into data-related ethics problems. If anything, it's likely to be the reverse since these large organisations tend to be more sophisticated in their use of data and the application of data governance than smaller, less data-oriented, organisations. It's just that ethical problems experienced by those smaller organisations are less likely to make the news.

While it's obvious that organisations want to avoid breaking data-related laws, doing things with data that seem unethical to many people – even if they are not explicitly illegal – can lead to bad publicity and an erosion of trust among customers, employees, and other stakeholders. That can, in turn, make customers less willing to buy from an organisation – especially if doing so involves providing additional data. It can also make potential employees less enthusiastic about working for an organisation.

Who is Responsible for Ensuring Organisations Use Data Ethically?

You may be thinking that you just want to be a data analyst or data scientist, or data-oriented subject matter expert, and that you'll leave the ethics to someone else. Unfortunately, that's really not possible. As Professor Agar notes, responsibility for data ethics must be:

> distributed throughout the entire organisation because when you say: 'Well look, our job involves data, but it doesn't involve ethics, so we just do whatever, but there's a separate department, the ethics department, and they'll check on it'. Well, if you have that approach, then you probably won't ever get checked on because that ethics department will probably be a bit too busy.

Further reinforcing the need for data ethics accountability to be the responsibility of everyone working with data is the fact that many organisations don't have anyone specifically in charge of ethics in general or data ethics in particular, and that even if/when there is they may not have enough expertise in the particular use and form of data to understand the full ethical implications of every application of data happening within that organisation. As with legal considerations, the volume of data now being collected, stored, processed, analysed, and used within most organisations tends to be too great to make it feasible for any single person or department to monitor it all for ethical transgressions. That's why it needs to be everyone's job.

How can you decide if a particular use of data is ethical?

So if everyone working with data needs to be thinking about ethical issues, how can you decide if a particular use of data is ethical?

A good starting point is what the UK's Office of National Statistics calls 'The Five Safes' (Stokes, 2017). Those are mainly privacy-oriented checks, and refer to having safe people, projects, settings, output, and data.

- Safe *People* focusses on ensuring the people working with data have the required skills to do so and have also committed to treating it with appropriate levels of confidentiality.
- Safe *Projects* focusses on the need to use data for a particular purpose. Most universities, and some government organisations and companies have ethics committees that evaluate particular data projects, but for reasons described throughout this section, it's wise for all organisations to do such an evaluation whether or not they have a formal committee for doing so.
- Safe *Settings* refers to where the data is used. The UK's Office of National Statistics and similar organisations in other countries require that data that includes identifying information be accessed in locations where it is not even possible to print it, copy it, or upload it to the Internet. While not every organisation has facilities that can prevent all of that, it is worth thinking about where people can access different types of data – especially in an era where more and more people are working outside of traditional offices.
- Safe *Output* refers to publishing analytical results in a way that prevents identification of individual people. That includes more obvious things like not including names and addresses, but also less obvious things like not publishing a result for such a narrowly defined group that even if a name is not provided it's possible to deduce the person to whom the data refers.
- Safe *Data* refers to blocking of personally identifiable information, even during the analysis process, so that even those involved with that cannot see unnecessary personally identifying information.

The earlier discussions about culture and ethics also provide some additional questions you can ask yourself to form your own considered judgement about whether a particular use of data is ethical:

- If the data is about people or things belonging to people:
  - Will the collection and use of data about them benefit them individually and collectively, and do they believe that themselves?
  - Are there potential individual or collective harms associated with the proposed use of the data? Have you checked with the people who will be affected to make sure no potential harm or unintended consequences have been over-looked?
  - Does use of the data benefit or harm people in some groups more than others?
- What other ways could data be collected, analysed, stored and used to address the same question, problem, or opportunity?

o   Would any of these result in data and data insights that are as high quality with greater benefit to the individuals involved or with less harm?

o   After fully evaluating the alternative options and hearing from the people who will be affected, do the benefits exceed the harms for the people who will be affected?

o   Are there ways to collect, analyse, store, and use the data that would reduce any disproportionate impact on a particular group of people?

It's important to consider both sets of questions because there is generally not just one way to address a question, problem, or opportunity with data, and often some ways are much more ethically problematic than others. That means that if we find that one way of address-ing a question, problem, or opportunity with data is ethically problematic we should not just give up on using data or accept doing something ethically questionable. Instead, we should look for an alternative that enables us to use data to address the question, problem, or opportunity, but in a way that's ethically acceptable. The Analytics in Practice section of this chapter provides some examples of this.

SUMMARY

Anyone working with data needs to be aware of laws and regulations that govern the col-lection, storage and use of data. Those laws vary by location and are changing over time, and it would be easy to collect, store, or use data in a way that's not permitted without even knowing it. There have been many examples of even large organisations running into legal problems because of the way their employees used, managed, or collected data.

Beyond just making sure your plans to use data for business analytics purposes are legal, it's important to ensure they are ethical and appropriate from a cultural standpoint. Perceptions about what is and is not okay to do with data vary by location and across cultures and time, so even if something was perceived as okay in one place at one time, it may not be in another. These issues are important in terms of doing the right thing, but they are also important even if all you care about is data accuracy. Failure to consider cultural perspectives and differences can lead to data quality problems. A good way to avoid such problems is to ensure that the people you are collecting data about are involved in designing your analytics project from the beginning. Being closer to the issue, they may be able to identify potential ethical or cultural problems or issues that could affect data quality that you can't.

It may seem that ensuring use of data is legal, ethical and culturally appropriate is some-one else's job, but the reason that it needs to be the job of everyone working with data is that analytics projects can be quite detailed, and without knowledge of every detail of a project, a high level observer may not be aware that something that's being proposed risks crossing legal boundaries or doing something that is ethically questionable or culturally inappropriate.

ANALYTICS IN PRACTICE

Opening New Zealand's data – thoughtfully

There are probably few people who spend more time thinking about how to use data both effectively and in a culturally sensitive way than Ngapera Riley. Ngapera is the CEO of Figure NZ, an organisation whose mission is 'to get the people of New Zealand using data to thrive' (see: https://figure.nz). Figure NZ makes data from Statistics New Zealand and other organisations available to the general public in a way that's easy for them to find and understand. Ngapera is a passionate advocate for high-quality, open data that people can use to improve their communities and organisations. That also makes her a champion of data literacy:

> Back in the day when only monks, or priests, and men, or rich people could read or write, there was no use for everybody else to even think about writing, or reading, or literacy of any kind. So you know, it was only just meant for the small portion, but you know and then it would be like: Okay, 100 years later and you have this awesome library of information, but then 97% of people can't even read, so this information stays unlocked. And I think that we're going to be the same or similar now with data literacy. We've got data everywhere, but unless we've got the skills to teach people how to use it and apply it...

In making data available and helping teach people how to apply and use data, Ngapera is acutely aware of the importance of doing so in a way that gives careful consideration to culture. In addition to her role at Figure NZ, Ngapera is part of the Māori[2] Data Sovereignty Network. They 'advocate for Māori rights and interest in data to be protected as the world moves into an increasingly open data environment' (see: www.temanararaunga.maori.nz) and are an integral part of the broader indigenous data sovereignty movement discussed earlier in this chapter. As part of their work, the Māori Data Sovereignty Network has developed a set of Māori Data Sovereignty Principles, covering how data about Māori people and things should be designed, collected, stored, and used.

In her role as CEO of Figure NZ, Ngapera has to make decisions about how to apply those principles to the large volume of data Figure NZ curates and publishes. For example, one of the principles says that: 'The collection, use and interpretation of data shall uphold the dignity of Māori communities, groups and individuals' (Māori Data Sovereignty Network, 2018). In keeping with this principle, Figure NZ has a whole site (https://maori.figure.nz) dedicated to data that are important to Māori:

(Continued)

---

[2]Māori are the indigenous people of New Zealand.

So we now have really awesome surveys that collect awesome Māori data: how many people are connected to their marae[3] ? Their Tūrangawaewae[4] ? How many people are speaking their languages? And so you know, from that sentiment of unhappiness with that, it has forced us to collect better data - different data. And this has been collected with Māori experts, and they have determined what is important for Māori.

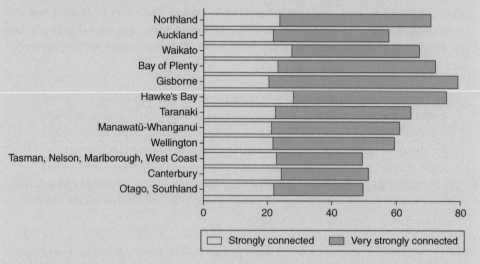

Māori people in New Zealand who feel strongly connected to their Tūrangawaewae

Figure 2.2 Strength-based data example (Tūrangawaewae means a place to stand)

Credit Line: Stats NZ

This proved so popular that other groups who have traditionally not seen themselves reflected in data, including Pacific Peoples, and the LGBTQ and disability communities have asked for similar sites of their own.

Another one of the Māori Data Sovereignty Principles says that 'Māori data shall be collected and coded using categories that prioritise Māori needs and aspirations' (Māori Data Sovereignty Network, 2018). Ngapera has been involved in a task force helping to achieve that when it comes to the needs of Māori businesses and Māori economic aspirations:

We're trying to come up with a Māori business definition. One does not exist. ... So when we're looking from a COVID strategy, post COVID strategy, economic position, we actually don't know how many Māori businesses exist. You know, and that means we don't know a lot, right? If you don't know how many Māori businesses exist, how can you calculate the worth of the Māori economy?

---

[3]Location where important Māori meetings and ceremonies are held.

[4]A person's 'place to stand' or place in the world.

New Zealand organisations in general, and government organisations in particular, have been receptive toward Māori Data Sovereignty, but reconciling that with existing data-related infrastructure, ecosystems, and privacy legislation has not always been easy. For example, coronavirus vaccination rates for Māori lagged behind those of other ethnic groups in New Zealand, and some community leaders and an organisation called Whānau Ora, which looks after the welfare of families, wanted data on non-vaccinated Māori people so that they could be approached and encouraged to be vaccinated to help reduce the spread of Covid-19 among the Māori community. This is in keeping with a Māori Data Sovereignty Principle that says: 'Individuals' rights (including privacy rights), risks and benefits in relation to data need to be balanced with those of the groups of which they are a part. In some contexts, collective Māori rights will prevail over those of individuals' (Māori Data Sovereignty Network, 2018).

The Ministry of Health initially declined to provide the information requested for a combination of privacy reasons and coverage grounds:

> If you think about that - currently the government is holding true, saying: 'we can't give this data out. This is IDI data. It's personalised information. You're asking for addresses. We can't give it out'. But the Māori health providers are going: 'But hang on - we really need this information. There's a really good reason to use it'. And so now you see - government trying to do the right thing by holding the data and protecting it, but now then you see the practical application of why you would need access to that information in this particular case.

Another challenge is providing data at a level of **disaggregation** (i.e., separating out data for one group from that of the whole) that would be most helpful to Māori. That would often mean providing data at the Iwi (tribe) or Hapū (sub-tribe or clan) level, since that is the level that is often most useful for decision-making. And yet, as Ngapera points out:

> It's so, so complex. We don't just have one Hapu. I have seven... If you're not equipped with the skills to use that data well, you could start doubling up on counts and things like that.

And even among those directly involved with Māori Data Sovereignty, there are still questions to resolve:

> When it comes down to the actual practical application, as much as, you know, that school of thought that says Māori should protect it, then you have to go down the route of: 'Well who? Who in Māori should protect it? Is it the Iwi Leader Data Group? Is it a democratic process? How do you do it?'

You can hear more from Ngapera in this video: https://vimeo.com/649353077/ba2049e8ee

RUNNING CASE STUDY: 4TE, PART 2[5]

Emily sat down with a cup of coffee on that cold January morning to start the process of analysing 4tE's current situation to provide the information she and Matt needed to make decisions about its future direction. She first went to the portal for their POS (Point of Sale) system. She wanted to pull some reports to get a sense of how things were trending and to think more deeply about what data they were collecting and if that should change.

Emily had been hearing things about something called GDPR going into effect in Europe and also about concerns related to privacy breaches in the US. She and Matt had both received notices about their data being compromised as customers of companies that had experienced security breaches. When Matt and Emily started 4tE they thought using commercial SaaS (software as a service) options would be easiest for them and they had been assuming they were looking after data security, but Emily realised they had never really had time to check into the details.

Emily and Matt also hadn't had time to change the default settings on the standard reports they could pull from the POS system, or to see what other types of data they could extract that might be useful. Over the next couple of days, Emily not only investigated that, but also all of the other places they were collecting data. They used a different software vendor for their accounting. They also used that system to track their employee's hours, vacation, and sick time. They used a separate analytics platform to track the number of people visiting their website, and what they were doing when they got there. Matt drew on his supply chain experience to create a complex Excel file tracking what 4tE had ordered from suppliers, when the order was expected, when it was actually delivered, and if any of the items that arrived were unable to be sold due to damage, spoilage, or anything else.

In addition to getting a better handle on what data was already available, Emily read up on GDPR and other rules governing the legal use of data as well as some articles about ethical issues related to storing and using data. Given 4tE was founded based on the desire to be more responsible toward the earth, Emily wanted to assure herself that they were being equally respectful toward their customers and the data about them. Since the business was still relatively small, they tried not to use lawyers unless they really needed to, but she also wanted to assure herself that everything they were doing now with data was legal and that any changes they made were on a sound legal footing.

---

[5]The 4tE case is fictitious.

EXERCISES

1 Search online to discover if your own personal data is covered by laws or regulations such as GDPR, and if so, what organisations can and can't legally do with your data.

2 Use this site: www.theguardian.com/commentisfree/2018/mar/28/all-the-data-facebook-google-has-on-you-privacy to see what information Google (Alphabet) and Facebook (Meta) have about you. Consider whether you believe their use of data about you is ethical or not, and if not, what aspects you feel are unethical even if they are legal.

3 Search online to discover if the indigenous people in your country have a stated position about the use of data for and about them, and if so, what it is. If you are in a country where the indigenous people are the majority group, consider whether there are any other groups of people within the population who may have concerns about how data about them is being used.

4 Identify an organisation in your local area and a question that they might have that could be answered using analytics.

   a What is the question?

   b Knowing what you know now, what do you think they would need to do to answer the question you identified? (i.e., What data would they collect, how would they collect, analyse, use, and/or report it.)

   c Are there any legal considerations you believe would need to be taken into account, or at least further investigated, before doing the things you identified?

   d Are there any cultural considerations you believe would need to be taken into account, or at least further investigated, before doing the things you identified?

   e Are there any further ethical considerations you believe would need to be taken into account, or at least further investigated, before doing the things you identified?

5 Identify an organisation based in another country whose goods or services you use (e.g., an online platform or retailer based in another country) and a question that they might have that could be answered using analytics.

   a What is the question?

   b Knowing what you know now, what do you think they would need to do to answer the question you identified? (i.e., What data would they collect, how would they collect, analyse, use, and/or report it.)

c   Are there any legal considerations you believe would need to be taken into account, or at least further investigated, before doing the things you identified?

d   Are there any cultural considerations you believe would need to be taken into account, or at least further investigated, before doing the things you identified?

e   Are there any further ethical considerations you believe would need to be taken into account, or at least further investigated, before doing the things you identified?

3
PREPARING TO WORK WITH DATA

WHAT WILL YOU LEARN FROM THIS CHAPTER?

1 Common categories and sources of organisational data.
2 How data is typically stored and structured.
3 How to identify missing data, and what to do about it.
4 How to identify bad data, and what to do about it.
5 Variable types.

COMMON CATEGORIES AND SOURCES OF ORGANISATIONAL DATA

So far we've talked about the context in which data is collected and analysed, but not so much about the data itself. We've also talked about data in a generic sense, but now let's get more specific about the categories and sources of data organisations tend to work with.

Let's start by thinking about data on two broad dimensions. The first relates to how the data is collected, and more specifically, whether the party providing the data is aware that they're doing it. When we're doing something like filling in a questionnaire or participating in an interview we know that we're doing it, and we are providing the data so that it can be analysed. That's **actively collected data**.

On the other hand, our phones and computers generate a large amount of data in the background as we work, play games, watch videos, or scroll social media. That data is needed to make those things work, but it can be analysed subsequently and used for other purposes, such as improving our apps, phones, or computers. That type of **passively collected data** can also be used to build up a profile of our overall pattern of behaviour that can be used by automated systems to do things such as decide what ad to show us or what song, tv show, or product to recommend to us. Loyalty programmes are another example of this. From the perspective of users, the purpose of loyalty programmes is to enable them to get discounts and earn free products and other rewards. But in doing so, it creates a passively collected dataset linking all purchases made by individual members of the programme that can then be analysed to better understand purchase patterns and customise future marketing efforts.

A second dimension that can be used to categorise data is whether it is qualitative or quantitative. Think of **quantitative data** as anything that starts as a number or is easy to covert to one. For example, numbers in a spreadsheet, answers to multi-choice questions, or data being generated by sensors on things like parking meters or electricity meters. **Qualitative data** covers a much broader range of forms, including text, audio, images and video.

When you combine the two broad dimensions just described, you end up with the four categories of data shown in Table 3.1, along with examples of common organisational sources of data within each category.

Table 3.1 Data categories and examples of common organisational sources of data

Actively Collected Quantitative Data	Passively Collected Quantitative Data
• Data collected via paper and online forms (e.g., registration data, HR forms). • Most survey questions. • Quotes from suppliers.	• Web and app analytics data (including data from experiments on digital platforms). • Transaction data. • Sensor data. • Product ratings.
Actively Collected Qualitative Data	**Passively Collected Qualitative Data**
• Responses from focus groups. • Responses from interviews. • Open-ended survey questions. • Customer feedback forms.	• Social media posts. • Product reviews. • Articles and documents. • Audio, video and images.

Traditionally, actively collected quantitative data was the most commonly used category of data within organisations. Examples include forms that employees fill in when they start a new job, closed-ended survey questions asking customers about things such as their satisfaction, and quotes from suppliers.

Many organisations also have a long history with actively collected qualitative data, though perhaps not at as large a scale as for actively collected quantitative data. Examples of actively collected qualitative data include things such as responses to exit interview questions, and remarks made by customers in focus groups, comment cards, and open-ended survey questions. Note that here the main form of data is words. Chapter 4 will describe how those can be converted to something closer to our conventional notions of data.

The availability of passively collected data has exploded in the digital age since so much data is captured in the course of other activities. Passively collected quantitative data includes things such as our actions as we use apps or websites, sales of products through digital platforms, the movements of vehicles as recorded by sensors, or customer ratings on a website such as Amazon. This is the type of data people are often thinking of when they talk about '**Big Data**'. See the Statistics Explainer in this chapter to learn more about Big Data.

Passively collected qualitative data includes things such as social media posts, product reviews, articles and documents, and even audio, video, and images. Of the types of data discussed so far, those probably seem least like what we typically think of when we think of data, but as will be discussed in Chapter 4, they can be converted into more traditional forms of data for analysis.

The examples just described are not meant to be an exhaustive list. Commonly used forms of data vary by context, but can generally be classified into these four categories.

STATISTICS EXPLAINER

Big Data

While exact definitions vary, most people agree that Big Data has high volume, variety, and velocity. Volume refers to the total quantity of data, variety relates to whether or not the data is of a consistent type, and velocity relates to how rapidly it is being changed or added to. There are no generally agreed standards for exactly what 'high' means when it comes to volume, variety, or velocity. Part of the reason for that is that they have traditionally been interpreted in terms of their computational load, and the ability of computers to manage data has evolved over time, so something that was perceived as Big Data when that term first started to be used a couple of decades ago might not be now because computers are so much better at storing and processing data.

Of the different categories of data discussed in this chapter, passively collected data is much more likely than actively collected data to be considered Big Data. Because it is being collected passively, it tends to come in more quickly and in greater volumes. Some of it, such as content being posted to social media, is also highly varied. For example, a post could include a combination of text, video, and emojis. Because Big Data is generally collected passively, it also generally represents a population rather than a sample (see the Statistics Explainer in Chapter 1 if you need a refresher on the difference). For example, an organisation using analytics to monitor equipment may have sensors on every piece of equipment and may be collecting all of the data from all of them. Even when an organisation has population-level data it might choose to sample from it (i.e., randomly select a sub-set of elements within the population) if it is Big Data because it might take too long or be too computationally intensive to do analysis on the full population-level dataset – especially if a carefully selected sample can give nearly as accurate a result.

Since business analytics evolved from and overlaps with a range of disciplines, each with its own terminology, multiple words are often used to describe the same thing. Actively collected data is sometimes called captured data and passively collected data is sometimes called data exhaust. Structured data is another way of describing quantitative data and unstructured data is another way of describing qualitative data.

As described in Chapter 1, analytics are used within most organisations to support the marketing/communications, HR, operations and finance functions. Any of the categories of data just described could be used in any of those application areas. As shown in Figure 3.1, combining the data categories with the application areas gives us 16 different business analytics domains. It's important to note that not all organisations will be using analytics within all 16 domains, and that for any given organisation, some will be more important than others and they may be better at some than others. Those differences result from a combination of what the organisation does, what data they have or can get access to, and their data-related capabilities. These differences will be explored more extensively in the discussion of analytics for each functional area in Chapters 6–9.

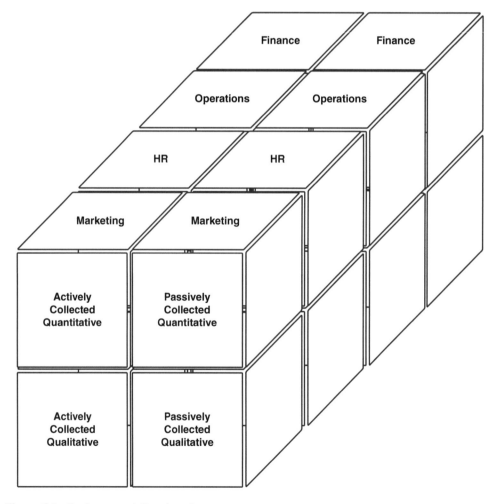

Figure 3.1 Business analytics domains

MATCHING DATA TO QUESTIONS AND PROBLEMS

Part of the reason that different organisations, and different parts of the same organisation, use different data sources and different types of analytics is that they have different questions and problems. Figure 3.2 provides an overview of how questions being posed – particularly relating to people – may lead an organisation to at least start with different data sources.

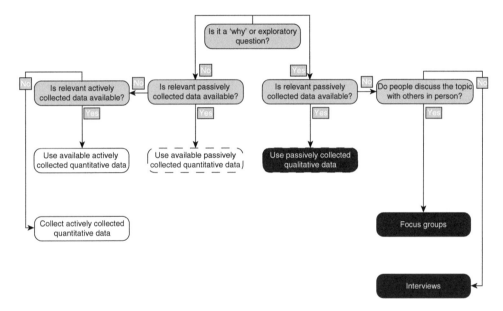

Figure 3.2 Matching data sources to questions

A good place to start when considering what source of data is likely to be helpful in addressing a particular question is to consider whether the question is a 'why' or exploratory type question. For example:

- Why have customer buying patterns changed?
- Why are our employees leaving our organisation after a shorter time, on average, than was the case previously?
- Why has the number of accidents in our factory increased?

As you can see, questions in this category often literally start with the word why; however they also include other exploratory type questions, such as:

- What types of new products might our existing customers be interested in? or
- How can we improve employee morale?

Generally speaking, questions that are in 'why' or exploratory form tend to be well-suited to qualitative data sources; whereas more definitive 'what', 'where', 'when', 'how' type questions tend to be better suited to quantitative data sources. For example:

- What is the most popular item on our restaurant's menu?
- Where do the majority of customers who visit our restaurant live?
- When is our restaurant busiest?
- How do the customers who visit our restaurant hear about us?

Notice that those questions have a limited number of possible answers that can be known in advance. That's what makes them more suited to being answered using quantitative data sources.

The next step after considering whether we have an exploratory type question or not is to determine whether passively collected data that could answer our question already exists and is available to us. If it is, we would generally choose to use that, at least in the first instance. The reasons for that are that its availability means that we could access it fairly quickly and often relatively inexpensively, and the fact that it is passively collected means that it is also likely to be population-level data, which removes the risk of an unrepresentative sample as well as giving us a lot of data to analyse.

If our question is an exploratory type question, but passively collected qualitative data is not available, we would then want to consider whether the question is something that people tend to talk to others about in person. If so, we could do a focus group, where we would have a discussion with a group of people. If not, we could interview them individually. Here we're trying to emulate the way people would naturally talk about something. That means giving them the opportunity to hear and bounce thoughts off others in situations where they would naturally do that or to have a private one-on-one interview for more sensitive topics that people would only be likely to converse with others about privately.

If our question is not an exploratory one, and relevant passively collected quantitative data is not available, we could see whether actively collected quantitative data, such as responses to a survey or experiment that someone did previously, exists and is available. If so, we could use that. If not, we could generate our own actively collected data using a survey, experiment, web form, etc. Part of the reason for exhausting other possibilities before these is that they often require more time and resources than other data sources.

As noted in Chapter 1, multiple questions often need to be answered to make a decision in an organisation, so often the different data sources described are frequently used in combination. It's also common for a single data source to provide a partial answer to a question but for additional data sources to be needed to fill in gaps or to provide additional confidence that what we learned from the first data source we investigated is correct, since each source of data has different advantages and disadvantages.

HOW DATA IS TYPICALLY STORED AND STRUCTURED

As shown in Figure 3.3, regardless of the source, data is often stored or given to us in a structure that looks like a spreadsheet. Data in that structure could be called a dataset, but it could also be called an analytics record or a database table. The term dataset will be used throughout the rest of this book.

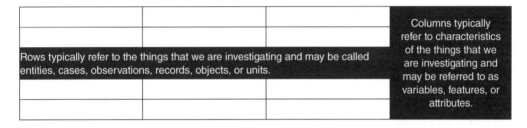

Figure 3.3 includes the following text within it:

Columns typically refer to characteristics of the things that we are investigating and may be referred to as variables, features, or attributes.

Rows typically refer to the things that we are investigating and may be called entities, cases, observations, records, objects, or units.

Note that:
- Analytics record is another name for a dataset.
- More complex projects and applications may involve multiple inter-related datasets (often called tables in a relational database).
- Big data projects often involve data stored in non-relational databases.

Figure 3.3 Dataset structure and terminology

The most common way of structuring a dataset is to have each row refer to one of the things we're investigating and each column refer to a characteristic of that thing. For example, a dataset for a course would generally have each student represented in a row and each column would show the marks for each student on one assignment. This is another situation where there are multiple names for the same thing. The general term for the students in that example may be cases, observations, entities, records, objects or units. And in other situations rather than those being students the things in the rows might be customers, employees, or planes owned by an airline. Whichever they are, in this book, the term cases will be used to describe the individual elements that we are investigating.

The columns – each representing one assignment in the course example – also have multiple names. Those with more of a statistical focus tend to call them **variables**, while those with more of a machine learning focus tend to call them features. Attributes is another name for them. You could also think of them as characteristics, but they will be referred to as variables in this book.

CHALLENGES IN BUILDING AND PREPARING A DATASET

People who work with data often talk about spending more time preparing their data than analysing it. This preparation is important though because we can't analyse data that we don't have, and the more messy our data is, the harder it is for us to see patterns, even if they are really there beneath the mess.

There are a variety of reasons that building a dataset can be challenging. There are some situations in which it's hard to know what variables to include in a dataset. For example, as described in Chapter 2, there is a trend now to want to be able to disaggregate data based on things such as race, gender and the combination of race and gender; however in many existing datasets race and gender have not been included as variables or those variables alone may be insufficiently granular for the purposes for which someone wants to use the data.

Other times it may be unclear what cases to include. For instance, people tracking use of apps and websites often have some minimum threshold of time people need to have used the app or website to count as a session or visit to allow for accidental taps and clicks, but there's no definitive way to know exactly what that minimum threshold should be. A small difference in where it's set could result in the inclusion or exclusion of some cases, and that could change the results.

It can also be unclear if the cases included in a dataset are representative of cases that are not included. This is often an issue with survey data. It's very difficult to be certain that the answers of people who do respond to a survey are truly representative of those who don't, even if we try to get a sample that's representative in terms of some basic demographic characteristics, such as age and gender, because people who have similar demographic profiles may have different attitudes about the issue being investigated.

Finally, it can be unclear if the variables included were measured properly. Both humans and machines can make measurement errors. In the case of machines, things like sensors can have hardware or software failures. They are also vulnerable to things such as power and Internet outages. Human measurement error can stem from unclear instructions, inadequate training, or just lack of motivation to record data correctly.

Chapter 1 described how data and judgement work together, and judgement guides the data preparation process. Those without adequate domain knowledge may fail to spot data that just doesn't look right or lack the institutional knowledge to know that a problem with some specific data may exist. That knowledge can also be helpful in deciding how to resolve inconsistencies or deal with missing data or bad data, which are discussed in the next section.

DATA CLEANING

Regardless of whether we have collected data ourselves or received it from someone else, before we can analyse it we almost always need to clean it up. That's true whether we're working with a really large dataset or a much more modestly sized dataset. Each dataset is unique, which means that the particular ways in which they're messy may vary, and the tools and particular approaches we use to clean the dataset may be different depending on the size of the dataset, software we're using, etc., but the basic tasks that we need to accomplish are pretty similar regardless of what the data is about or the size of the dataset. The next sub-section describes why datasets often need cleaning, and the two after that discuss what to do about two common issues that come up when cleaning datasets – missing data and bad data.

Why Datasets Need Cleaning

Datasets are subject to a variety of possible sources of messiness. For example, values for some variables for some cases may be missing. For instance in the earlier example of a dataset with marks for students on each assignment in a course, if a student skipped an assessment there would be no mark for them in a cell in a column where most other people do have marks. We need to take that into account later when we analyse the data. There are some situations in which we would want to treat that value as a zero (e.g., in calculating that student's grade) and others in which we would want to treat it as a missing value (e.g., in calculating the average mark for the assignment among students who submitted it). For that reason, a convention used in many datasets is to use a specific value (e.g., -99) or symbol (e.g., '.') to designate a missing value and to distinguish it from zero or a cell that is just blank because the real value was subject to a data entry error or accidental deletion.

Exact or inexact duplicates are another possible source of messiness in a dataset. For example, if you've purchased from retailers using multiple e-mails or addresses you may appear to be two people in their dataset. This can also happen if there is any ambiguity about what your first and last names are or if you sometimes abbreviate one or more of your names. My name is Mary Ellen Gordon, but at various points it has been recorded by different organisations as Maryellen Gordon, Mary-ellen Gordon, Mary Gordon, Mary Allan Gordon, Mary Ellen and Ellen Gordon. That can make me appear as two (or more) separate cases in a dataset. The process of removing duplicates is often called de-duping. It's easy when there are exact duplicates in a dataset that shouldn't have them, but it's harder when there are records that are very similar, but not exactly the same. For example, two records for Adam Smith at the same physical addresses but with different e-mail addresses could belong to a father and son living in the same house or to one person with two e-mail addresses.

Another source of dataset messiness is data for the same variable being recorded inconsistently. Going back to the example involving student marks, in a course taught by two different people one person may record raw marks and the other may record the percentage of available marks a student earned for that assignment. Inconsistencies such as this can also arise when things like dates, names, or phone numbers are recorded using inconsistent formats. Data can also be bad because it has been intentionally or unintentionally entered incorrectly or changed accidentally.

How to Identify Missing Values, and What to do About Them

It's common for datasets to have missing values for a variety of reasons. In a small dataset, we can find them by scrolling through and doing a visual inspection. In a larger dataset that's not feasible, but in those situations we can do counts of how many cases have values for a particular variable (this is covered in Chapter 4), and if that is less than the number of cases (or the number of cases that are relevant for a particular piece of analysis) then we know there are missing values. Excel also has a function called countblank that will count empty cells. Just type '=Countblank()' with the range of cells for where you want to count blanks between the parentheses. You will have a chance to practise doing that in subsequent chapters.

For survey data, some software allows questions to be required and it will also record whether a response is complete. If we require all questions to be answered, and we know that the response is complete, then unless there was a problem with the coding of the survey, there should be no missing values. If we require all questions to be answered and a result is incomplete, then we know that all of the missing values are at the end of the survey after the point where the person quit responding.

It's one thing to find missing values, but the next thing we need to do is consider what to do about them once we find them. Probably the easiest way to deal with missing values is to exclude cases that contain missing values if we've got enough cases that don't have any missing values. That makes our life easy, but before we make that decision it's good practice to check to see if there are systematic differences between cases that do and don't have missing values.

We can do that using data we have for both groups. For example, if we have data on the whole population of interest (e.g., all customers, or all employees), we can check to see if the number of missing values varies systematically by demographics as opposed to being random. For example, perhaps there are many more missing values for young people than for older people. When the missing values follow a pattern rather than being random, we need to think much more carefully about whether to exclude cases with missing values. For instance in some situations we may have added a new field to our data at some point in time, and if we exclude all of the cases without a value for that new field we will be excluding all of the cases recorded before that point in time.

Another example would be a situation in which the values are missing because we did a survey and didn't include any response options for a particular question that would be appropriate for people in that particular group. Therefore, if we delete their responses the overall result for that question will be at least misleading because it will appear to cover all possible relevant responses, when in fact it doesn't. It could also create problems for the rest of the survey because we may be reducing or eliminating responses from one specific group. If the characteristic that defines that group is related to other questions in the survey – which is often the case – then the results for those other questions will also be misleading.

If we can't eliminate cases with missing values because there are too many of them, it would leave too few responses to analyse, or doing so would skew the remaining sample, the most simple option is to use the cases for which we have values for each variable needed for analysis even if that means the total number of cases used in our analysis may vary depending on what variables are included in a particular piece of analysis. This means we don't lose any data, but in some situations it can make the results confusing to people because the reported sample size may keep changing.

For example, if we were gathering data from machines and we sometimes have 100 machines contributing data and sometimes 75 and sometimes 50 because not all machines are used at all times, someone looking at the data to answer a question about how many machines are broken or have a certain rate of output is likely to think about those things in terms of percentages, but that will be hard because the denominator will vary depending on exactly what analysis is done. At best, that may not be particularly user-friendly, and at worst it could cause confusion that could undermine confidence in, or understanding of, the data overall.

Another option when we can't remove cases with any missing values is to impute or fill-in the missing values. See the Statistics Explainer that follows to learn more about how that works.

STATISTICS EXPLAINER

Imputation

One way of dealing with missing values is to impute them, or to estimate the missing values from data that we do have. One way to do that without making any assumptions is to replace missing values with the **mean** for the variable for which the value is missing. That won't skew the mean for that variable one way or another, but it's also not particularly precise.

We can try to make imputed values more accurate by estimating them using other known answers. For example, for data about people, we may know the age and gender of a person for whom the value of a particular variable is missing. In that situation, we could replace the missing value with the average value for the variable among people who are the same age and gender.

(Continued)

An alternative approach is to find the missing values in other datasets. For example, if an employee omitted his or her role when filling in a survey, we could fill it in for them using HR records. In that type of situation, the data would be likely to be very accurate, but there are situations in which data from another data source does not exist, it's not possible to match observations across the two datasets, or there is reason to question the accuracy of data being used to fill in the missing values.

How to identify bad data, and what to do about it?

There can be situations in which data for a given observation on a given variable exists, but that data is bad for one of a variety of reasons. Starting with passively collected data, things like machines and sensors can lose power or Internet access, or be poorly calibrated or inconsistently calibrated. If a machine or sensor breaks or loses power or Internet access for an extended period of time, the data will just be missing, but intermittent power, a brief Internet outage, or poor or inconsistent calibration can result in bad data.

One of the first things to check for with any type of data is values that shouldn't exist or are very unlikely. For instance, if we looked at **app analytics** data and saw negative values for the amount of time or money spent by app users it would be a clear indicator there's some sort of problem since negative values should not exist for those variables.

In addition to checking the values for individual variables, we should also check for patterns that are impossible or very unlikely. For example, a machine or a sensor repeating the same value over and over and over may be an unexpected pattern for something like electricity usage at all times throughout a day. When we do observe something that is very unexpected given the nature of the situation, it's important to investigate more closely. In the previous example for instance, we could turn things that use a lot of electricity on or off and observe whether the electricity usage recorded changes as a result.

Judgement from subject-matter experts can be helpful in a situation like this because they may know enough detail about how the data was collected to be aware of a problem or the possibility of one and they also may be able to identify less obvious unusual and unexpected patterns in the data. For instance, in the electricity example, perhaps an engineer who is familiar with the wiring of a building may know that the usage records we are seeing only relate to one part of the building where usage is constant, but not to other parts of the building where electricity usage varies more throughout the day and week.

Actively collected data may also be bad for a variety of reasons. Sometimes the people providing it just don't care enough to provide accurate data. For example, people doing a survey might just fill in random answers as quickly as possible if an incentive is being offered and they are more motivated to get the incentive than to provide accurate data. Similarly, sometimes people are required to collect data from others as part of their jobs, but they are either not aware of why having accurate data about that particular thing is important, or it's not something they personally care about, and so they might not do a very careful job of it.

Even when people have good intentions, they don't always understand exactly what information is being requested, and therefore they answer the question that they think was asked rather than the one that was intended. Other times people don't want to provide the correct information. This can be due to social desirability bias, which is wanting to be perceived positively by the person asking for the information.

Once again, it's also a good idea to check for patterns that shouldn't exist or are very unlikely. So, for instance, if a survey asks a whole series of questions where people rate things on something like a one to five scale, and someone has given exactly the same answer for all of them, that's called **straight-lining** and that type of pattern is considered to be very unlikely. The same is true of patterns that form a perfect diagonal or criss-cross. Impossible or very unlikely patterns in actively collected data can be indicators that people don't understand what is being asked or are not willing or able to provide accurate information.

One indication that someone may have provided bad data in a survey is how long it took them to answer the questions and how that relates to the length of time it took other people to answer them. Unrealistically fast completion times may indicate that the person did not read the questions carefully and answer thoughtfully. It's also useful to check answers to open-ended survey questions (e.g., how could our service have been improved?) and see if they suggest that the person provided a considered response. There can be responses to open-ended questions that are essentially gibberish or something that is not responsive to the particular question asked. In those sort of circumstances, we might question whether the person really understood what they were doing and took it seriously.

What makes this tricky is that very often no one indicator can definitively identify a bad case. In those situations, we can use some sort of points or flags system where we allocate points or flags for different possible issues. So I might give one flag for a fast completion time, another for incomplete or irrelevant answers to open-ended questions, and so on, and then exclude cases that exceed a certain threshold number of those flags or indicators. If you are using a certain number of flags to detect bad cases, you can create a new variable that reports the number of points or flags that somebody has. Then instead of deleting bad cases, you can use that new variable to filter out cases that exceed your threshold. That gives you flexibility in deciding whether or not to include the potentially bad cases, and provides a good reminder of what flags were used in case you need to remember that later.

It also enables you to backtrack easily if needed. For example, maybe two minutes seemed to be an unrealistically fast completion time so you initially thought a case with a shorter completion time was bad, but as you get into your analysis you realise that there was a certain situation in which people were allowed to skip a whole bunch of questions and for people in that circumstance, two minutes may be a reasonable completion time. If that's the case, you could then just remove the flag applied originally and use the case in question.

There are situations in which we may decide to exclude only part of a case – for instance sometimes everything else seems okay, but someone's answer to an open-ended question suggests that they just didn't understand what they were being asked in that particular question. The problem there is the same as for keeping a case and just not using it for analysis involving the variables with missing values. That is that the size of the sample, or sub-group of it, will keep changing across different types of analysis, and that can be confusing for people.

Tips for Getting Your Data into the Format Needed for Analysis and Visualisation

We often need to spend quite a bit of time getting the data into the format that we need it to be in to analyse or visualise it. That's true for people just starting to work with data and for seasoned professionals, but here are some tips for doing it more efficiently and effectively.

1   Any time you're reformatting or reformulating data, it's good practice to work on a copy and leave the original. That enables you to backtrack if you make a mistake or need to reconstruct what you did.
2   Document exactly what you do during the cleaning process. That may be important, but hard to remember in a few days, weeks, or months.
3   Make sure that your **metadata** is correct. Metadata is the data about the data – for example, when and where the data was recorded.
4   Check to make sure your data is structured and formatted the way that it needs to be for the analysis that you plan to do.
5   Check for missing values, and decide how to deal with them on a variable-by-variable basis.
6   Check for bad data, and decide how to deal with that on a variable-by-variable basis.

TYPES OF VARIABLES, AND WHY THIS MATTERS

As mentioned previously, we usually use columns to represent the variables that we're investigating, and we might call them features, attributes, or characteristics instead of variables. There are several generic types of variables, including: **ratio-scaled**, **interval**, **ordinal**, **nominal**, **binary**, and **string**. It's important to understand the differences between them and to know which you have because the type of variable you have influences the type of analysis you can do.

Using the wrong type of analysis for the available variables or using the wrong type of variable for a particular type of analysis are some of the most common problems people have when they start working with data. With modern software, you can often do that and get an answer without the software highlighting any problem, but the answer won't make any sense and there is a risk of trying to interpret numbers that are not meaningful at all for any purpose.

Numeric Variables

The type of variable most people may think of when they think about analytics is numeric, and many analytical techniques require numeric data. There are two forms of numeric data. One of them is ratio-scaled, and the other is interval-scaled.

Ratio-scaled variables are things like money that have a true zero. What I mean by that is that you can have a complete absence of money and that makes things like ratios and fractions meaningful. For example, if you have $200 and spend $100 you have half as much as you did before. Or if you owe £1000 on your credit card and you pay off £500 you only have half as big a negative balance as you did before.

In an interval scale the order is meaningful, as it is for ratio-scaled variables, and the interval is fixed, as it is for ratio-scaled variables, but the zero point is arbitrary. That means that ratios, fractions, and multiplication are not meaningful. Temperature is a good example for illustrating this point. We know that the freezing point in Celsius is zero and we know that the freezing point in Fahrenheit is 32 degrees, so that shows us that the choice of where zero is is arbitrary because it's in a different place in those two different scales but the temperature still feels the same on a chilly morning in Minnesota. We can also see that by multiplying them each by two and finding that would still be zero for Celsius, but 64 for Fahrenheit.

Ordinal Variables

The second major category of variables are ordinal variables. The easiest way to think about ordinal variables is as rankings. They, and other ordinal variables, have an order but not necessarily equal intervals. You can prove this to yourself by thinking about how you would rank your top five favourite books, songs, or TV shows of all time. Those have an order, so you can tell me which is your #1, #2, and so on, but the interval between your #1 and #2 may be different than between your #4 and #5 or my #1 and #2. You may have a clear #1, but your #4 and #5 may be nearly a tie, as my #1 and #2 may be. That shows us that we're working with ordinal data rather than interval data.

A lot of ways of summarising data, such as taking an average, are not appropriate with ordinal data whereas they do work with numeric data. Instead, what we can do is count or calculate the proportion of people who gave a particular thing a particular rank. For example, what percentage of people have a particular TV show in their top 5 or in the #1 slot. We can also compare that proportion or number to those for other groups, other time periods, and so on. For example, what percentage of GenZ have a particular show in their top 5 compared to Millennials, GenX, or Boomers? Or how has the proportion of people who rank a particular song as the greatest of all time changed over time?

There is a situation in which many people treat an ordinal scale as though it's an interval scale. That is the case for **Likert scales**. Even if you haven't heard that name before, you've almost certainly seen many Likert scales because they are very common in surveys. Any time you've answered a question on a survey where you are given response options that range along a continuum – for example, from strongly agree to strongly disagree or from very important to very unimportant – you have been answering on a Likert scale.

The reason that those scales are ordinal is that we can't be sure that the differences between points on the scale are perceived equally even by the same person, let alone by different people. For instance, suppose you were asked how likely you are to recommend the course you are currently taking to a friend on the scale between zero and 10, where 10 means that you definitely would recommend it and zero means that you definitely would not. To be a true interval scale, the way you perceive the distance between a 0 and 1 needs to be exactly the same as your perceived distance between 5 and 6 and your classmate's distance between 8 and 9. Those assumptions are almost certainly untrue, so technically, we should not be doing things such as calculating an average for how likely everyone in your class is to recommend it to their friends.

Nonetheless, Likert scales are often treated as interval scales because it's useful to be able to do things such as calculate averages for variables such as satisfaction or intention to recommend and to compare those averages across groups or over time. That's useful, but if/when we do it, we should focus more on those overall patterns than precise values since we can't be sure the intervals are perceived as equal.

Nominal Variables

It's definitely not correct to calculate averages if your variable is the next type, which is nominal. They are also called categorical variables because an arbitrary value is assigned to a given category. For example, airlines assign numbers to flights flying a specific route at a specific day and time, but the assignment is arbitrary. As long as everyone knows that a particular flight is scheduled to take off in Montreal and land in Vancouver at a particular time on a particular day, it doesn't matter if the number given to that flight is 301 or 103. And while it would be possible to take an average of flight numbers 301, 103, and 311 in any spreadsheet or statistical software package, the resulting number – 238 – does not mean anything. It would also be different if a different number was assigned to a given flight even if the flight was going to the exact same place at the exact same time. When we have nominal data, even ranking isn't appropriate. For example, flight 103 could easily refer to a longer route than flight 311 on many airlines and flight 311 may leave before flight 103. Therefore, the main things we can do with nominal variables are counts and proportions.

Binary Variables

Binary variables are a special form of nominal variables that have only two categories, which are usually coded as one if a particular characteristic is present, and zero if it's not. So for example, we could have a variable that is coded 1 for flights that begin in Montreal and 0 for those that do not. As with other nominal variables, we can summarise binary variables with counts and proportions – for example, the number or proportion of flights that originate in Montreal – but they also have a special role in regression analysis that will be discussed in Chapter 4.

String Variables

The final type of variables are string variables. They are usually represented as text rather than numbers. For example, a string variable may be a Tweet, a response to an open-ended survey question, or a product review on Amazon. As those examples show, in their original form, string variables are quite different from other types of variables, but as we will see in Chapter 4, they can be used to create nominal variables by categorising them. That's useful because then they can be used in subsequent quantitative analysis. For example, we could categorise the Tweets, survey responses, or product reviews as positive, negative, or neutral and then count the number or calculate the proportion that are positive, negative, or neutral.

SUMMARY

The foundation of any business analytics project is ensuring the data being collected and analysed is relevant to the questions that need to be answered to inform decisions. Once data has been collected it needs to be compiled into a dataset for analysis and that process involves checking for missing data, bad data, inconsistently formatted data, and duplicate data.

It's also important to be aware of what types of variables your dataset contains: numeric, ordinal, nominal, binary, or string. The reason that's important is that it influences what types of analysis can be done with your data. With modern software, it's possible to run analysis on data that's not appropriate for that form of analysis or to run it with bad data, but in both of those situations the results will not be useful. Worse, they could be misleading because you will have what appear to be results and may not be aware that they are meaningless.

RUNNING CASE STUDY: 4TE, PART 3[1]

Having spent her first few days of the year trying to get a handle on what data 4tE had, the capabilities of the platforms they were using, and some of the major developments related to data privacy and ethics, Emily was both enthusiastic and daunted. She could see that while they had been busy just trying to ensure 4tE survived the past few years, it had accumulated a lot of data that could now help her and Matt manage 4tE more proactively. She could also see that this was a bigger project than she thought it was going to be when she started it a few days before. Fortunately at one of their family gatherings over the holidays, Emily had been chatting with Matt's cousin Ben, who was in his last year of an analytics degree. Emily remembered Ben saying that his classes didn't start up again until February. She called him, and he agreed to put in a few weeks working with them to get their analytics set up to support 4tE into the future.

The following Monday when Ben started he mentioned that he had learned how important it is to make sure data is in good shape before analysing it. That had been stressed in his classes and he also learned it the hard way when he had to redo a lot of work on one assignment after discovering some bad data when he thought he was almost finished with his analysis. Ben thought the best place to start would be with the customer data from the POS system.

At the time they set up 4tE, most people Matt and Emily knew paid for things using debit cards, credit cards, or app payment systems. Since few people seemed to be paying cash, and dealing with cash seemed like a pain, 4tE had never accepted cash. 4tE also had a loyalty card system in which people who signed up for a card received a $5 credit for every $100 they spent on purchases made using their loyalty card number. Emily had instituted the loyalty card scheme based on her experience in marketing. She thought the credits would be attractive to customers and that linking purchases to loyalty card numbers would enable them to better understand purchase patterns and to offer targeted promotions. While they hadn't had time to do those things yet, she really wanted to get going on them in this new phase of their business.

[1]The 4tE case is fictitious.

Ben found the loyalty card numbers very useful as he started inspecting the customer data. He could use them to aggregate all of the purchases made by each customer, which would be very useful when they started implementing some of Emily's plans. The loyalty card numbers were also the key needed to connect purchase data to customer information provided when people signed up for loyalty cards. That was stored in the **web analytics** software 4tE used, and included things such as customers' names and e-mail addresses. Those could be used to send those targeted promotions Emily had planned. Customers signing up for loyalty cards also answered questions about things such as the number of people living in their household and dietary restrictions and preferences of household members. There were also some questions about how the customer heard about 4tE and how important they believed different factors are in choosing where to buy their groceries.

One of the tasks Ben set for himself was to see if the set of customer numbers in the POS system matched the set from the customer information he extracted from the analytics platform. He found that all of the numbers in the POS system matched to a number in the customer information file, but that there were numbers in the customer information file that never appeared in the POS data. There were also transactions in the POS system with no loyalty card number attached to them.

Ben also checked the customer information file for duplicate e-mail addresses, and found five e-mail addresses that were connected to two different loyalty card numbers and one e-mail address that was connected to three different loyalty card numbers. He noted that down on his growing list of issues to talk over with Emily and Matt.

EXERCISES

Suppose that you are a business analytics consultant, and the institution from which you are taking this course has e-mailed you to ask your advice about the best data source for answering the following questions. Draft a reply recommending what you believe to be the best source of data for answering each question and your rationale for recommending it.

1 What percentage of people who enrol at our institution successfully complete their degrees?
2 Why do some people decide to stop studying at our institution before completing their degrees?
3 On average, how much time does the average student spend each week on each course they are taking?
4 How can we get more students to engage more fully in the courses they are taking?
5 Based on what you've learned about 4tE and its data so far, use Figure 3.2 to consider what data sources are likely to be most useful to it for answering the questions posed in part 1 of the 4tE case.

4
ANALYSIS
FUNDAMENTALS

WHAT WILL YOU LEARN FROM THIS CHAPTER?

- How to quantify qualitative data.
- What analytical techniques to use for answering different types of questions.
- How to implement different analytical techniques in Excel.
- How to use some basic statistical tests in Excel, and when they are necessary.

This chapter provides an overview of some of the most common categories of questions business analytics are used to answer, and the most fundamental approaches to answering them. In doing that, it touches on the basics of statistics, but it does not address more nuanced statistical complexities. Instead it focusses on techniques that are very common and are fairly forgiving, even when strict statistical requirements are not fully satisfied. It is intended to give you enough practical understanding to start analysing data and to provide enough of a conceptual foundation to act as a springboard for deeper learning for those who want that.

HOW TO QUANTIFY QUALITATIVE DATA

Let's start our discussion about analysing data by talking about how to work with qualitative data. That's because while sometimes we work with qualitative data in its original form, often we convert it to quantitative data so it can be used in many of the types of analysis that we'll talk about subsequently, so we first need to understand how to quantify qualitative data.

As discussed previously, we can think of qualitative data as anything that doesn't start out as a number or isn't easily converted to a number. That includes things such as open-ended survey responses and other text-based content, such as documents, news articles, Tweets, and other social media posts. It also includes non-text forms of content, including audio, photos, and video.

There are many situations in which working with qualitative data is advantageous. One of those is when we don't have enough understanding of a situation yet to know what quantitative information to collect and analyse. That is often the reason for open-ended questions on surveys, but it's also sometimes the reason people use other sources of free-text, such as Tweets or other social media posts.

Another advantage of qualitative data is that there are fewer constraints on inputs. Besides text, qualitative data can include things such as images and sounds. That freedom from constraints may enable us to uncover options or perspectives we weren't aware of previously. It also enables people to express things in their own words and that, in turn, can give us a better understanding of what they really mean. It can also be a better indication of what's truly important to people. Last but not least, qualitative data just feels more human to some people and it's a better fit for the preferred communication style of some cultures.

Unfortunately, there is no such thing as a perfect tool, technique, or data type. Everything has advantages and disadvantages. As just discussed, a benefit of qualitative data is having fewer constraints on inputs, but there are also drawbacks to that. It can make the data inconsistent, incomplete, and difficult to consolidate or summarise.

There is subjectivity involved whenever we work with data, but there is arguably more subjectivity involved in working with qualitative data than with quantitative. That's because we are making choices about what to pay attention to, and also how to classify information into categories, and different people may make different choices about those things.

A big difference between quantitative and qualitative data is that it's much easier to scale analysis of quantitative data than qualitative. Within the limits of the computing power of the device we're working on, adding additional quantitative data usually doesn't add much analysis time, but increasing the volume of qualitative data can add a lot of time because at the very least someone needs to review it, and they also often need to classify it. As we'll soon see, computers can help with that job, but at least for the time-being, getting them to do it well typically requires human input too.

There can also be situations in which qualitative data on the topic we're interested in for the population we're interested in is just not available. For example, it's easy to find out what people who are on Twitter and Tweet a lot think about a given topic, but it can be much harder to get the opinions of people who don't provide such convenient access to them or such a clear signal that they have an interest in a particular topic.

As that Twitter example shows, there can be situations in which the people creating qualitative data on a given topic may not be representative of the population of people affected by that topic. For instance, we could use things such as social media posts or articles in traditional media publications as qualitative inputs, but it's likely that opinions expressed by people writing in those places are not representative of the opinions held by people not posting to social media or writing for traditional media.

Most ways of analysing data involve summarising or aggregating the data in some way. When it comes to qualitative data, some of the ways we do that are to summarise the sentiments being expressed. In other words, are the comments generally positive or negative? Are they angry or joyful?

We can also summarise qualitative data according to topic or theme. For example, we could look at the submissions that come to a governmental organisation considering a policy change and see what issues people arguing for or against the changes raise most often. Categories of topics or themes can be determined ahead of time or derived organically from the text.

Another way of summarising qualitative data is according to the source. That could be by the specific creator or some category of creators, such as by role: for example, if an open-ended comment on a survey or a social media post came from a student, a staff member, or an alumnus of an institution. Other source-related data that's sometimes used to classify qualitative data include things such as location or the time when the content was created.

Images, which are another form of qualitative data, tend to be classified based on whether or not they include specific features. For example, we could classify photos in your favourite photo app according to whether or not they show people, animals, food, or scenery. Similarly, we could classify audio data according to things such as whether the audio is speech, music, or a different type of sound or by its pitch or volume.

We typically code all of the different types of qualitative data I've just described using a binary variable that is one if the characteristic is present, and zero if it's not. Sometimes only the ones are recorded and empty cells are left where zeros would otherwise be. That's done to save storage space, but for analytical purposes it's much easier to record the zeros. That also lets us more easily distinguish between missing values and zero values.

So now we know what data we want recorded, but how do we achieve that? There are three main options. One is having humans do all of the coding. There, individual people review the content and assign codes. Ideally three people would review each piece of content and assign codes, and then discrepancies in codes assigned by different people would be discussed and resolved.

Alternatively, we could have machines do the coding. These days, there are sophisticated algorithms that can find patterns even if the data is in the form of text, images, or video. So in that case, the machine would both determine the categories and then assign values to individual observations on those categories.

There are also a variety of ways of getting humans and machines to work together to code the data. Those can range from having the computers search for keywords identified by humans to human-coded data being provided to computers as training data for machine learning algorithms. Humans can also check and refine machine-coded data.

There are a large, and growing, variety of options for technological assistance with coding qualitative data. Excel can do things such as search for keywords and count the number of times they occur (you can do that using the 'CountIf' function which records a 1 if a value or string you have specified appears in another cell that you have specified and a zero if not). There is also software, such is NVivo, that helps track codes assigned by humans. There are a number of free and paid options for software that does more of the classification work, but the paid versions are generally more sophisticated and more trainable. Some of these options integrate with other statistical software, such as SPSS and SAS, whereas others are stand-alone text analytics software. These approaches use a combination of statistics and linguistics to do their classification.

Whether it's done by humans, machines, or a combination, classifying and summarising qualitative data can be hard for a number of reasons. People may disagree both about the overall category structure and how to classify a particular piece of qualitative information. Different conclusions may also be reached by different automated systems, and there is generally no clear test to identify the 'correct' structure or category assignment.

Classification across multiple cultures and languages is especially challenging. Direct translation may not work because cultural differences can give rise to different category structures and different understandings of words.

ANSWERING DIFFERENT TYPES OF QUESTIONS WITH DIFFERENT TYPES OF DATA

'How Many' or 'What Percentage'?

A surprisingly large number of questions organisations want to address with data boil down to counting how many of something there are or calculating what percentage of records have some characteristic. For example, a museum might want to know how many people visited last month, and what proportion of visitors were children. Or a restaurant might want to know how much revenue it took in last month and what proportion of that came from drinks.

One reason for quantifying qualitative data is that it lets us answer these 'how many' and 'what percentage' type questions. For example, a company may want to know how many social media accounts mentioned them in a given week, and what proportion of those mentions were positive. Or a legislative body considering a new law or regulation may want to know how many individuals and organisations made a submission about it and what proportion of those were supportive of the proposed law or regulation. While individual submitters may be making different arguments for or against the proposed legislation, or individual social media posters may be making different points, it's often still very useful to know if a given perspective is widely held or idiosyncratic.

Answering these 'how many' or 'what proportion' type questions involves simple arithmetic rather than any kind of complex maths, and this form of question can be answered with numeric, interval, ordinal, and nominal data as well as qualitative data that has been converted into quantitative data, as described in the previous section. Nonetheless, 'how many' and 'what proportion' type questions can still have challenging twists. Those typically relate to the definition of the thing we're counting or calculating a proportion of.

For example, suppose we are part of a start-up that recently launched a new app. Our investors might want to know how many users we have. We can easily recognise that as a 'how many' type question and know that we just need to count users. That seems simple until we start thinking about exactly what it means to be a user of an app. Does it just mean someone who downloaded it? Do they need to have opened it? Do they need to have had it open for a certain period of time? Do they need to have used it within a given period of time? If I have the app on both my iPad and my iPhone, am I one user (because I am one person) or two (because the app is being used on two devices)? The answer to the question of how many users the app has depends on the answer to all of those questions about what we mean by a user. Changing the answer to any one of the questions about what we mean by a user is likely to result in a different answer to the question of how many users the app has.

Many 'how many' and 'what proportion' type questions have similar definitional challenges as do other types of questions business analytics are used to answer. Coming up with really clear definitions about exactly what we're measuring can seem pedantic, but it's also vital. Without that, we can come up with conflicting answers to the same question or observe something that appears to be a pattern in the data, but is in reality just a reflection of a difference in exactly what was being measured.

Sometimes when we answer a 'how many' or 'what proportion' question, the variable of interest is binary, and there are only two possible things that could have happened. For example, if we wanted to know how many people came to a staff meeting, we could just count the number of people in the room or on the Zoom call. If we wanted to know the proportion of staff that represented, we could then divide that number by the total number of all staff.

Many times though, a variable can have many possible values. For example, we might have a nominal variable representing countries where one number is arbitrarily assigned to each country. In those situations, it can be useful to know how many or what proportion of observations have each value. So in that country example, we would total the number of people that came from each country, or if our question was about proportions, calculate the proportion who do.

We can also consider the proportion of observations that have each value, or group of values, of a **numeric variable**. The result is often referred to as a **frequency distribution**, if shown in table form, or a **histogram** if shown graphically. Examples of these are shown in Figures 4.1 and 4.2 respectively. Those examples show prices of houses sold in the southern suburbs of Wellington, New Zealand in the second half of 2021.

Wellington is New Zealand's capital city and sits at the very bottom of the country's North Island. Because it is almost entirely surrounded by ocean and hills, land is at a premium and during the second half of 2021 house prices were rising rapidly, making it both important and challenging for home buyers, sellers, developers and others to understand the factors that help predict the price a house would sell for. Wellington's South Coast is close to Cook Straight, between New Zealand's North and South Islands, but it is also close to the central business district, which is home to New Zealand's Parliament and many government organisations as well as many private sector businesses.

Distribution of prices for sales of residential housing in southern suburbs of Wellington in the second half of 2021

Price range	Frequency
$ 0 - $100,000	0
$100,001 - $200,000	0
$200,001 - $300,000	1
$300,001 - $400,000	0
$400,001 - $500,000	2
$500,001 - $600,000	2
$600,001 - $700,000	7
$700,001 - $800,000	8
$800,001 - $900,000	10
$900,001 - $1,000,000	12
$1,000,001 - $1,100,000	9
$1,100,001 - $1,200,000	10
$1,200,001 - $1,300,000	11
$1,300,001 - $1,400,000	8
$1,400,001 - $1,500,000	8
$1,500,001 - $1,600,000	2
$1,600,001 - $1,700,000	5
$1,700,001 - $1,800,000	2
$1,800,001 - $1,900,000	2
$1,900,001 - $2,000,000	1
$2,000,001 - $2,100,000	0
$2,100,001 - $2,200,000	1
$2,200,001 - $2,300,000	2
$2,300,001 - $2,400,000	1
$2,400,001 - $2,500,000	0

*Data source: TradeMe Property insights. Data is for all houses in these suburbs for which sales prices were available (which includes most houses sold during this time period).

Figure 4.1 Frequency distribution example

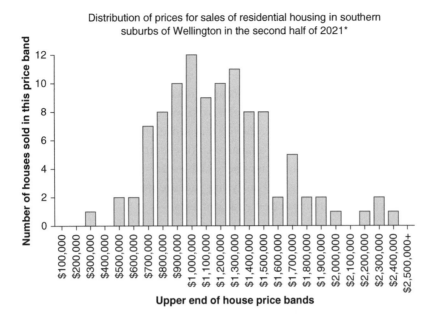

Distribution of prices for sales of residential housing in southern suburbs of Wellington in the second half of 2021*

*Data source: TradeMe Property insights. Data is for all houses in these suburbs for which sales prices were available (which includes most houses sold during this time period).

Figure 4.2 Histogram example

When there are a relatively small number of possible values to show in a frequency distribution or histogram, then each possible value can be shown individually, but when there are a larger number, values are shown in groups, which are sometimes referred to as bins or buckets. The number of bins or buckets shown tends to be a function of the data itself (i.e., how many observations there are and how varied they are) and also the question the data is being used to answer. More bins or buckets tend to be used when more granularity is required due to the nature of the problem, whereas fewer bins tend to be used when all that is needed is a high-level overview.

Looking at a frequency distribution and/or histogram can help us answer a lot of questions. For instance, we can look at those for the examples shown and answer questions about things such as how many houses sold for more than a million dollars or what proportion sold for less than $500,000. That might help an organisation based in that area to know how much its employees would need to be paid to be able to afford to live in the local area, and how much choice they could expect to have in the housing market depending on their salary.

Examining the data this way can also be a helpful transition between data cleaning and more complex forms of analysis. For example, if we saw a lot of houses that appear to have sold for between $100,000 and $200,000, we might realise that's very surprising given local market conditions. A surprising result like that should prompt us to go back and look at our data to see if we made a mistake, such as accidentally omitting a zero. There are some cases where looking at a frequency distribution or histogram may reveal a value or values that are just not possible – for example, a value of 8 on what is supposed to be a 1–5 scale. That is a clear indicator of something like a data entry error, and it's useful to catch those early before we have incorporated an inaccurate data point into other analysis.

Even if all values are accurate, it's useful to know their overall range and shape and if some are surprisingly high or low. Having that sense of our data will help us plan and reality-check more advanced forms of analysis. For example, as discussed in the Statistics Explainer, many forms of analysis assume variables are distributed in a particular way. Also, some ways of aggregating and analysing data are more or less sensitive to extreme observations, which are often referred to as **outliers**.

STATISTICS EXPLAINER

Normal distributions

When we look at the shape of a distribution, we can also consider how close it comes to the classic bell- or normal-curve shape, which is superimposed on the house price data in Figure 4.3. In distributions that follow that shape, many observations are fairly close to the mean, with fewer and fewer the further away we get from the mean.

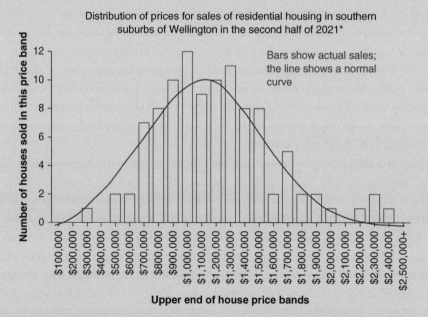

*Data source: TradeMe Property insights. Data is for all houses in these suburbs for which sales prices were available (which includes most houses sold during this time period).

Figure 4.3 Normal curve

Here we can see that the pattern of prices is somewhat bell-like in that it's shorter at the ends and taller toward the middle. It's not perfectly bell-shaped though. For example, we can see that more houses than would be expected based on the bell curve sold for between $800,001 and $900,000 and few sold for between $1,500,001 and $1,600,000.

Having a bell-like, but not perfect, bell shape is very common. Going into the details of the characteristics of normal distributions is beyond the scope of this book (if you want more information, see any introductory statistics book), but for now I just want to mention that we don't tend to see that perfect bell shape unless our sample is reasonably large and the variable that we're looking at is continuous. If a variable is continuous, any value within a given range - including fractions - is possible. Because we don't normally sell a tenth of a house, the distribution in our example would always have a shape that looks more like steps than a smooth curve. The only questions are how big and even the steps are.

Many statistical methods assume a normal distribution, but fortunately, many, including all of those discussed in this book, are pretty forgiving, even if distributions aren't perfectly normal. Nonetheless, it's always worth considering why a distribution might be a bit abnormal. For example, if we restricted our focus to one type of dwelling (e.g., only stand-alone houses, with no apartments, townhouses, or any other type of housing), the distribution of sales would probably come even closer to what would be expected based on a normal curve. If a distribution is very different from the normal distribution, different methods are needed. Those are beyond the scope of this book, but are discussed in detail in many statistics texts.

What's Normal or Typical?

Another common question about data is 'what is normal or typical?'. For example, an emergency department at a hospital might want to know how many patients are normally admitted on Saturday nights to help with staffing, or someone managing a supermarket's supply chain might want to know how many packs of toilet paper are sold in a typical week.

Three common ways of describing what is normal or typical are the mean, **median** and **mode**. Mean is the more formal way of saying average. To get it we add the values for all observations of a variable and divide by the number of observations. The median is the value of a variable that's at the exact midpoint of all observations for that variable sorted from highest to lowest. The mode is the most common value for a variable.

Sometimes, the mean, median, and mode are all very similar, but that's not always the case. For example, the number of patients admitted to a hospital's emergency department on a Saturday night might have been far greater during the height of a Covid outbreak than for most Saturday nights. That could increase the value of the mean a lot because the total for that night would be added to all of the others, nudging up the average. On the other hand, even if the number of patients admitted that Saturday night were far greater than ever before, the median number of patients would barely move. One additional number would be added at the top of the frequency distribution, but it's the values at the middle of the distribution rather than either end that determine the median. The mode would be completely unaffected by that extreme Covid-fuelled Saturday night in the emergency room because it's an outlier, and therefore unusual, while the mode is the most common value.

In situations where there are extreme values, the median tends to be considered the best way to talk about what is normal or typical; however the mean is probably the most common way of talking about that – in part because many forms of analysis incorporate the mean in one way or another. Modes can be useful in some situations, such as when designing or promoting products. In those situations it can be helpful to understand the most common user experience.

How Much Variation is There?

Beyond wanting to know what's normal or typical, we also want to understand the extent to which individual observations vary from what is normal or typical. If we're trying to use information about the normal number of Saturday night admissions to the emergency department to schedule staff or to use information about the number of packs of toilet paper our supermarket sells in a typical week to order from our suppliers, we not only need to know what's normal or typical, but we also need to understand the extent to which we may go over or under that in some weeks so as to ensure we are not short-staffed or faced with empty shelves. On the other hand, we also don't want to be paying many more medical personnel than our emergency department needs or to have so much toilet paper on hand in our supermarket that we run out of space to store it.

We can get a sense of how much variation there is by looking at a histogram. Sometimes we may notice that most observations fall within a very narrow range of values around the mean, whereas other times they may be far more spread out. Two terms that are commonly used to talk about that type of variation more formally are the **variance** and the **standard deviation**. As will be discussed in the next section, Excel and other software can calculate both of these measures for you, but it's useful to have a general understanding of what they tell us.

Variance is calculated by taking the difference between each observation and the mean for that variable, multiplying that difference by itself (squaring it), then adding up all of those squared differences and dividing by the number of observations. Some observations will be larger than the mean (e.g., toilet paper sales at the start of a lockdown period) and others will be smaller (e.g., toilet paper sales once everyone had hoarded toilet paper at home). That means that some differences will be positive and others will be negative, but squaring them makes them all positive so that the positive and negative differences don't cancel each other out.

Because it's squared, the units in which the variance is expressed are hard to understand in relation to the mean, which is where the standard deviation comes in. That's just the square root of the variance. Taking the square root converts the units back to making more sense in relation to the mean. For example, if an emergency room gets an average of 35 patients on a Saturday night, a standard deviation of 2 would tell us that the variation from one Saturday night to another is much less than would be the case if the standard deviation were 5. When a variable is distributed normally (see the Statistics Explainer earlier in this chapter if you want to know more about what that means), about 68% of observations are within one standard deviation above or below the mean, about 95% are within two standard deviations above or below the mean, and nearly all are within three standard deviations. So if the standard deviation in the emergency department example was 2, it would tell us that around 95% of Saturday nights have between 31 patients (35–(2*2)) and 39 patients ((35+(2*2)), whereas if the standard deviation was 5, to make sure we had adequate coverage 95% of the time, we would need to plan for anywhere between 25 patients (35–(2*5)) and 45 patients ((35+(2*5)).

How Does This Compare to That?

Many questions answered using analytics involve looking for differences. Based on what we've covered already, we can start to think more specifically about various types of differences. Many of those related back to things that have already been discussed.

Besides just wanting to know 'how many' or 'what proportion' of something there are, we often want to understand if or how that varies by group. For example, is the number or proportion of men in the class you're taking right now different from the number or proportion of women? In that situation, we are either comparing total counts across groups or comparing proportions across groups. We could also compare the proportion of men and women in your class to the proportion in your university to see if the gender balance in your class is about the same as it is in your university as a whole as opposed to being more skewed towards a particular gender than the rest of your university. When we do that, we're investigating whether one nominal variable is proportionately distributed across another (i.e., if 50% of students at your university are women, is that the same for this class?). Another name for that is a **cross-tab**.

Another common task in analytics is checking to see whether the mean for a variable or variables is similar across groups or not. In that situation, we're still doing a comparison between groups (which comprise a particular nominal variable), but the variable being compared across groups is numeric, which is why we are comparing averages rather than proportions. For example, we might want to compare the average mark or points men in your class earned on the last piece of assessment to the average mark or points earned by women to see if one is greater than the other or they are about the same. We can also compare means for more than two groups – for example, to find out whether the grade point average for students majoring in one subject is greater than others.

We might also be interested in other types of differences between means – in this case the difference between means on two variables (as opposed to two groups). That would help us answer questions such as 'on average, do people in this class get more points or marks on the final than on the mid-term?'. Or in the case of a retail store or fast food outlet, is the average value of orders this year more or less than it was last year? It's easy to get confused between this and the type of difference just described, but the key is that here we are comparing the average *for everyone* between *two different variables*, whereas before we were comparing the average for *different groups* on a single *variable*. Either way though, since we are comparing averages, the variable or variables being compared must be numeric.

Yet another type of difference we could look for involving means is the difference between the mean for a variable and some sort of reference value. This comes up a lot in the context of the environment – for example, whether the amount of carbon dioxide in the air is under a specified limit – but it can also apply in other contexts. For instance, sticking with the example of your class, was the average score on the most recent assessment at least equal to some benchmark score that might be some sort of institutional standard? For this type of comparison, our analysis focusses on just one numeric variable in our data.

Is This Related to That?

In the previous sub-section, the focus was on analysing differences, but another common category of questions in analytics relates to whether one variable is related to others. Another word for this type of relationship is an association.

One of the most simple forms of association is a **correlation**. Again, as will be discussed in the next section of this chapter, Excel and other software can measure correlations for you, but it's important to understand when they are used and what they mean. They're normally used to see whether there is an association between two or more numeric variables (though there is a separate type of correlation focussed on ordinal variables). Correlation coefficients are expressed as values between -1 and 1. A value of 0 means that the two variables are completely unrelated. For example, there is no reason to suspect your grade point average to be related to your height, so we might expect the correlation coefficient measuring the relationship between height and grade point average to be somewhere near zero. On the other hand, we might expect there to be a positive association between the amount of time you spend studying and your grade point average. What we mean by positive association or relationship is that when one variable increases in value, so does the other one. So if people's grade point averages do indeed tend to go up as the amount of time they spend studying goes up, the correlation coefficient measuring that association would be positive, and the more related those two things are the closer the correlation coefficient would be to one.

There are other situations where two variables are highly correlated but the correlation is negative, meaning that as the value of one variable goes up the value of the other goes down. For example, perhaps there is a negative correlation between grade point averages and the average number of minutes each week students spend gaming. If so, the stronger the relationship between those things, the closer the correlation coefficient would be to negative one.

What is Expected or Predicted?

Often we don't just want to know if two or more variables are related, but instead we want to use the value of one or more variables to predict the value of another. One of the most basic techniques for making predictions like that is regression analysis. There are many versions of regression analysis, and other related techniques, but let's focus on the most basic one. With that, we can use one or more numeric variables, supplemented, if we wish, by binary variables, to predict the value of another numeric variable. For example, we might want to predict a student's grade point average based on the number of hours per week they spend studying, the number of hours per week they spend gaming, and perhaps other variables too. Consider what other variables you think might help predict Grade Point Average (GPA).

Using a combination of variables to predict the value of another variable can often lead to a more accurate prediction, and even with just one variable regression analysis gives us the formula we need to generate a prediction for what the value of a dependent variable will be given specific values of the independent variable(s). For example, it would give you an estimate of how your GPA would be expected to change if you spent an additional hour studying every week or spent one less hour gaming. As that example shows, it can be very helpful for 'what if' type examples. For instance, an organisation could estimate the additional sales it could expect if it spent an extra $10,000 on advertising a new product compared to an extra $10,000 on research and development for a new product.

HOW TO IMPLEMENT DIFFERENT ANALYTICAL TECHNIQUES IN EXCEL

'How to' examples in this book focus on Excel. Note that even in Excel things may look different or be in slightly different places depending on your computer's operating system and the version of Excel you are using. If things look different in your version, just try looking around or using the search function. The same features should be available – possibly just in a different place in the menus or ribbons; however, note that the cloud-based versions of

Excel have more limited features than the desktop versions do, so if you're having trouble finding something and are using a cloud version of Excel, try it on a desktop version. Other statistical software, such as R, SPSS and SAS, and general programming software, such as Python, can also do the same things as discussed, but exactly what things are called, and the steps required to find and implement them vary.

Data Analysis Menu

There is an Excel Add-in that does a lot of forms of analysis that previously required special statistical software. If you have a modern version of Excel, it may already be enabled. That is the case if you can see a little icon like the one shown in the top right corner of Figure 4.4 somewhere in Excel, though exactly where that is may vary depending on your version of Excel. Try using Search if you are having trouble finding it. You can also check by going to Tools/Excel Add-ins. Once there, check to be sure Analysis ToolPak is checked. If not, add it.

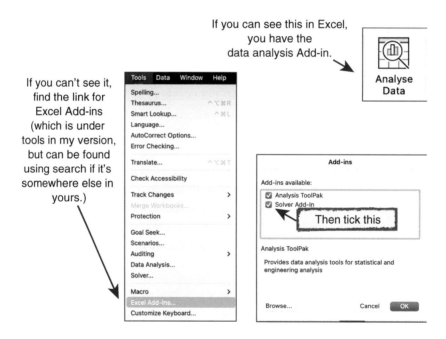

Figure 4.4 Excel data analysis add-in

This add-in does many of the things already described, and more. Let's start with the descriptive statistics option. As shown in Figure 4.5, if you select that option you will be able to input a range where the columns for the variables for which you want descriptive statistics are located. Including the names for those columns and selecting the 'Labels in first row' box will make it easier to keep track of which variable is which if you have more than one. Also tick 'Summary statistics'.

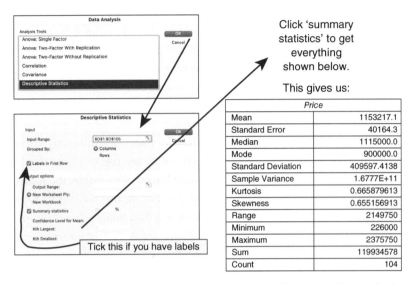

Click 'summary statistics' to get everything shown below.

This gives us:

Price	
Mean	1153217.1
Standard Error	40164.3
Median	1115000.0
Mode	900000.0
Standard Deviation	409597.4138
Sample Variance	1.6777E+11
Kurtosis	0.665879613
Skewness	0.655156913
Range	2149750
Minimum	226000
Maximum	2375750
Sum	119934578
Count	104

*Data source: Trade Me Property insights. Data is for all houses in these suburbs for which sales prices were available (which includes most houses sold during this time period).

Figure 4.5 Descriptive statistics from the data analysis menu

Figure 4.5 shows what happens when you generate summary statistics for the Wellington, New Zealand housing data used to generate Figures 4.1 and 4.2. We get a count of the number of observations, which is good way of checking that all of those that should have been included have been. We can also see the sum of the values of all of those observations for each variable selected. In this example, that is the sum of the prices for all properties sold in the relevant set of suburbs during the relevant time period. We can see the minimum value for that distribution, as well as the maximum and the range (the difference between the minimum and maximum). We can see the standard deviation and the variance, which are the more formalised ways of describing the variability in the variable we are investigating. We can also see the mean, median, and mode; however, note that there may be more than one mode, but descriptive statistics in Excel will only show us one. We can see if there is more than one mode by looking at the frequency distribution or histogram, which we will see how to generate next. Before getting to that though, note that the descriptive statistics option in the data analysis menu also gives you some additional measures, which are beyond the scope of this book, but may be familiar to you if you have taken a statistics course.

There are at least two ways to generate histograms in Excel, but let's start with the one that uses the data analysis menu because that gives us the most control over how the histogram is generated. That's because it allows us to specify what bins or buckets to use. As you may recall, the bins are the groups we want the values for the observations of the variable categorised into. If there are only a small number of them, such as responses on a 1–5 or 1–10 scale, we can just use the individual values. But for something like our house price example, doing that would result in a very large number of rows in the frequency distribution table or a very large number of columns in the histogram, and that would not be very helpful. So in a situation like this, we need to choose how big or small we want those bins, buckets, or categories to be. In the examples in Figures 4.1 and 4.2, they are in increments of $100,000, but that's an arbitrary choice. It could be $50,000 or $250,000. The choice comes down to a combination of the data itself and how we plan to use it, so we may need to experiment with larger and smaller groupings to see what's most useful in a particular situation.

To specify those bins, we create a list somewhere in Excel (it can be anywhere – it does not need to be in the same tab or worksheet as the data we use to create the histogram). The list shows the upper limit of each of our desired bins. For example, the list used to create Figures 4.1 and 4.2 would be $100,000, $200,000, etc. all the way up to $2,500,000, as shown in Figure 4.6. After doing that, we can open the data analysis menu from wherever it is in our version of Excel and click histogram. There are some versions of Excel that may not have that option, and we'll come to an alternative solution for those shortly.

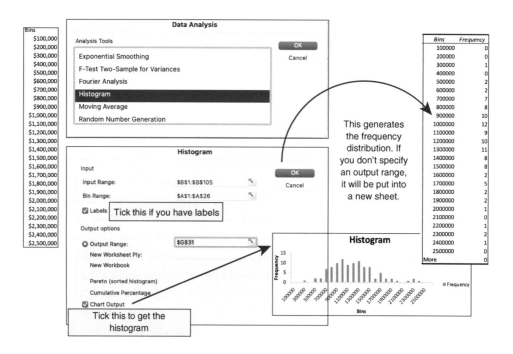

Figure 4.6   Generating a histogram from the data analysis menu

As shown in Figure 4.6, when we click on histogram, we will be asked to enter the input range. That is where the data for the variable that we want a histogram or frequency distribution for is. It will also ask us for the bin range, so we select the list of cells we created for our bins. If we choose labels, both the input data and the bin range need to be labelled. Click chart output to get the graphical histogram rather than just the frequency distribution. You may also indicate where you want the output to go. If you don't, it will be put in a new worksheet. Doing that generates output like that shown to the right of Figure 4.6.

Histograms can also be generated using charts in Excel, so that's the solution for anyone using the cloud version or who, for some other reason, does not see an option for histograms on the data analysis menu in their version of Excel. As shown in Figure 4.7, to generate a histogram using the chart part of the menu, select the data for the variable you want a histogram for, and then click insert/chart/histogram. That's obviously easier than first having to make bins; however, the downside is that when Excel makes bins for you it may not make the same choices about them as you would. In particular, the bins may start or stop in places that are not particularly logical, as the example in Figure 4.7 shows. You can click on the columns in the first histogram it makes and use the 'format data series' screen to make some modifications to the bins. You can only specify the number of bins or the width of the bins, whereas using the data analysis menu you can make the bins be whatever makes the most sense for your data, even if that means having bins of unequal width or that start with a number lower than the lowest value in your data or end with a value higher than the highest value in your data to make the bins start and end with round numbers or to enable the same axis values to be used over time as the data changes.

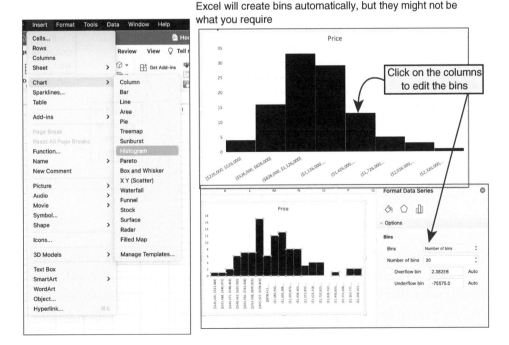

Figure 4.7 Generating a histogram by inserting a chart

More help using the data analysis menu in general is available by going to https://support.microsoft.com/en-us/office/use-the-analysis-toolpak-to-perform-complex-data-analysis-6c67ccf0-f4a9-487c-8dec-bdb5a2cefab6 or searching 'Use the Analysis ToolPak to perform complex data analysis' and clicking on the Microsoft link.

Pivot Tables

Pivot tables in Excel are useful for doing many of the forms of analysis discussed in this chapter. All versions of Excel can do pivot tables, but the exact placement of where they are in the menu structure varies by Excel version and operating system, so yours may not be exactly in the same location as it is in the example in Figure 4.8, and you may need to look around a bit to find the icon. If you can't find it, click help and type in pivot table.

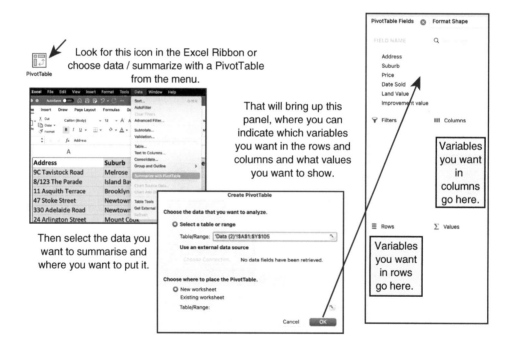

Figure 4.8 Making pivot tables

To make a pivot table, you first need to select the cells with the data for the variables that you want to include. It's helpful to copy just the data you want to work with to a new worksheet before doing this. That will make creating your pivot table simpler because you won't have to keep looking through a long list of variables to find the variables you want to work with.

Besides selecting what data you want to include in the pivot table you need to 'tell' the software where to put the table. The default option is in a new worksheet. Once you've done that and clicked okay, an interactive panel will appear. You can use that to indicate what variables you want in the rows and columns by dragging them into the appropriate position in the panel. You can have more than one variable in the rows or columns and the order will influence how they appear. It's a good idea to draw a prototype of how you want the data to look so you just need to replicate that, but you can also use a trial-and-error approach to structure the data in a way that works well for your purpose.

The values part of the pivot table panel is where you 'tell' Excel what metric you want to show in the cells of your table. By default, it will show the sum of the variable(s) that you pull into that position, but often it's not the sum that you want. For example, Figure 4.9 shows the house price data, and if we use a sum it will show us the sum of the prices of all houses sold in a suburb in the time period covered by the data, but that's not particularly useful for most purposes.

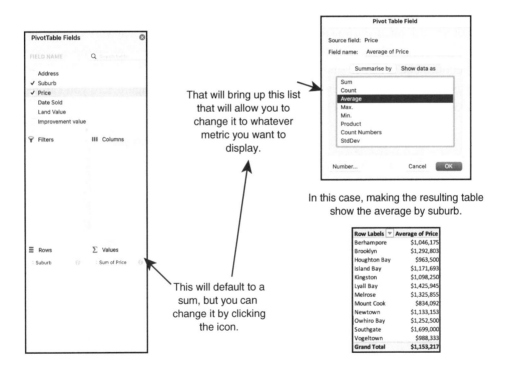

Figure 4.9 Changing the metric shown in pivot tables

By clicking on the icon in the values field (which is an i symbol in Mac versions of Excel, but an arrow in at least some PC versions), we can change to a different metric, including all of those we have discussed so far. In fact, you can drag a variable into that values field more than once to show two or more different metrics for the same variable.

One of the best ways to learn about pivot tables is just to experiment, but Microsoft also has tutorials and templates if you want more help with them. Those are available at: https://support.microsoft.com/en-us/office/excel-video-training-9bc05390-e94c-46af-a5b3-d7c22f6990bb or by searching Excel video training – support Microsoft and clicking on the Microsoft link.

Formulas

Another way of generating the types of metrics discussed in this chapter using Excel is through the use of functions or formulas. Those insert a specific metric, such as an average, into a specific cell of a spreadsheet. That can be useful in situations where that number is then used as part of another calculation or shown in context, such as showing an average changing over time.

There are many formulas in Excel. You can see them by clicking on formulas in the menu or by clicking insert/function (the exact placement of those may vary depending on the menu structure of your version of Excel). When you do either of those things, you will see categories like the ones shown in Figure 4.10. The formulas discussed so far are all in the statistics category (which, in the version of Excel shown in Figure 4.10 you can get to by clicking on 'More functions'), along with many others.

Figure 4.10 Inserting a function or formula in Excel

If you're not sure what you're looking for, you can also click insert/function and that will bring up a search box. That will allow you to type in what you are trying to do and Excel will search for the relevant functions. It also 'tells' you what information is needed for each function and in what format, since that varies a bit for each function. Figure 4.11 shows the formulas for doing the things discussed so far. As shown there, for most of the things that have been discussed so far, you just need to type an equal sign, then the name of the function, then put the range of the cells to which you want to apply the function in parentheses; however, correlation is slightly different. That starts out the same, but within the parentheses you need to separate the ranges of the two variables for which you are checking the correlation.

MEASURE	FUNCTION	FORMULA
Mininum	MIN	=MIN(location of the data)
Maximum	MAX	=MAX(location of the data)
Mean	AVERAGE	=AVERAGE(location of the data)
Median	MEDIAN	=MEDIAN(location of the data)
Mode	MODE	=MODE(location of the data)
Variance	VAR	=VAR(location of the data)
Standard Deviation	STDEV	=STDEV(location of the data)
Correlation	CORREL	=CORREL(location of variable 1,location of variable 2)

Fill in the Excel cell references for your spreadsheet in place of the text shown in blue

Figure 4.11 Commonly used Excel functions

HOW TO USE AND INTERPRET SOME BASIC STATISTICAL TESTS IN EXCEL, AND WHEN THEY ARE RELEVANT

You've probably heard the term 'statistically significant' before. This section discusses what that means, when it's relevant, and how to determine statistical significance for the types of analysis that have been described in this chapter.

What are Statistics?

The different metrics we have been discussing, such as means and standard deviations are examples of statistics. As we've already discovered, they help us synthesise, summarise, and describe data. That's true whether we are working with a population or a sample (see the Statistics Explainer in Chapter 1 if you are not clear on the difference between those), but a lot of statistical theory and a lot of what is covered in many statistics courses focusses on using data from a sample to make inferences or estimates about a population. For example, customs agents at an airport might open and check a sample of bags to find out what percentage contain restricted items that were not declared and were not picked up by x-ray screening, and based on that make an estimate of the total number of restricted items that are being missed by current screening processes. That is useful because in a situation like that it may be expensive or unfeasible to conduct a thorough check of every bag. It's also useful in other situations, such as quality control processes, where testing may damage or destroy something.

When are Statistically Significant Inferences and Differences Relevant?

When we're trying to generalise from a sample to a population, it's important to try to control for the possibility that something may be true of our sample, but not of the population to which we are trying to generalise. Statisticians have developed a variety of procedures and tests for doing that. The general idea is to establish that it's very unlikely that the thing we're observing — whether that's a difference in proportions or some other type of pattern like a correlation or a difference in means – appears to be true based on our sample, but really isn't because we were just unlucky and ended up with a highly unusual sample that's not representative of the broader population. When we talk about something being statistically significant what we really mean is that it has passed those tests. The procedures and tests that apply to the different forms of analysis that have been discussed in this chapter are described in the remainder of this section; however before getting to those procedures and tests it's important to note three things:

1 The statistical tests that will be described are most relevant when working with a sample and trying to generalise to a population. When we are already working with population-level data, as we often are in business analytics, any result that we observe is a 'real' result (assuming we have followed good practice in collecting and analysing the data).

2 Statistical significance is not the same as practical significance. There can be results that are statistically significant, but are still not meaningful or useful for anything an organisation is doing.

3 Much of the theory about statistical significance (particularly in relation to the tests discussed next) is based on the idea of random sampling and each element of the population having a known, non-zero, chance of inclusion in the sample. Those assumptions are easy to meet when it comes to inanimate objects, which were the subject of a lot of the original research establishing tests for statistical significance. Things get much more difficult with humans. It's often hard to know who all of the people in whatever population we are interested in are, and people often have the ability to opt out, so they could have a zero chance of inclusion or their chance of inclusion could be unknown because we don't know the real denominator for our population. That's not to say that these same ideas aren't useful for dealing with

data that has been actively collected from humans, but we need to understand these underlying assumptions because the more we start to deviate away from them, the more we need to avoid getting a false sense of security about how accurate and precise our results really are.

Testing for Statistically Significant Differences in Proportions (Chi-Square Tests)

The test we do to see if a difference in proportions is statistically significant is called a chi-square test. Its basic assumption is that one variable is proportionately distributed across another. That would mean that the two variables are independent of one another. The chi-square test checks to see if the difference in proportions that we see in our real data is different enough from what we would expect if the two variables were completely independent of one another to reject that assumption and conclude that the distributions are not proportionately distributed across each other.

In order to do the chi-square test we need to have matched sets of actual and expected results. For example, suppose I want to find out if the gender proportions for a business analytics class I taught in 2020 was the same as it was for my institution as a whole. I could get the actual counts from student records for my class and use a pivot table to get counts of students in my class who identify as men and women. I could compare that to counts by gender for students enrolled in my university from data that the university submits to the government and then subtract the number of men and women in my class from those totals to find the number of students by gender who were enrolled in the undergraduate programme at my university, but were not in my class. I could also include a count of non-binary students or students who prefer not to state a gender, but since all of the students in my class in 2020 identified as men or women, I am just including those gender identities.

Then I have to calculate the expected numbers for each cell. As shown in Figure 4.12, I do that by dividing the total for the row the cell is in by the total for all rows and then multiplying by the total for the column the cell is in. I could also divide the total for the column the cell is in by the total for all columns and then multiply by the total for the row the cell is in. The answer will be the same either way. So in Figure 4.12, I am dividing the number of women (in my class and not in my class) by the total number of all men and women and then multiplying by the total number of men and women who were in my class. That gives me the number of women who would be expected to be in my class if my class had the same proportion of women as my university as a whole. So here we can see that the expected number of women would be 92 if my class had the same gender distribution as the university as a whole, but the actual number of women in my class was 76. We repeat that same procedure to calculate the values for the other cells.

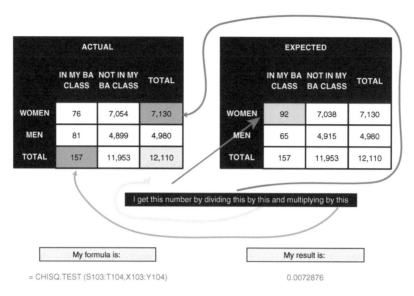

Figure 4.12 Chi-square test example

Just by looking at the cells, we can see that the numbers don't match. There are more men and fewer women in my class than would be the case if my class had the same gender distribution as the university as a whole. In this situation, that's really all we need to do. The reason is that those actual counts were the counts of all of the students in my class in 2020 and all of the students enrolled for undergraduate degrees in my university in 2020. That means I am working with population level data, so those are all of the students.

If, however, those actual numbers represented results for a sample of students rather than the full population, I could go on to use a chi-square test to see if the difference is statistically significant. To do that, I use the chi-square function in Excel, which is =CHISQ. TEST(Range for the actual results, range for the expected results). Note that when you include the ranges for the actual and expected results, you don't include the totals – just the cells that show the counts for the combinations of the variables in rows and columns.

As you can see from Figure 4.12, the result for this example is 0.0072876. That very small number means that there would be a very small chance that the proportion of women in my class appeared in a sample to be this much lower than the proportion of women in the university as a whole if it wasn't really true that the proportion really is lower. Often the default we look for in this type of situation is whether the value is below .05. If it is, we would say the result is statistically significant.

Levels of statistical significance, whether in proportions or anything else, are affected by a number of inter-related things.

One of those is sample size. Generally speaking, the smaller the sample size, the larger a difference needs to be to be statistically significant. For the chi-square test, this also applies to the count of observations within individual cells. The general rule of thumb is to try to have at least five observations per row*column combination, which sometimes may mean combining categories (e.g., creating an 'other' category to group rows or columns with only small numbers of observations in them). This imperative to have at least five observations per row*column combination was the reason for excluding non-binary people from the example.

Another thing that we want to consider are the consequences of being wrong. As previously mentioned, when we test for statistical significance, we often look for a value of less than .05 which means we're willing to live with a chance of being wrong of less than 5% of the times when we do a test like this. In this case, being wrong would mean concluding that my class has a smaller proportion of women than the university as a whole if it really didn't. That threshold for being wrong is an arbitrary choice though, and in some circumstances a 5% chance of being wrong would be unacceptable – for example if it's something like a new drug we may need to insist on a lower chance of being wrong if being wrong means people could experience severe detrimental effects if we conclude it's safe based on data from a sample when it really isn't.

Testing for Statistically Significant Differences Between or Among Groups (ANOVA and Independent or Two-Sample Sample t-Tests)

As with proportions, if we observe that the mean for a particular variable is different for two or more different groups, and we have data for the entire population, there is no need to do a test to see if that difference is statistically significant because we are measuring the population itself rather than generalising from a sample to a population. If; however, we calculated means from a sample and want to generalise to a population, we need to test to see if any difference we observe from the sample is likely to hold for the population as a whole.

If we are comparing means among more than two groups, we need to use ANOVA, which stands for Analysis of Variance. There are multiple forms of ANOVA available in the Data Analysis menu of Excel, but we will just focus on single factor. That allows us to calculate the means for different groups and also to test to see if differences in means across groups within a sample are statistically significant. It does that by taking into account both the mean itself and also the standard deviation. That's because it's less likely that a given difference between means found in a sample will hold for the population as a whole if there is a lot of variability around that mean than when the vast majority of observations within each group are very close to the mean for that group.

Using ANOVA in the Data Analysis menu of Excel almost always requires changing the way your data are structured. That's because it needs data for each group you are comparing to be in its own row or column and for those rows or columns to be adjacent to one another (whereas usually all of the data for one variable would be in one column). The groups don't need to be exactly the same size, and those rows or columns do not need to be the same length as one another. An example is provided in Figure 4.13 for the house price data used in some previous examples, though note that that is population level data so this is a situation in which testing for statistical significance is not necessary.

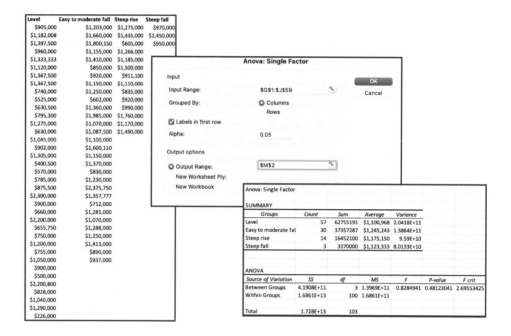

Figure 4.13 ANOVA example

In that example, the goal is to check to see if the average price of houses varies depending on whether the land a house is on is flat or upward or downward sloping. The easiest way to get your data into the required structure is to copy the relevant data into a new worksheet and then sort it according to group – in this case based whether the land is flat, rising, or falling. Once it has been sorted you can copy the variables you want to calculate averages for across the different groups into the required position, as shown.

Once the data are in that structure, we can select Anova: Single Factor from the Data Analysis menu and 'tell' Excel where to find the data. That range may include empty cells since there may be more observations in some groups being compared than in others.

When we do that, we will get output like that shown in Figure 4.13, giving us the count, sum, mean, and variance for each of the groups we are comparing. We can look at that, and see that in that example the average selling prices for houses on all four categories of properties was above 1.1 million; however, somewhat surprisingly, the average sales price was lowest for houses on level ground and highest for those on land with an easy to moderate fall.

In this particular example, we have population-level data (data for all of the houses sold in these suburbs in this time period), therefore those differences are a reflection of sales prices for that area in that time frame. If the prices shown were from only a sample of houses sold rather than all houses sold, we could check the p-value to see if it is less than .05. In this example, it is well above that, meaning that if this had been a sample, we could not be confident that average sales prices really do vary based on land contour as shown (in part because of the amount of variability in prices within each land contour grouping).

If we only wanted to compare averages for two groups – for example, to compare average selling prices just between houses on level ground to those on ground with an easy to moderate fall – we could use a two-sample or independent sample t-test. Figure 4.14 shows the results for that example, and how they were generated in Excel. That was with what's called the two-sample t-test assuming unequal variances. As you will see, there are multiple versions of t-tests in Excel. In this case, we are using two-sample because we are comparing two groups, and we know from the ANOVA example that the variances are unequal. With real-world data unequal variances are much more common than equal variances anyway, so if in doubt, use this option, but you can also use Excel to test to see whether the variances are or are not equal.

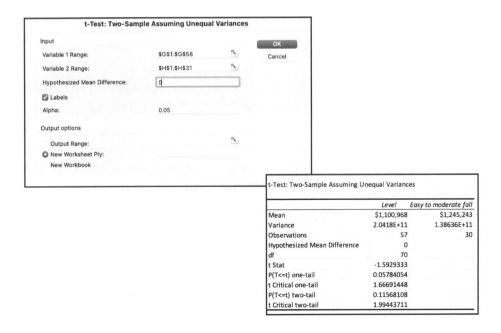

Figure 4.14   Two sample t-test example

When you open the menu for that test, you will see that you need to input the ranges for the two groups you are comparing. Those do not need to be in adjacent locations. We also need to enter the hypothesised mean difference. That's often zero, which means we are testing the assumption that there is no difference between the mean for the two groups. There may be situations in which we want to change that. For example, some houses on hills in the suburbs where this data comes from have views out to the sea, so perhaps historically they have sold for a premium compared to houses on level ground, which tend to have less scenic views. If that's the case, we might want to test the assumption that the difference between the means is some value other than zero, such as $100,000 or $200,000.

The means and variances calculated using a two-sample t-test are exactly the same as they were for ANOVA, as they should be. They would also be the same if we had calculated them with a formula or pivot table. But we can also see that the statistical output we get is different. In this case, that is not particularly relevant since we have population-level data rather than sample data.

If we were working with sample-level data and wanted to know if the difference we observe between these means is likely to hold for the population as a whole we would again look at the p-value, but what we would notice is that there are two of them. With a one-tail test, we go in with a clear idea of which group we think will have a greater mean, whereas with a two tail test we are just looking for any difference with no prior expectation about which way around it will go. We can see from the output in Figure 4.14 that while neither p-value is less than .05, the one for the one-tail test is close – in part because now we are just testing the difference between the two most extreme average values, which also represent the largest groups.

Testing for Statistically Significant Differences in Means Between Variables (Paired Sample t-Tests)

As discussed previously, sometimes rather than comparing averages across groups within variables we want to compare them across variables. For that, we need a paired sample t-test. For instance, Figure 4.15 shows an example comparing the mean for the price a house sold for to its rateable value in the Wellington house price data we have been examining. The rateable value is the estimated value of the house used by local government for tax purposes, so what we are investigating here is whether, on average, that value is the same as the prices houses are really selling for.

This works in a very similar way to the (non-paired) two-sample t-test in Excel. We select the data that we want to compare (in this case for two different variables rather than two different groups). We can also specify whether we expect the difference to be zero or something else. For example, in Wellington rateable values are only updated every three years, so toward the end of that period we may want to check to see whether

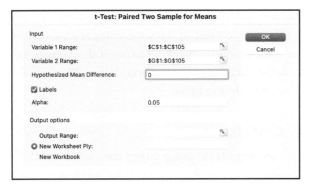

t-Test: Paired Two Sample for Means

		Price		Rateable value
Mean	$	1,153,217	$	1,151,538
Variance		1.6777E+11		1.46448E+11
Observations		104		104
Pearson Correlation		0.970590068		
Hypothesized Mean Difference		0		
df		103		
t Stat		0.171668208		
P(T<=t) one-tail		0.432017602		
t Critical one-tail		1.659782273		
P(T<=t) two-tail		0.864035205		
t Critical two-tail		1.983264145		

Figure 4.15   Paired sample t-test example

average prices are over rateable values by a certain amount. Once again, we can see both one- and two-tail results and choose which one to review based on whether or not we have a pre-determined expectation about whether one mean will be greater than the other by more than the difference specified. In this case, both p-values are well above .05, which would lead us to conclude that if these had come from a sample rather than the whole population we could not be sure that the difference we see between the two means would hold for the population as a whole. Even with these averages coming from a population rather than a sample, we can see that the absolute difference between them is quite small.

Testing for Statistically Significant Differences Between a Mean and a Benchmark Value (One Sample t-Test)

If we want to compare the mean from a sample to a single specific value, we do that using a one-sample t-test. The Data Analysis menu in Excel does not offer a specific option for doing this (some statistical software does), but it is possible to do using a small hack of the two-sample t-test in Excel. All we need to do is perform that as described previously in this section, but make all of the values of the second group just duplications of the test value. It doesn't matter how many there are, and the interpretation is exactly as described for the two-sample t-test. If we were comparing data from a population to a single specific value – for example, checking to see if the average house price in the suburbs we have been investigating is over a million dollars, then we would just look at the difference and not need to do the t-test.

Correlation

We can check to see if two variables are correlated using either correlation in the Data Analysis menu or the CORREL function. If we do it from the Data Analysis menu, the data need to be contiguous because, as shown in Figure 4.16, there is only one box for the input range. The correlation coefficient will be in the off-diagonal cell of the output. In this example, correlating land value and improvement value (the value of the land a house sits on and the value of the house and any other structures respectively), that's positive, but much closer to zero than to one. So that tells us that the correlation between the value of a house and the land the house sits on is very weak, meaning that at least in these suburbs in this time period, there may be expensive houses on small plots of land and small houses on properties that are large or desirable for other reasons, such as their view.

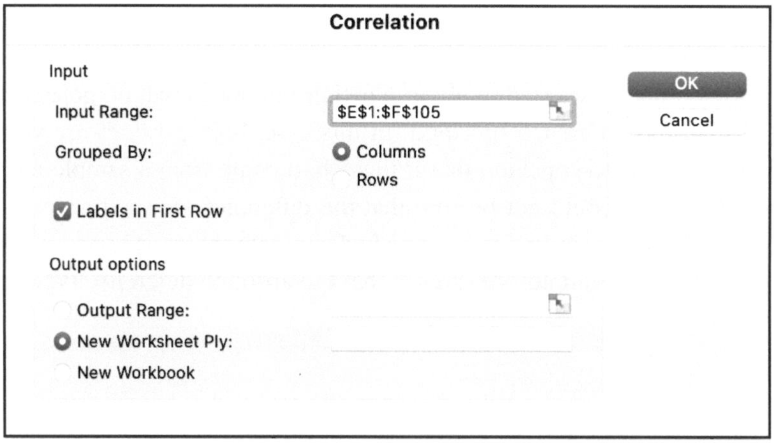

	Land Value	Improvement value
Land Value	1	
Improvement value	0.064497398	1

Figure 4.16 Correlation example

Regression

We've already discussed how correlations can tell us which variables are related to one another. Regression is another way of measuring associations and it builds on the idea of correlations, but offers some advantages that we don't get with just correlations. Regression allows us to make a prediction for the value of a variable based on the values of multiple other variables rather than just one. Prediction is one of the most common objectives of data projects, making regression and related techniques very useful.

The terminology for what we are trying to predict and the data we use to do that vary. Those coming from a statistical perspective tend to think of the thing that we are trying to predict as the dependent variable and the variables that we are using to make the prediction as independent variables. People coming from a machine learning perspective tend to talk about the thing being predicted as the target and the things used to make the prediction as attributes or features. Another way of thinking about these things is as inputs and outputs, with the output being the thing we are trying to predict and the inputs being the things we use to make the prediction.

One of the most common uses of prediction in business analytics is for forecasting — often of sales, but also of other things, such as the weather or share/stock prices. Predictions are also used to estimate when machinery will fail or malfunction so maintenance can be done before that happens, but not unnecessarily early. Predictions are also used to model disease risk. We saw examples of many countries using those types of predictions to make decisions about Covid-related restrictions.

To see how this works, let's go back to our house price example. Suppose a developer wanted to buy land in Wellington's southern suburbs to build houses on, and was trying to decide what type of land to buy in that area and what type(s) of housing to build to generate the greatest profit from selling finished housing units on that land.

Since sales price is what we're trying to predict, that is the dependent variable. While there are many forms of regression, in the most common form, which is called ordinary least squares, the dependent variable has to be numeric. Essentially what we are trying to do with regression – including in this example – is explain the variability in the dependent variable to understand it and/or make future predictions.

We've already seen the variability of house prices that we are trying to explain in this example in Figure 4.2. From that, we saw that in the second half of 2021, houses in Wellington's southern suburbs sold for as little as between $200,000 and $300,000 and as much as between $2.3 and $2.4 million, with most selling for somewhere between $600,000 and $1.5 million. That's a wide range, and whether you are a developer, a landlord, or a potential home-owner, it would be helpful to have a more precise estimate of how much a specific house is likely to sell for.

The things we think will help us predict house prices are the independent variables.

Those that are already in numeric format can be used directly. Nominal, ordinal, and string variables would need to be transformed into binary form to use. Another name for those in this context is **dummy variables**. They are coded as 1 if a characteristic is present, and 0 if not. For example, with the house price data we could create a new variable coded as 1 if a house has a sea view and zero if not. Or we could create another variable coded as 1 if the house looks out onto bush and zero if not. We use regression to figure out which of the potential independent variables are useful in predicting home prices and which are not.

There is a regression option in the Data Analysis menu in Excel. Once you click it, enter the location of the data for your dependent variable where it asks for the y range and enter the data for the independent variables in the x range. For now, we are just going to use one independent variable, but when we move on to using more, they will need to be in adjacent columns, so this is another one of those times when it can be useful to copy your data to a new worksheet before you start your analysis. Click the labels box so you can keep track of which variable is which.

Figure 4.17 shows regression results using sales price as the dependent variable and the number of bedrooms as the independent variable. One of the first things people tend to look at in results of regression analysis is the R-square (R^2). This will be a number between 0 and 1 that can be interpreted as the percentage of variability in the dependent variable that can be explained by the independent variables collectively. So in this case, about a third of variability in house prices can be explained just by knowing how many bedrooms a house has.

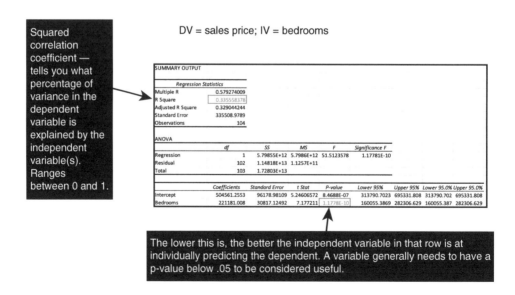

Figure 4.17   Regression example with one independent variable

Another thing that we can look at is the significance of the F statistic. The F statistic tells us the statistical significance for the model as a whole if the data for it came from a sample rather than a population. As usual, when looking at significance results, lower p-values are better. While it may not look like it initially, this number is very small. That E-10 at the end of the value is scientific notation, meaning that there is a decimal point, then nine zeros (one less than the number after the minus sign), then the number before the minus sign. So in this case, that makes it well under the 'less than .05' level that we often default to. This tells us that even though explaining about a third of variability doesn't sound like a lot, knowing the number of bedrooms gives us a far better estimate of the price a house will sell for than we would have without knowing that.

We can also look at the p-value for each independent variable. In this case, there is only one, so the p-value for it is exactly the same as it is for the F statistic, but, as we will see, these p-values for individual coefficients become important when we have multiple independent variables.

Figure 4.18 shows how we can use the output we just saw to make a prediction for the price of a house with a given number of bedrooms. All we need to do is multiply the coefficients in the first column after the labels by the values for the thing we are trying to generate a prediction for: in this case a house with two bedrooms.

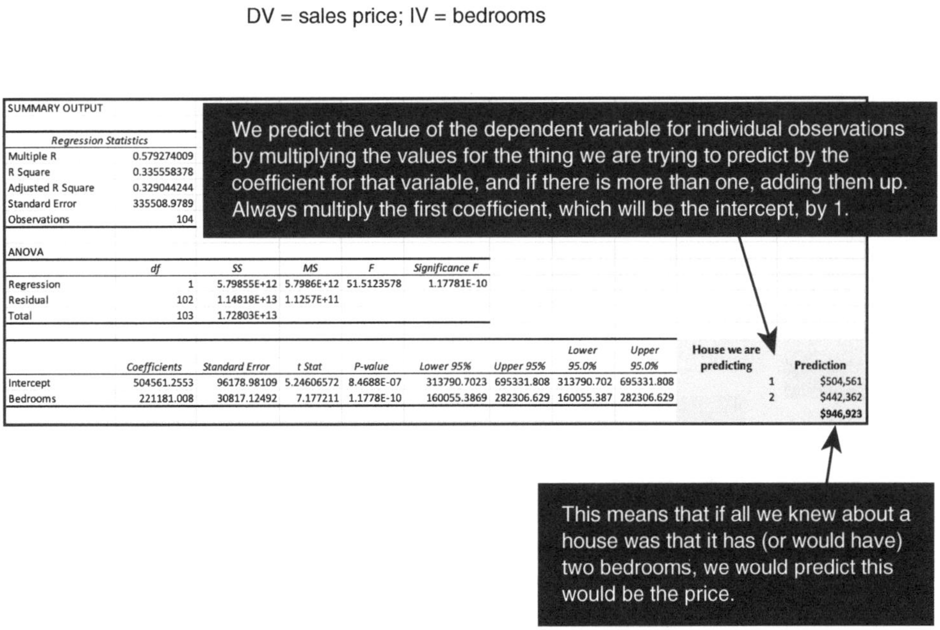

DV = sales price; IV = bedrooms

Figure 4.18   Generating a prediction with one independent variable

The first coefficient is the intercept. We won't go into detail about exactly what that is other than to say we always multiply it by one in generating our prediction. Then the next coefficient is for the first independent variable, which in this case is the number of bedrooms the house has. If I want to estimate the price of a two-bedroom house, I multiply the coefficient for bedrooms by two. You can see that value in the last column shown here. Then I just add those numbers in the last column together to get an estimate of just under $947,000 for a two-bedroom house in Wellington's southern suburbs in the second half of 2021.

Now, instead of just using the number of bedrooms to predict the price a house will sell for, let's add a number of other variables: the number of bathrooms, the floor area, the land area, the number of garage parking spots, and the number of off-street parking spots. As you may recall, with a single variable we could explain about a third of the variability in house prices, but we can see by looking at Figure 4.19, adding those other variables resulted in a big improvement in the amount of variability in house prices that we can explain, with that growing to nearly 60%. Given that, we shouldn't be surprised to see a very small number, representing very great significance, for the F statistic's p-value.

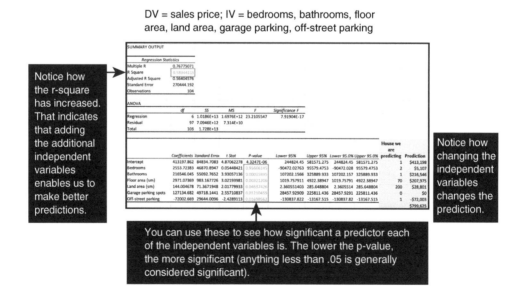

Figure 4.19 Generating a prediction with six independent variables

But what's more interesting, now that we have more variables, is to look at the p-values for the individual coefficients. As usual, smaller values mean that a coefficient is more significant, and we often use a default cut-off of .05 to say that everything below that is significant and anything at that level or above is not. Using that criterion, the coefficients for all of the independent variables are statistically significant except one. Somewhat surprisingly, that is for bedrooms which was significant when just tested on its own.

The reason it's not in this situation is that the variability it was explaining on its own is now being captured by the other variables. What I mean by that is that the number of bedrooms a house has tends to be related to the floor area of the house in particular, and to a lesser extent other things such as the number of bathrooms a house has. For example, it would be very uncommon to find a house with only one bedroom but a very large floor area or a house with a very small floor area and five bedrooms. Similarly, it would be very unusual to find a house with two bedrooms and five bathrooms.

Even with this greater number of independent variables, we use the exact same method to make a prediction as we did with one variable. We multiply the coefficient for the intercept by one, multiply each of the other coefficients by the value of the type of house we want to make a prediction for, and then add up all of those values we calculated. So, for example, if the developer in our example were trying to figure out how much smaller houses in Wellington's southern suburbs might sell for, we could input the values for a 70 square metre house that would have two bedrooms, one bathroom, no garage, but off-street parking on a 200 square metre section, we would estimate the house would sell for just under $800,000, as shown in Figure 4.19. Note that there is a reasonably large difference between this and our estimate based on the number of bedrooms alone, and based on the R-square this is likely to be the more accurate estimate.

Sometimes the variables we want to include are nominal or categorical variables, but it's important to keep in mind that we can't use those in regression analysis unless or until they are in binary or dummy form. That means they are coded as one if the characteristic is present and zero if it is not. For example, we could create dummy variables for particular suburbs by coding an observation as one if the house it represents is in the particular suburb and zero if it's not. For reasons that are beyond the scope of this book, the most we can include in the regression is one less than the total number of suburbs. The same one less than the total number of categories rule is true for any other nominal variable representing mutually exclusive categories. An easy way to create these dummy variables in Excel is to create a new column for each new variable and use the 'CountIf' function to fill in a one if that row has the characteristic (in this case whether the house is in the specified suburb) or zero if not.

For example, a developer considering building new houses in Island Bay might want to understand if locating them in that suburb, which is at one end of a proposed rapid transit system, could be expected to result in prices that are higher or lower than in the surrounding suburbs. As you can see from Figure 4.20, adding a variable to indicate whether or not a home is in Island Bay makes very little difference in our ability to accurately predict how much a house in Wellington's southern suburbs will sell for. We can see that based on the very small difference in R-square compared to what it was without the variable representing whether a house is in Island Bay and also based on the fact that the coefficient for the variable indicating whether a house in Island Bay is well above the .05 threshold.

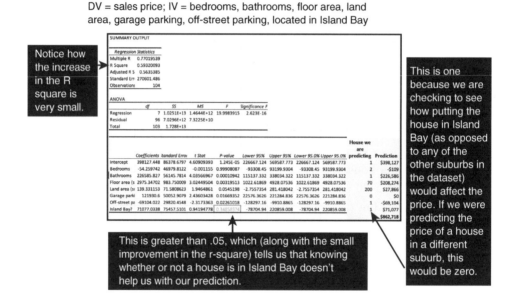

Figure 4.20 Generating a prediction when a binary variable is included

When we have this type of dummy variable and want to generate a prediction for a new observation, we do everything as we did before, but multiply the coefficient for the dummy variable by one if we want to make a prediction for an observation that has that characteristic and zero if not. So in this example, we would multiply by one to make a prediction for a house that is in Island Bay and zero if we wanted to make a prediction for a house that is in a different one of the southern suburbs.

That prediction we just made comes in between the previous two. Figure 4.21 shows how even though our predictions have bounced around a bit depending on exactly which independent variable we use to make the prediction, that bouncing around is still within a fairly narrow band of the overall range of prices for houses in Wellington's southern suburbs.

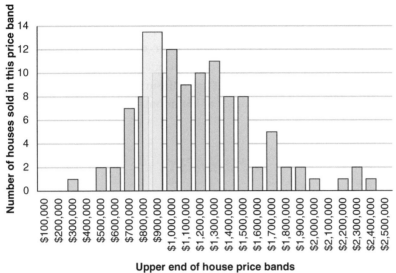

Figure 4.21 How regression helps narrow an estimate

So even though the best we can do is explain just short of 60% of variability in house prices with the variables we have tried so far, that still enables us to make much more accurate predictions than we could without considering those explanatory variables.

There are many different forms of regression that differ in their specifics, but they and other related techniques all predict future outcomes based on historical data. That's fine if and when the underlying conditions are fairly stable, but may result in poor predictions when the underlying conditions have changed.

Some changes to underlying conditions may result in changes to the value of specific independent variables as predictors. For example, if there was a large shift to people using active and public transport, the predictive value of parking spaces in garages and off the street might diminish over time.

In other cases, the same set of predictors may still be useful, but differences in their relative importance may make their coefficients change. For example, as more people started working from home in response to the pandemic, the value of having additional bedrooms to use as offices may have increased, and if that was the case it would appear in our data as a larger coefficient for bedrooms.

If underlying conditions have changed, it's also possible that the collective predictive power of the independent variables could diminish. One reason that can happen is if a variable that has not been included in the model increases in importance as a predictor. For example, insurance companies are starting to increase prices for insuring coastal properties or refusing to insure them at all because of expectations of increases in claims due to sea level rise and more frequent and extreme storms. If many houses on Wellington's south coast suddenly became much more expensive to insure or can't be insured at all, that would almost certainly affect their prices, with insurable houses being likely to sell for a lot more than houses that are uninsurable, even if they are the exact same size and have the exact same number of bathrooms and parking spaces.

SUMMARY

We covered a lot of different analytical approaches in this chapter, so Figure 4.22 provides a summary of which techniques are suited to which questions and data types.

QUESTION	ANALYSIS	DATA
How many	frequencies / counts	All
What is normal / typical	mean, median, mode	Numeric
How varied is ...	standard deviation (and variance)	Numeric
How does this compare to that?	compare means or proportions	• Any (for comparing proportions • Numeric (for comparing means)
Are these variables related to one another?	correlations	Numeric
Do these variables influence / explain / predict that one?	regression	Numeric (plus nominal converted to dummy / binary independent variables)

Figure 4.22   Summary of which types of questions use which types of analysis and data

We've covered which analytical techniques can be useful for answering which types of questions, but in all of those cases it's important to pay attention to details. We need to make sure that the data that we're using exactly matches the way the question was asked, so it's important to pay attention to things like definitions to make sure we've got exactly the right variable and not a somewhat similar variable, but not quite the right one.

We also need to pay attention to things like timeframes. Sometimes questions are framed in such a way that we really need to get data from a particular time period because of the nature of the problem. For example, in early 2022 there was a downturn in the Wellington housing market, so using data from 2021 to predict the price of a house in 2022 would have resulted in a much less accurate prediction than it would have in 2021.

We might also need to pay close attention to geographical locations. For instance, we could not draw conclusions about house prices in other parts of the world, other parts of

New Zealand, or even other parts of Wellington from the data we worked with for many examples from Wellington's southern suburbs.

Details like those can make the difference between the data we have really doing a good job of answering a particular question versus not being useful at all.

RUNNING CASE STUDY: 4TE, PART 4[1]

Once he was satisfied that 4tE's data was as clean and well-structured as he could make it, Ben was excited to use some of the skills he had been developing in his degree to analyse it. He thought he would start with the customer-oriented data since he knew that Emily and Matt wanted to get a clear picture of their current customer base before making decisions about things such as possibly expanding their product offerings, opening a new store, or expanding the delivery area for online orders.

Ben had used the portal for the POS system to calculate sales by loyalty card number by year and appended the results to the customer data pulled from the web analytics portal. To start to build a picture of the 4tE customer base he calculated how many loyalty card customers had spent anything in 2020, 2021, and 2022. He also calculated the average amount active customers spent in each of those years.

The next thing Ben checked was the proportion of customers who made purchases in one year, but did not make a purchase in the next. He knew that would be the case for some customers. Some people might have moved out of the area, and a small number of customers could have died, but he wanted to make sure the percentage was not high enough to signal dissatisfaction. He thought the amount spent would be another indicator of how satisfied 4tE customers were, on average, so Ben then checked to see if the average amount individual customers were spending was changing over time. To round out his picture of spending patterns, Ben calculated the average number of transactions per year by customer.

To summarise information about the demographics of 4tE customers, Ben calculated the average number of people living in their households, the proportion in different age brackets and gender categories, and the proportion with different dietary preferences. He also explored their answers to the questions about grocery shopping collected when they signed up for loyalty cards.

It seemed likely that the amount customers spent, and their answers to the questions about things such as dietary preferences and grocery shopping attitudes may vary by age bracket or number of people in the household, so he also checked to see if that was the case.

Regression was one of the things Ben found most interesting in his classes, so he also built a regression model to see if he could predict the amount of money customers spent in a year based on the number of transactions they made and the number of people living in their household.

---

[1]The 4tE case is fictitious.

EXERCISES

1   Check to see if the proportion of men and women in your class is similar to the proportion for your institution as a whole. You may be able to count the number of men and women in your class, but if not you could ask your instructor for those numbers. Then find the number of men and women enrolled in your institution. This information is often available on the web, but if not your instructor may have it. See what you learn by comparing those proportions.

2   Check to see if the proportion of men and women in your institution is similar to the proportion for both genders in the same age bracket in the area where your institution is located. You should be able to get the number of men and women in the relevant age bracket for your local area by searching online for census information. See what you learn by comparing those proportions.

3   Find house price data for 50 houses that have recently sold in your local area similar to that shown in this chapter for Wellington New Zealand. That type of information is often available from local authorities as well as through sites such as Zillow.com, Redfin.com, Zoopla.co.uk, Honestdoor.com, propertyvalue.com.au, homes.co.nz. Once you have that information, make a histogram to show the distribution of sale prices. Then use any of the methods described in this chapter to:

   i   Calculate the mean selling price.
   ii   Calculate the median selling price.
   iii Calculate the standard deviation in selling prices.

   Based on all of that information, what could you tell someone who just moved to your local area and wanted to buy a house about what they should be prepared to pay?

4   Use the data described in the previous question to create a regression to generate an even more precise estimate of what the person who is new to your area should be prepared to pay for a house.

   i   What variables did you use as independent or predictor variables?
   ii   How much of the variability in house prices was explained by your predictor variable(s)?
   iii Make a prediction for how much your new acquaintance is likely to pay for a house in your local area that meets their requirements in terms of bedrooms, bathrooms, etc. (which you can make up for your fictitious new friend).

5
COMMUNICATING ANALYTICAL RESULTS

WHAT WILL YOU LEARN FROM THIS CHAPTER?

- How to tailor the way you communicate analytical results to the audience with whom you are communicating.
- How to tailor the way you communicate analytical results according to the specific objectives of the project you're working on.
- General data visualisation principles.
- Which common forms of data visualisation are best suited to different types of data, audiences, and objectives.
- How to make data communication more interesting and engaging.
- How to assemble a collection of results from data into an accurate, insightful, coherent and actionable narrative.

KNOW YOUR AUDIENCE

It's easy to think of data as being definitive, and therefore to believe that the way you communicate analytical results should be the same regardless of your audience; however, as you will learn in this chapter, communicating data-oriented results effectively means tailoring them to the intended audience. That's because different people come to the results with different levels of familiarity with, interest in, and assumptions about the domain to which they apply. It's also because different audiences have different data-related knowledge, experience, and expectations.

What Does Your Audience Know and Think About the Domain?

As you think about your audience, first consider what your audience knows and thinks about the domain to which your results apply. The domain might be a business, an industry, an ecosystem, a specialised area of healthcare, laws or regulations pertaining to a specific type of activity, or really any subject area. Domain knowledge can vary between experts and lay people and between people who are new to an organisation and those who have been with an organisation for decades. For example, consider the difference between presenting climate-related data to an audience of climate scientists versus to the general public. The climate scientists would have extensive background knowledge about things such as where and how much climate change has already occurred, factors that influence the rate of climate change, and how climate change is expected to unfold in the future under different scenarios. All of that would mean that you could get into the specifics of your analysis without providing a lot of background information. On the other hand, if you were presenting the same analysis to members of the general public, you might need to provide a lot more background about what specific terms mean, why they are important, and how they relate to how those people may experience climate change.

Similarly, in other professional contexts, people who have worked in a particular field for a long time have shared understandings of things, such as common problems and industry-specific terminology and acronyms, and may feel annoyed or patronised if those things are explained to them before getting to analytical results. On the other hand, those who are new to a field may not understand the analytical results unless those contextual and definitional issues are explained in advance.

People who work in a given domain also typically have assumptions about how things work. For example, a car sales person will have assumptions about what types of people buy what types of cars and a doctor will have assumptions of what types of patients will respond best to treatment. Assumptions often drive people's decision-making even if they're not aware of it. Often data supports decision-makers' assumptions, but sometimes it doesn't. People's assumptions tend to be grounded in their own experiences, but are subject to biases and to limitations in the number of experiences any one person can have of a broader phenomenon. There are also situations in which people's assumptions are correct as they relate to things that have happened in the past or in specific contexts, but not correct as they relate to the current time or to other contexts. As will be discussed further later in the chapter, it's important to understand whether the results you will be presenting affirm, refute, or are unrelated to assumptions held by your target audience because that needs to be taken into account when thinking about how best to communicate your results. In order to tailor the presentation of the results based on the assumptions of the target audience, you first need to know what those assumptions are.

What Does Your Audience Know and Think About Data?

Just as it's important to ground communication of analytical results in an understanding of what your audience knows and thinks about the domain to which they apply, it's also important to tailor them based on what the audience knows and thinks about data. That includes their baseline knowledge of statistics and other quantitative methods and their level of understanding of how specific metrics are defined and calculated.

An audience's baseline knowledge of statistics and other quantitative methods needs to be considered when deciding whether results should be presented in a way that includes a lot of statistical detail or perhaps using visualisations that faithfully represent statistical findings, but include no actual statistics. It also needs to be considered when deciding whether to build up results gradually or to present them in a consolidated form that packs a lot of information into a single chart or table.

To illustrate those points, suppose that we were presenting the results of the regression analysis shown in Figure 4.20 to two different audiences: a property developer planning what types of housing would be most profitable for them to build in Wellington's southern suburbs and an academic economist studying housing affordability. Most academics have some understanding of quantitative methods and economists in particular are typically trained in econometrics, which involves applying statistical techniques, including various forms of regression analysis, to economic data. On the other hand, while property developers deal with financial data and with data related to construction, we probably can't assume that they have been exposed to, and remember the details of, regression analysis.

Because of those differences between property developers and academic economists just described, we would not want to communicate our results to the two groups in the same way. The data could be communicated to the academic economists in more or less the same format shown in the main table in Figure 4.20 without any annotation because people in that target audience have the background needed to understand all of that and would want to see at least most of that detail. If, on the other hand, we used that format to communicate the results to property developers, many people in that target audience would not understand it at all. For them, we might want to take the results of our analysis and convert them into a more intuitive graphical format, and to take a more staged approach to describing them.

For example, from the regression results shown in Figure 4.20, we know that the price a house sells for is associated with both the number of bedrooms it has and its total floor area. So when presenting the data to developers, we might want to start by showing them Figure 5.1, which just shows the average price based on the number of bedrooms in the house. From that, even without knowing anything about regression analysis, it's easy to understand that at least on average, the more bedrooms a house has, the greater the price it sells for.

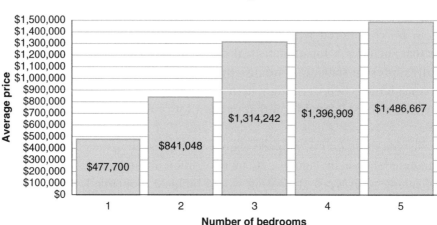

Average house price by the number of bedrooms
in southern suburbs of Wellington in the second half of 2021*

*Data source: TradeMeProperty insights. Data is for all houses in these suburbs for which sales prices were available (which includes most houses sold during this time period).

Figure 5.1   Example of using a chart to show a statistical result

Having shown that price is related to the number of bedrooms, we could make a slightly more complex chart that includes two variables – the number of bedrooms and floor area represented by three size groupings (less than 90 square metres, 90–125 square metres and 126 square metres or more). Once again, just by looking at the chart in Figure 5.2, someone could see that price increases with the number of bedrooms, but now they would also be able to see that this does not hold for houses that are over 125 square metres, all of which had at least three bedrooms. They could also see that for a house with a given number of bedrooms – for example, 3 – the price increases as the floor area increases. Note that both this graphical way of presenting the data and the statistics-driven way are accurate representations of the data, but the graphical representation is likely to be more useful to the developers and the statistical representation is likely to be more useful to the economists because of their different relationships to data.

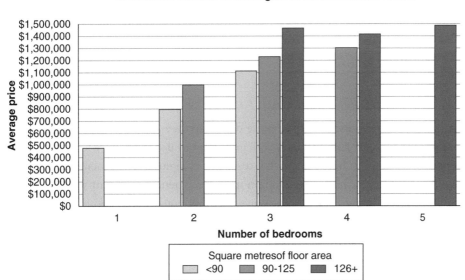

Average house price by the number of bedrooms and floor area in southern suburbs of Wellington in the second half of 2021*

*Data source: TradeMeProperty insights. Data is for all houses in these suburbs for which sales prices were available (which includes most houses sold during this time period).

Figure 5.2 Example of using a chart to show a statistical result

Beyond having a sense of your target audience's familiarity with the domain and with analytical methods generally, it's useful to know how familiar they are with domain-specific data. Even people who have a good general background in statistics or are very familiar with the domain to which analytics are being applied may not be familiar with how some of the metrics are calculated. For instance, words such as 'new users' or 'monthly active users' are often used in discussing analytics related to apps or websites and they seem intuitive. Yet perhaps because they seem so intuitive, many people do not understand precisely how they are calculated in a specific context, and that can lead to misunderstandings about what results actually mean. For example, does the term 'users' refer to people, devices, or web browsers? Does 'new' mean that the user has never visited a website before or that they have not visited within a given period of time, such as the past year? Does 'active' mean that they have engaged with the app or website at least once for any amount of time or is the threshold for counting active use higher?

If there is any doubt about whether members of a target audience know how specific metrics are defined and calculated, it's useful to provide that information. On the other hand, if everyone in the audience is very familiar with those things, then providing that detail may create visual clutter or be perceived as condescending. Of course, an audience can include both types of people, which can complicate things. In digital forms of data communication that can be resolved by including links to things such as definitions and details of calculations. In static formats, that type of information could be included in glossaries or appendices.

What Does Your Audience Care About?

These days, many organisations have more data than they can even fully analyse, let alone communicate in detail. That makes it very important to use your knowledge of what your audience cares about to help select what results to communicate to them and what results to give the greatest emphasis to. Common mistakes when people start working with data are to present too many results and to give them all equal emphasis. In a way these are understandable mistakes. People often present too many results because they want to show all of the work they have done in analysing the data. Giving all results equal emphasis can feel thorough and unbiased. But doing those things may mean that the most important results are not given the attention that they deserve because they are buried within so many other results or not highlighted.

Even in social situations, you've probably noticed that different people care about different things. Even with friends or family, you may notice that certain people always get animated when certain topics are raised. The same is true within organisations. Different people are in different roles and have different priorities and those are likely to mean that some things are more important to them than others. Insights about what your audience cares about should influence what analytical results you communicate and highlight. Different people also have different personalities, interests, and hobbies, so if your audience is relatively small – for example, one decision-maker or a board – you may know about their personalities, interests, and hobbies, and you can use that information to inform the selection of examples, analogies, and metaphors used to describe analytical results. Those won't affect the results, but they may increase the chances that your audience will really pay attention to the results as opposed to tuning out.

BE CLEAR ABOUT YOUR OBJECTIVE

Just as your approach to communicating analytical results should be adjusted based on your audience, it should also be tailored based on the specific objectives of the project that you're working on. Many analytics projects fall into one of three categories: 1) informing, 2) persuading, or 3) monitoring or evaluating. An example of a project with an informing-oriented objective would be one using transaction data to profile or **segment** customers to answer the general question of what types of people buy what types of products. An example of a project with a persuasion-oriented objective would be using data on the failures of city infrastructure, such as networks of water pipes, to persuade local politicians to allocate a budget to upgrade the network to improve its reliability and reduce the chances of outages or water becoming contaminated as a result of aging pipes. An example of a project with a monitoring-oriented objective would be the HR part of an organisation monitoring employee attrition and looking for variation by location, job category, etc. to see if some parts of the organisation experience particularly high or low rates of attrition.

One way to think about your objective is as an 'inform (or persuade or monitor)-that-because' statement. The first part is the overall nature of the objective – informing, persuading, or monitoring – as described in the previous paragraph combined with the target audience. For example, inform the leadership team, persuade the board, or monitor on behalf of the communications team. The second part (the 'that') is the beliefs about the domain you want the audience to have after viewing your data-driven deliverable. For example, the 'that' for an informing objective might be that the majority of employees prefer to have the option to work from home at least three days a week. The 'that' for a persuading objective might be that the organisation should invest in a new cybersecurity system. The 'that' for a monitoring objective might be that public sentiment about an organisation is stable. The 'because' part of the statement is the evidence you are providing to demonstrate why your audience should believe what you're telling them. That would mean the full versions of the examples discussed in this paragraph might be:

- Inform the leadership team that the majority of employees prefer to have the option to work from home at least three days a week based on the results of an employee survey.
- Persuade the board that they should approve an investment in a new cyber security system because of the results of a threat analysis.
- Monitoring on behalf of the communications team shows that public sentiment about an organisation is currently stable based on sentiment analysis of social media data.

This way of framing your objective can help you plan and curate your data communication. This includes everything from how the information will be communicated, to what is and is not included, to the order in which information appears, and to what gets the most and least emphasis. It's important to keep coming back to your audience and objective as you develop your data communication to ensure that everything that is being included is relevant to both the objective and the target audience. While that may seem obvious, too often extraneous information ends up being included. Sometimes that's to show all of the work that was done in the analysis process, sometimes it's 'just in case' someone wants that information, and sometimes it's because the person preparing the deliverable has just lost sight of the audience or objective. But, whatever the reason, including that extraneous information makes it harder for the audience to absorb the main points the deliverable is being created to convey in the first place.

GENERAL DATA VISUALISATION PRINCIPLES

While it's possible, and sometimes desirable, to communicate analytical results using only words or numbers, data visualisations are often a useful alternative or supplement to those ways of communicating. The most important rule to keep in mind is that you should only use a visualisation when it helps achieve the particular objective with the intended target audience. This is another one of those things that seems obvious, but is too often not the case.

Sometimes people think that including a visualisation will add literal or figurative colour to an otherwise dry and boring report, but if text is the best way to communicate the information, the real answer there is to make the report less dry and boring. Other times people think including a visualisation will enhance understanding, but then make poor choices about the type of visualisation or how it is executed and end up confusing or misleading the target audience rather than enhancing their understanding. This section describes some general principles that apply to many types of visualisations and then the following one describes some of the most common forms of visualisation and the types of situations each is best suited to.

Use of Colour

You probably have experience making charts in Excel or other software. When you've done that in the past, have you just used whatever colours the software selected by default? Most people typically just stick with the colours selected by the software, but that's rarely the best choice. Colour is an important part of your visualisation. First, consider the overall set of colours you will use in your visualisation. Your organisation may require that all communications use a particular set of colours, in which case whatever colours you select have to be part of that set.

It's also important to think about the natural associations people have with colour and about consistency. For example, it has become common to use traffic light colours to convey things like good and bad or stop and go, whether on actual traffic lights or on infographics. Organisations also often have colours associated with them because of their own logos and branding and, whenever possible, it's helpful to pick up on those conventions in data visualisations. Even if your audience has no natural associations between the things that will be represented in your visualisation and particular colours, once you have used a particular colour to represent something you should try to use it consistently. For example, if one division is blue on the first slide in your presentation, that same division should still be blue on the tenth slide and in your presentation next month, but if you are just using the software defaults there is a good chance that won't happen automatically. Once you've developed those colour choice standards, it's a good idea to document them so they are easy for you to remember and to share with others creating deliverables for the same target audience.

One complication when it comes to picking up on people's natural associations with colour is that various conditions make it hard for some people to see colour well, and often the colours they find hardest to see are red and green, which are of course, the traffic light colours. The UK Office of National Statistics has good recommendations about how to deal with that issue in particular and how to think about colour and deal with accessibility issues more generally (see: https://style.ons.gov.uk/data-visualisation/using-colours/using-red-and-green/). They use actual traffic lights to point out that colour is not the only feature of traffic lights that give people information. The red is always at the top and the green is always at the bottom, which means that even colour blind people know whether they need to stop because they can look at the position of the light that's on, even if they can't see its colour. They suggest following that same type of logic in other situations and using other indicators such as textures or symbols to communicate things such as groupings instead of or in addition to colour. They and many others advocate use of grey scale (black, white, and the shades of grey in between) since it is visible to most people as well as the use of blue, which is still visible to people with many visual impairments.

Use of Order

Just as many people present data in charts in whatever colour their software uses by default, many also leave data series and groupings within a chart in whatever order the software put them in (which is normally a function of their order in the source data). That is often a mistake. We can use the order in which things appear in charts to convey a lot of information and to create a situation where the audience can really focus on what the data is trying to tell them rather than looking around to figure out where things are.

There is no single best order. Instead, the ordering should be a function of the objective and audience. Often this means showing values from highest to lowest or lowest to highest. For example, charts showing many sports statistics would be ordered from highest to lowest in many cases since in many sports more of something (goals, runs, etc.) is better, but it might be the reverse for things like golf or running where fewer of something (shots or seconds) is better. And what's better may depend on the audience. For instance, in the house price example used in Chapter 4 and earlier in this chapter, prices being high might be good if we are presenting to an audience of developers or existing home owners, but bad if we are presenting to an audience of people hoping to buy their first home, and we would want to adjust our order accordingly.

Common ways of ordering data in visualisations include:

- highest to lowest or lowest to highest value
- highest to lowest or lowest to highest difference (between groups, time periods, etc.)
- alphabetically
- chronologically
- geographically
- putting data for a particular group (e.g., the organisation for whom the data is being analysed) first and then having other groups follow based on one of the previously described orders.

Which of these is best will depend on the particular situation, so it's important to carefully consider order on a case-by-case basis. Once you've done that, it's good to stick with the same order when presenting data about that same topic to that same audience unless there is a really good reason not to. Again, that's not something most software will just do by default. You either need to structure your source data in the order that will generate the chart the way you want it or manipulate it once it's in the chart if the software you are using will allow that.

Labelling and Legends

Another very common type of mistake people make when creating visualisations is not labelling things at all or not labelling them as clearly as possible. For example, an axis might show numbers, but not the units the numbers are in. It's a shame to spend a lot of time collecting and analysing data only to have it presented in a way that makes people uncertain about exactly what they're seeing. That makes it very important to label everything, and even more so when communicating analytical results to an audience that might be unfamiliar with conventions about how a particular thing is measured. Exactly what needs to be labelled and how (e.g., values versus percentages) varies by audience, objective, and chart type, but in general it's far better to err on the side of over-labelling than under-labelling. This also ties back to a point previously made about colour. Some people have difficulty seeing some colours, so don't just use colour to indicate something like a particular group. Use a label too.

It's also often useful to use a **legend** or key showing what colour, symbol, etc. is used to represent each data series. When you do, it's helpful to orient the legend to match the chart. In other words, if your chart is a series of vertical columns spread horizontally across the page, then your legend should also be laid out horizontally whereas if your chart is a series of horizontal bars spread vertically on the page then your legend should also be laid out vertically. That may seem unnecessary since a legend typically has both a label and a colour so, apart from potential issues with visual impairments, people should be able to figure out which data series or group is which. But taking those extra few minutes to make your legend match your chart means that your audience will spend a tiny bit less time trying to figure out your chart and a tiny bit more thinking about the implications of the results it's showing. On complex charts, the legend can also be used to provide even more orienting information. For example, the legend of a chart with two y axes can be used to indicate which axis is associated with each data series.

Sketch it Out

The one thing that most people could do to improve their visualisations is to sketch them out first. Too often people go right from their analysis to using software to make charts and graphs, often even letting the software recommend what type of chart to make. But the software doesn't know your audience or objective and so the chances of it generating the very best type of chart for your particular audience, objective, and data are very slim. You are much better off getting a tablet, whiteboard, or piece of paper and sketching out what type of visualisation would best convey the results you have in a way that serves your overall objective and is appropriate for your particular target audience. Your drawing doesn't need to be perfect. Since you're just sketching, try out a couple of different options. Maybe change what data is shown in different positions. Once you have what you think is the best version, make choices about ordering and colouring, and add labels. Doing those things takes very little time, but can greatly improve the impact of your visualisations. It also simplifies the actual execution of the visualisation because now you just need to reverse engineer your sketch using your software of choice and your actual results.

Edit!

It's hard to get visualisations right on the first try, so even once you've executed your visualisation in software, look at it carefully through the eyes of the target audience — or even better, have someone who is in the target audience look at it — and see if you can find ways to fine-tune it to make it even more effective. Even small changes can make a big impact on the ability of your audience to understand the data you are trying to communicate and therefore to take action based on that information.

COMMON FORMS OF DATA VISUALISATION

This section describes some of the most common and useful types of data visualisations that can be executed in many different types of software.

Grouped Column and Bar Charts

The first types of charts are **grouped column and bar charts**. The terms column and bar have specific meanings in the context of data visualisations: columns are vertical and bars are horizontal. The grouped part of the name for these types of visualisations can be obvious in some situations as they are often used to compare groups, for example, to show if/how men differ from women or one age group differs from another. One thing that can be confusing about this type of chart though, is that it is still called a group bar or column chart even if data is only being shown for a single group. The group part of the name distinguishes these charts, in which one column or bar represents one group – even if that group includes everyone – from **stacked column and bar charts**, which will be discussed next.

Grouped column charts are useful for showing difference over time, as you can see in Figures 5.3 and 5.4. They're also useful for showing differences between groups, as shown in Figure 5.3, which illustrates differences in average CO_2 emissions per person for high-, medium-, and low-income countries. It's easy to scan the chart and understand that people in high-income countries tend to generate vastly greater emissions than people in medium-income countries, and that people in medium-income countries generate far more emissions than people in low-income countries. One of the reasons it's easy to see that is that the data is shown as an average per person rather than an overall total. We could still show total emissions for high-, medium-, and low-income countries using a grouped column chart; however, it would be far less meaningful since the number of people living in countries within each grouping may vary.

Notice this is being expressed per capita.
Per capita CO_2 emissions
Metric tons per capita
12
10
8
6
4
2
0
2011
2012
2013
2014
2015
2016
2017
2018
Low income
Middle income
High income

Figure 5.3 Grouped column chart example - full axis

Data source: https://databank.worldbank.org/source/environment-social-and-governance-(esg)-data

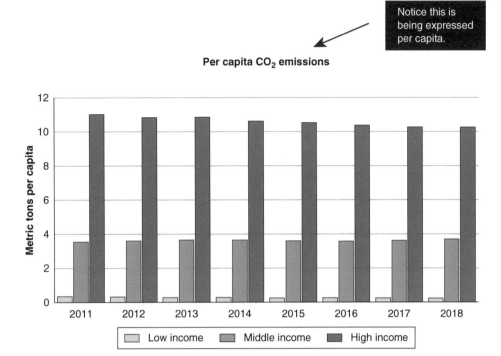

Per capita CO_2 emissions for high income countries
Metric tons per capita
11.5
11.3
11.0
10.8
10.5
10.3
10.0
2011
2012
2013
2014
2015
2016
2017
2018

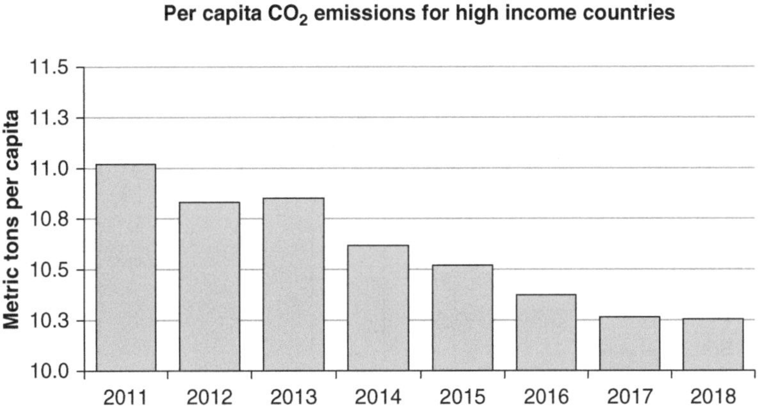

Figure 5.4 Grouped column chart example - truncated axis

Data source:https://databank.worldbank.org/source/environment-social-and-governance-(esg)-data

Grouped column charts work well in situations where we have short labels, and either a lot of groups or a lot of data points in a series. That's because we can show quite a few of them in a relatively small space, as shown in Figure 5.3.

One important thing to think about when making grouped column or bar charts, or for that matter, many other types of charts, is where to start the axes. You can see why that's important by comparing Figures 5.3 and 5.4. They show the exact same data, but Figure 5.4 has the y (vertical) axis truncated to only go from 10–11.5 metric tons per capita, and that has the effect of exaggerating differences and making it appear that high-income countries have reduced their emissions to a far greater extent than is actually the case. It's good practice to start your axes at zero unless there's a really good reason not to because it shows the data in its true context. For example, when we look at Figure 5.3, we can still see that average emissions per capita have been declining in rich countries, but we get a much more realistic sense of the rate of decrease and the gap in per capita emissions between the more and less affluent countries.

Something else to keep in mind with group column charts is that long labels can be a problem. The labels in Figures 5.3 and 5.4 are fine because they are just four-digit years, but if instead there were really long names along the x (horizontal) axis, they could be hard to squeeze in. That's where grouped bar charts come in. They can be used for similar purposes as grouped column charts, but they are flipped on their sides, as shown in Figure 5.5, allowing more space for longer labels.

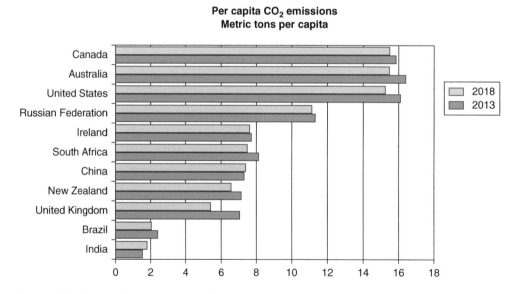

Figure 5.5 Grouped bar chart example

Data source: https://databank.worldbank.org/source/environment-social-and-governance-(esg)-data

Stacked Column, Stacked Bar, and Pie Charts

Unlike grouped bar and column charts, in which each bar or column represents one thing, the columns in **stacked column charts**, like the ones shown in Figure 5.6 and 5.7, and the bars in **stacked bar charts**, like the one shown in Figure 5.8 are broken into slices.

Often the slices represent different possible values for the same variable. For example, the different slices in the columns in Figures 5.6 and 5.7 represent different age groups, as do the slices in the bars in Figure 5.8.

Stacked bar and column charts are good for showing individual and cumulative proportions. What I mean by that is if I wanted to know, for example, what percentage of people are younger than 5 I can just look at the white slices in Figures 5.6 and 5.8, but I can also see what percentage are younger than 14 by looking at the white slices and the lightest grey slices in combination. In order to do that, I need to show the data as percentages rather than as counts. You can see why by comparing Figures 5.6 and 5.7. They are displaying the same data, but Figure 5.6 shows the data as percentages while Figure 5.7 shows the data as counts. Showing the data as counts in that and other situations makes it hard

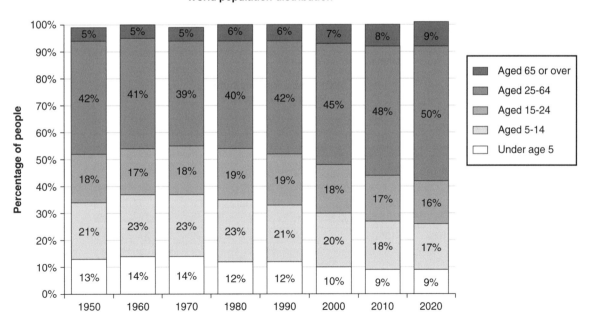

Figure 5.6 Stacked column chart example based on percentages

Data source: https://ourworldindata.org/age-structure

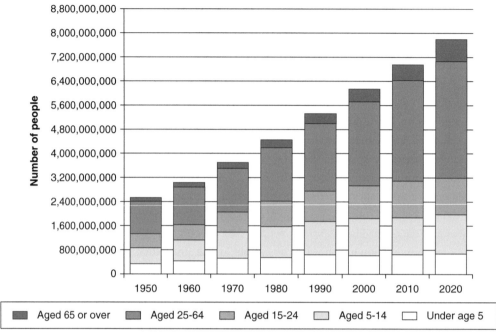

Figure 5.7 Stacked column chart example based on counts

Data source: https://ourworldindata.org/age-structure

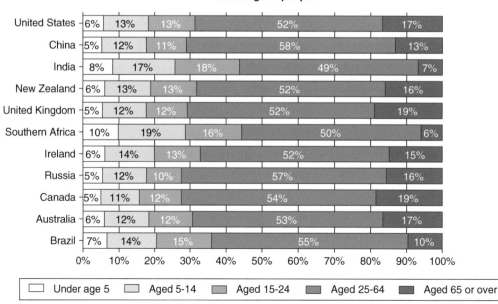

Figure 5.8 Stacked bar chart example based on percentages

Data source: https://ourworldindata.org/age-structure

to see if a change in the size of a slice is due to the total height of a column or length of a bar changing (reflecting an overall change in whatever is being measured) or a change in the proportion represented by that particular slice. Showing the data as proportions removes that problem.

Stacked bars and columns both require mutually exclusive and collectively exhaustive categories. That means that each observation must be included in one slice (even if it's something like an 'other' category), and no observation can be included in more than one slice. That's what allows the proportions to be meaningful. If observations can be included in more than one category – for example, in data from a 'select all that apply' type survey question, then stacked bars or columns are not an appropriate choice for visualising the data. The same applies to pie charts, such as the one shown in Figure 5.9.

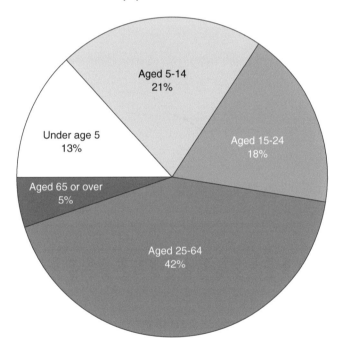

Figure 5.9 Pie chart example

Data source: https://ourworldindata.org/age-structure

As with stacked columns and stacked bars, **pie charts** are good for showing the proportional breakdown of something. But generally speaking, pie charts are better when you've only got a few of those categories that you want to break something down into. Up to five or so categories in a single pie chart is fine. If you want to be able to compare across a number of years, variables, groups, etc., as Figures 5.6 and 5.7 do by year and Figure 5.8 does by country, stacked bars or columns generally work better than pie charts because it's much easier for people to scan vertically or horizontally to see if particular boundaries between slices change than it is for them to scan across different pies to see if the size of a particular slice of pie is changing across pies.

Line Charts and Double y axis Charts

Line charts are another common form of visualisation. They're useful for showing trends over time, as shown in Figure 5.10. As that example illustrates, line charts show lines connecting data points plotted on two axes. Line charts work best when the data can be arranged in a logical order on both axes, and there are a reasonably large number of data points.

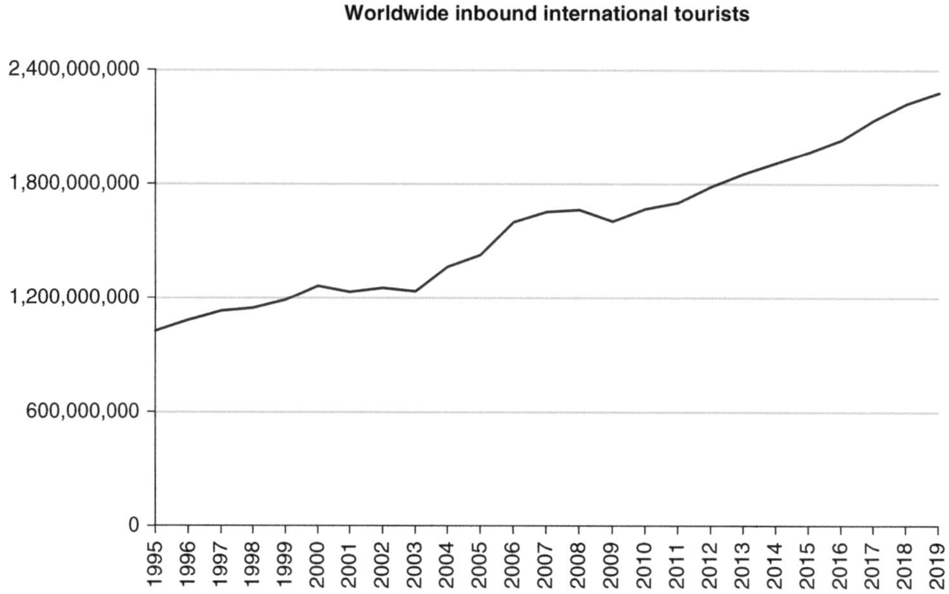

Worldwide inbound international tourists

Figure 5.10   Line chart example

Data source: https://data.worldbank.org/indicator/ST.INT.ARVL

As you can see, the visualisation in Figure 5.11 also features lines, but it's a **double y axis chart** for the obvious reason that it has two y axes. In this particular example, the data for the series associated with each axis is a line, but that's not always the case. For example, often the data associated with one axis is represented using columns with the data associated with the other axis shown as a line. The distinguishing feature is just that there are two y axes, regardless of how the data associated with each axis is displayed.

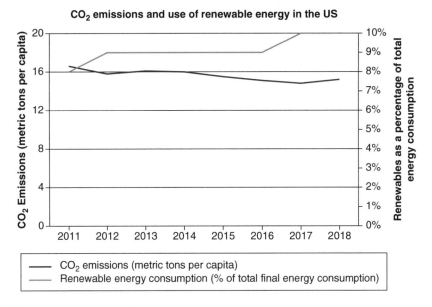

Figure 5.11   Double y axis chart example

Data source: https://databank.worldbank.org/source/environment-social-and-governance-(esg)-data

Double y axis charts are good for showing the relationships between variables. For instance, the visualisation shown in Figure 5.11 shows data for both US CO_2 emissions and the use of renewable energy by year. We can't show both of those data series on the same axis because one is a number (metric tons of CO_2 emissions per person) and one is a percentage (renewable energy as a percentage of total energy consumption). We could show each data series on its own using a traditional line chart, but showing them together makes is easy to see any relationship between the two data series. For example, it appears from Figure 5.11 that as renewable energy is gradually growing to make up a greater percentage of total energy consumption, average CO_2 emissions per person are gradually dropping.

Scatter Plots and Bubble Charts

Scatter plots and **bubble charts** are also common types of visualisations. Those two types of charts are very similar to one another in that both display data on two dimensions. The distinction is that bubble charts also add a third dimension by varying the size of the marker for each data point in proportion to the value of a third variable.

For example, the visualisations in Figures 5.12 and 5.13 both show GDP per person and the percentage of the population that has completed tertiary education in OECD countries, but in Figure 5.13, the size of the bubbles is modified to reflect the size of the workforce in each country. As you can see from the example in the figure, that works well for a relatively small number of data points, but with a large number of data points large bubbles end up obscuring other data points so they don't work as well when someone is very interested in being able to see specific data points rather than just a more general pattern.

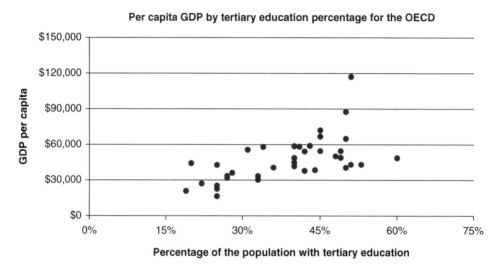

Figure 5.12   Scatter plot example

Data source: https://stats.oecd.org/Index.aspx?DataSetCode=EAG_EARNINGS and https://stats.oecd.org/Index.aspx?DataSetCode=PDB_LV

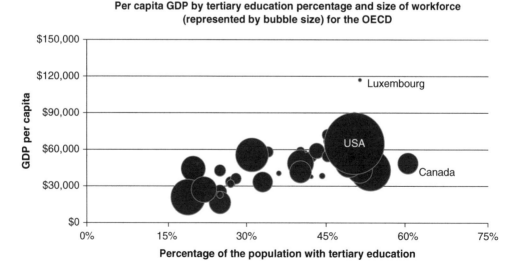

Figure 5.13   Bubble chart example

Data source: https://stats.oecd.org/Index.aspx?DataSetCode=EAG_EARNINGS and https://stats.oecd.org/Index.aspx?DataSetCode=PDB_LV

You can show the relationship between two variables with a scatter plot, and three with a bubble chart. You can even add a fourth or fifth dimension by varying the colours of the bubbles and/or the pattern of the bubbles. Doing that allows us to compress information about five variables into one chart, which is great for a concise presentation to a data-savvy audience, but may be overwhelming to an audience that is less familiar with data or with the specific domain.

Tables and Heat Maps

When we think of data visualisations, we don't tend to think about **tables**, but tables are a form of data visualisation, and they're especially useful if we're going to show a large number of data points that would be hard to show in a chart. Displaying data in a table is especially useful if people need to be able to look at the specific values rather than just looking at the overall pattern of values. Tables are best suited to situations such as written reports, where people can study them in their own time and go back and refer to them again if necessary. They often don't work as well in presentations because there may be too much information for people to absorb in the time a single slide is shown.

One way to make a table easier to digest in general, and in presentations in particular, is to consider adding conditional formatting. For example, the table in Figure 5.14 shows average annual wages over time in OECD countries. That would be useful if someone was reading the report and wanted to look up the average wage for a particular country in a particular year, but in its current form, the table doesn't really help us identify any trends in average wages across countries and time. What could help us with that is using different colours or shading to show countries that had above or below average wages or wage rate increases for each year.

Using conditional formatting in the way just described creates one form of **heat map**. In that example, we are using colours or other symbols to highlight patterns and differences in a table, but in other situations we might use something like a map or another type of image. For example, heat maps are sometimes used to show what part of a website people tend to hover over or what part of an ad they tend to look at.

Heatmaps are helpful if there are clear patterns in the data and it's the overall pattern that we're interested in rather than the specific data points. For example, the visualisation in Figure 5.15 gives us a good sense of where the highest emitting countries are, but does not show us the exact volume of emissions for each country.

Average annual wages (2020 constant prices, USD PPP)

Country	2015	2016	2017	2018	2019	2020
Australia	$53,636	$53,724	$53,437	$53,515	$54,021	$55,206
Austria	$52,686	$53,170	$53,136	$53,325	$53,690	$53,132
Belgium	$55,427	$55,526	$55,130	$55,388	$56,022	$54,327
Canada	$52,968	$52,019	$52,765	$53,730	$54,119	$55,342
Chile	$27,082	$28,252	$27,605	$28,574	$29,579	$26,729
Czech Republic	$25,660	$26,575	$27,931	$29,421	$30,355	$29,885
Denmark	$56,960	$57,043	$57,355	$57,794	$57,967	$58,430
Estonia	$24,633	$24,932	$26,417	$27,920	$29,948	$30,720
Finland	$45,194	$45,588	$45,339	$45,771	$46,249	$46,230
France	$45,680	$46,214	$46,852	$46,867	$47,112	$45,581
Germany	$51,172	$51,902	$52,454	$53,221	$54,041	$53,745
Greece	$26,886	$26,268	$26,418	$26,680	$27,010	$27,207
Hungary	$20,872	$21,062	$22,586	$23,721	$24,471	$25,409
Iceland	$58,377	$62,949	$69,051	$72,466	$70,391	$67,488
Ireland	$47,134	$47,812	$48,376	$48,586	$49,509	$49,474
Israel	$35,627	$36,921	$37,903	$38,811	$39,537	$39,322
Italy	$39,878	$40,193	$39,934	$39,985	$40,145	$37,769
Japan	$37,265	$37,810	$37,972	$38,462	$39,041	$38,515
Korea	$38,143	$39,266	$40,216	$41,624	$42,297	$41,960
Latvia	$23,742	$25,154	$26,128	$27,107	$28,645	$29,876
Lithuania	$23,715	$24,982	$26,382	$27,572	$29,695	$31,811
Luxembourg	$66,247	$66,393	$67,393	$67,448	$66,840	$65,854
Mexico	$16,516	$16,322	$16,277	$16,637	$16,771	$16,230
Netherlands	$58,403	$58,604	$58,171	$57,581	$57,475	$58,828
New Zealand	$41,503	$42,862	$43,148	$44,121	$45,092	$45,269
Norway	$55,404	$54,224	$54,117	$54,691	$55,753	$55,780
Poland	$25,854	$27,145	$28,294	$30,212	$31,959	$32,527
Portugal	$26,855	$26,699	$26,820	$27,263	$27,978	$28,410
Slovak Republic	$20,771	$21,430	$22,072	$22,692	$23,438	$23,619
Slovenia	$36,636	$38,049	$38,706	$39,377	$40,533	$41,445
Spain	$40,072	$39,845	$39,326	$39,033	$39,055	$37,922
Sweden	$44,719	$45,423	$45,681	$45,917	$46,418	$47,020
Switzerland	$65,910	$65,453	$65,151	$64,963	$65,906	$64,824
United Kingdom	$46,647	$47,181	$47,146	$47,229	$47,937	$47,147
United States	$63,845	$63,942	$64,618	$65,303	$66,383	$69,392

*Data source: https://stats.oecd.org/viewhtml.aspx?datasetcode=AV_AN_WAGE&lang=en

Figure 5.14 Table example

Average per person 2018 CO$_2$ emissions

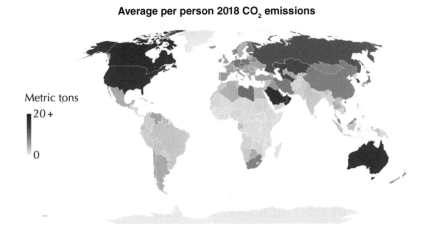

Figure 5.15   Heat map example

Data source: https://databank.worldbank.org/source/environment-social-and-governance-(esg)-data

ASSEMBLING A COLLECTION OF RESULTS INTO AN ACCURATE, INSIGHTFUL, COHERENT, AND ACTIONABLE NARRATIVE

Plan What to Include

Normally we don't just communicate a single analytical result, but instead we assemble a collection of results into a report, presentation, dashboard, infographic or some other type of data-driven deliverable. As we plan our deliverable, one of the first things to consider is what to include. We want to make sure that the results that are included are:

- statistically and methodologically valid (to the best of our knowledge)
- representative or proportionate
- relevant to the objectives and the target audience, and ideally interesting to the target audience.

By this point in this book, you should be aware that collecting and analysing data well can be challenging, but we still should be aiming to present results that are as statistically and methodologically valid as possible. While that may sound obvious, many people who work with data have had the experience of being pressured to present questionable results to advance a particular point of view or because they are the only ones available.

Something that may be less obvious is that we should avoid presenting results that are accurate, to the best of our knowledge, but not representative or proportionate. What I mean by that is we don't just want to pick a result that's true but doesn't accurately portray our overall findings. For example, suppose we conducted a customer satisfaction survey that included a question in which people rated their satisfaction on a 5-point scale, followed by an open-ended question in which people could explain their rating. One way of presenting the results from those questions would be to show quotes from responses to the open-ended question. That can be useful because we get to see customers' perspectives in their own words; however, if we presented the most negative comments among a set of largely positive comments and ratings, or the most positive comments among a set of largely negative comments and ratings, we could leave our audience with an incorrect understanding of the data even though we were just reproducing exact word-for-word quotes from the selected survey respondents.

Think About How to Make Your Deliverable Interesting

Knowing our audience well and being clear about our objective should help us identify which results are and are not relevant. Understanding our audience's assumptions can help us anticipate what's most likely to be interesting to them.

A very useful way of thinking about this is presented in an old article that's still very relevant for our purposes called: 'That's Interesting' (Davis, 1971). The basic idea is that people tend to find things interesting when they challenge some, but not all, of their assumptions. For example, people who are very familiar with a domain may believe that one thing influences another, but we may have results that show that the two things are independent of one another or that both are caused by a third variable. Or they may think that some phenomenon is completely random, but we may have used something like a regression model that can make reasonably accurate predictions using a set of independent variables no one had ever thought about in relationship to our phenomenon of interest. The point of all of this is to show results that give people new ways of looking at a familiar phenomenon. That can open up opportunities no one had previously considered or offer fresh insights about how to solve familiar problems.

Davis (1971) contrasts this situation where we are challenging some assumptions, and in doing so piquing the interest of our audience, with three others. One of those is a situation in which all of our results affirm our audience's assumptions. When that's the case, the results may be perceived as obvious, and therefore uninteresting. Another situation is one in which our results don't speak to any assumptions held by our target audience. In that situation, the results will rightly be perceived as irrelevant. A third possibility is that our results challenge all of our audience's assumptions, in which case they may perceive us to be absurd and ignore us completely.

There is really no excuse for presenting results that are irrelevant to our target audience. We should make the effort to understand the audience and their assumptions well enough to avoid that. It's harder to avoid presenting results that are obvious to our target audience because sometimes the results just do affirm their assumptions, and that's especially true in situations where we are reporting on the same results regularly – for example, analytics that need to be reported on a monthly or quarterly basis. Even in those situations though, we should always be challenging ourselves to consider new ways of analysing the data that may produce a result that challenges the assumptions of our audience and is therefore interesting to them.

The most difficult situation for people reporting analytical results may be one in which they have to present results that challenge many assumptions of the target audience, and therefore risk being perceived as absurd. This can happen when the assumptions of the target audience have been formed based on their own personal experiences without much grounding in data, and their assumptions are being tested with objective data for the first time or in situations where conditions have changed but the assumptions of the target audience have not. In those situations it's important to consider whether it's possible to package results in a way that the results being presented are still accurate and proportionate, but so that the results that challenge the audience's assumptions are presented amongst at least some other (legitimate) results that affirm the audience's assumptions. Those strategies may reduce the risk of the information being presented being perceived as so contrary to the audience's world view that they write it off as being absurd.

Options for Communicating Analytical Results

Once we understand our audience, we're clear about our objective, and we've thought a lot about what to include, then we can get to work actually planning the detail of our deliverables. There are many options for communicating data, and the choice should be determined with the audience and objective in mind. This section discusses the main options and the situations to which each is best suited.

One thing to note before describing those options is that some people really prefer to have a face-to face-conversation, others might want a formal presentation, and some might want a written report. Preferences and norms for how analytical results are communicated also vary by culture and by organisation.

We won't always be able to accommodate those preferences, but it's good to know what they are to see if we can accommodate them. It's also important to understand our audience's preferences and expectations around the length and level of detail of the communication. This can go wrong either way in the sense that if somebody really just wants a quick answer to a question and you give them a 20-page report, they probably are not going to be happy about that, but similarly if they were expecting a very detailed report and you just shoot them an e-mail with a few bullet points, they're not going to be happy about that either. So consider your audience and whether they just want the big picture or a lot of detail or something in between.

Also, think about the content of the communication and the audience's preferences and organisational norms about that. Does your audience mainly like to read a lot of text or do they like to look at a lot of images or quotes? What about charts and tables? This should, to a large degree, be driven by what sort of analytical results you are presenting, but it can also be shaped a little bit based on the preferences and norms for that particular audience.

Another thing to consider is the level of formality. This can vary by organisation. Some expect results to be presented in a very formal way, while in other organisations it might be the opposite. Either way, we want to clearly communicate accurate results, but if we do that in a style that's the opposite of what is expected, it can be really jarring for the audience and make it less likely that they'll take results on board and act on any recommendations presented. Another thing to think about is whether your audience expects the results to be provided in a way that's self-explanatory or prefers someone to walk them through the findings.

Finally, there may be legal considerations when deciding how to communicate analytical results. Public sector organisations in most countries are subject to official information requests and private companies may be concerned that analytical results could be subpoenaed if the company were ever involved in a lawsuit that relates to them in some way. Those sorts of situations tend to produce preferences for material being provided in any written form to be mainly factual, with subjective opinions about the implications of those facts communicated verbally.

Reports

One of the traditional ways of communicating data, and still one of the most common, is through a written report. This form of communication is well-suited for situations in which a lot of results need to be communicated or a lot of details need to be provided for results to be properly understood. Either of those situations assumes a highly engaged audience who are willing and able to put in the time to go through all of those results or absorb all of those details since without that the information will not be received by the intended audience. Unfortunately, that is what happens in many situations. A lot of time, and in some cases money, is spent collecting and analysing data and writing up results in a long report only to have the report describing those results go unread – at least in its entirety – by all or most of the target audience.

That makes it extremely important to ensure everything going in a written report really is relevant to the intended target audience and that members of that target audience will be able to understand the information just reading it on their own. Often people want to communicate analytical results to multiple target audiences and put all of the information in one report, but even though it may take a bit more time, the results are much more likely to be absorbed and acted upon if reports are customised for each target audience. Even then it's important to carefully edit reports with the specific objective and target audience in mind. Many written reports are longer than they need to be, and rather than adding value, that additional length tends to have the effect of obscuring the most important information.

Presentations

Presentations are another very common way of communicating analytical results. Presentations allow members of the target audience to both see the information being communicated and hear about it, and to ask questions as the information is presented. Those characteristics can help promote both engagement and understanding among target audiences where one or both of those things may be lacking.

A downside of presentations is that members of the target audience may miss or forget things, but that can be mitigated by providing access to the presentation after the fact as either slides or a recording. As with reports, many presentations of analytical results are too long, so once again it's very important to do a careful edit with the target audience and objective in mind.

Infographics

Infographics are like reports in that they are a static, written format; however, they are typically just a single – often over-sized – page. That has the advantage of not requiring a great deal of time on the part of the intended target audience. That makes them a good option for target audiences that are not particularly engaged, but it also makes it important to think very carefully about every single element going into an infographic. Because the space available is so limited, only the most important information can be included, and it has to be presented in as clear and concise a way as possible.

Dashboards

Dashboards are a newer way of communicating analytical results. They are interactive digital displays of information, and are best-suited to information that changes frequently. Examples of that type of data include things like sales data, sensor data related to the performance of machines, and rapidly changing financial data such as stock prices and exchange rates. Digital displays can easily accommodate rapidly changing information like that, whereas if it were communicated in a static format such as a report or infographic it would be out of date almost immediately. The dashboard format can also better accommodate the needs of different target audiences than something like a report. This is because dashboards can be constructed so that people who want more detail about something can simply click to drill down into it whereas in a written report that type of navigation to audience-specific results would require more effort from the reader to find the relevant chapter, appendix, table, etc.

Informal Communications

Not all communication of analytical results requires the more formal types of deliverables just described. Depending on the objective and target audience, the best means of communication may be a quick e-mail or a chat over coffee and a spreadsheet.

Ordering and Emphasis

Once you have a good sense of what you want to communicate and the general format that you're going to use to do that, it's time to think about what insights and information should get leading versus supporting roles. I think about this like casting a movie. In a movie, everyone doesn't get equal screen time. Certain characters are featured, and we see them a lot; others are present, but often in the background. They are important to giving us the whole experience, but they are not central to the storyline.

The same is true for your data – there are going to be certain insights and information that are extremely important and there will be others that are less important, and we really need to treat them that way when we communicate our data. We also want to think about the order of information and insights that are going to be most useful for serving our objectives given our target audience.

As with any story, it's important to consider where to begin. The start of a movie sets the scene and grounds us in the world of the characters. Where we start our data-driven deliverables should depend on our audience. If we are communicating our results to an academic, technical, or scientific audience, they will typically want to see the detail of our methodology first because that's very important to them, and if we convince them that we have approached that carefully, then they will be more interested in what we have to say after that. Frustratingly for anyone who has tried to make a single data-driven deliverable for multiple audiences, if we are communicating with other audiences, such as business people or policy makers, and we start with the methodology, we are likely to lose them before we even get to the results. For those non-technical audiences, it is better to start with the problem we are trying to address with our analytics. They need to see that we understand the domain and the challenges within it in order to be convinced our insights will be useful to them.

Having set the scene, we can present our results. We're trying to create a coherent and engaging narrative and, as with a movie, if the exact same content was arranged in a different order, we might have a very different experience and be left with a different impression. This is one area where people who are new to data often make mistakes. They are tempted to walk through every result – possibly in the order that they did the analysis, or maybe based on the order of variables in a dataset. That may seem logical, but it's often not very useful to the audience because it's not telling any kind of a story. It's not giving them any guidance about what's important and what's not or how things fit together.

Helping an audience to understand the data and see connections and patterns within the results is especially important if the audience isn't particularly data-savvy or if the results are complex. For instance, in Figures 5.1 and 5.2 we saw how we could gradually build out the insights we derived from regression analysis in a way that would make them understandable even to people who have no background in statistics. Building out a data story like that can also be a great way of demonstrating to an audience that you understand them, which will increase the chances that they pay attention to and act on the results. For example, try to anticipate what questions members of your target audience may have about your data and structure the way you present your results accordingly. For instance, you may anticipate that when you present a general result part of your audience may be thinking something along the lines of 'well that might be true in general, but not for these people or in this situation', but then if your next slide shows that the result also does apply to the specific types of people or situation the person has in mind that can help increase their confidence that you understand the domain and that your results are trustworthy.

Edit!

It can be tempting to show how much analytical work you've done by including everything you explored, but it's very important to consider whether that's adding value to your audience or not because adding more content can often detract from the most important insights or cause your audience to tune out if what you're presenting seems obvious, irrelevant, absurd, or even just redundant. The care you take in editing your deliverable can make the difference between your audience fully absorbing the key insights your analysis revealed and missing them entirely.

EVALUATING DATA-DRIVEN COMMUNICATIONS

Once you've created your deliverable, the last step is to do some additional analysis on it to ensure it meets your original objective as effectively as possible and to get ideas for making your future data-driven deliverables even better. This starts with giving yourself time to at least set your deliverable aside overnight and to look at it with fresh eyes the next day. A couple of days later is even better. That's because when we're immersed in our data and creating our deliverables we know what we're thinking about and intending to do, but sometimes something we had in our mind didn't make it into the deliverable or what made it into the deliverable isn't quite what we intended. It's easier to spot that kind of thing once we have some distance from it.

Next, and still before it is released to its intended audience, it's good to have someone else take a look at your deliverable. This could be a person within the target audience but, if that's not possible, someone as close to that in terms of domain and data knowledge as you can find. Ask that person to look at the deliverable and tell you what they take away from it. See if their main takeaways match your intentions or not. Also make sure they haven't misunderstood anything. For example, after they have given you their unprompted feedback, if they have not said anything about important charts or tables ask them what they think the data in those means to make sure they can understand them correctly.

Now it's time to release your deliverable to your intended audience. Depending on the type of deliverable and audience, this may be another opportunity to get feedback. For example, if you are doing a presentation of the results to the audience, what questions do they ask? What parts of the presentation do they seem most interested in? Are there parts where they seem confused? Are there parts of your presentation when they are looking at their phones and appear not to be paying attention? All of that's information about what your audience knows and cares about that you can use in creating your next deliverable.

For some types of deliverables, you will also be able to monitor if and how your deliverable is used. For example, if it's something that needs to be downloaded or accessed in digital form, you may be able to track how frequently it is downloaded or viewed online. If it's something like an interactive dashboard, you may be able to track which parts of the dashboard are most and least frequently accessed. In many cases content from data-driven deliverables is used by members of the target audience for deliverables of their own. For example, it may be used in Board papers, policy documents, reports, or presentations for external audiences, etc. If the nature of your deliverable means that it *could* be used that way, is it being used that way? If it is being used, are the results and any associated caveats being described correctly? All of that information is also helpful in understanding the extent to which you've hit the mark with your target audience in the current deliverable and how you can improve future deliverables.

SUMMARY

I hope this chapter has helped you understand that creating effective data-driven deliverables requires far more thought and effort than just letting your software choose a chart to make using the default settings. That will result in a chart, but almost certainly not the best visualisation for your objective and target audience, and probably not an even particularly good visualisation.

Making good visualisations and data-driven deliverables starts with understanding your audience well and being clear about your objective. When it comes to making visualisations, sketching them out freehand before even starting to execute them in software very often ends up saving time and almost always produces a better end result. Paying attention to things such as order, use of colour, labels, and which type of chart to use can make a big difference in the extent to which your audience is able to absorb and interact with your results as opposed to just trying to figure out what you mean.

A set of individual visualisations gains impact by being curated thoughtfully into a broader narrative. That narrative should be grounded in the concerns and assumptions of the target audience; build at a pace that is appropriate for them, and ideally anticipate questions they may have so that they can be addressed as the narrative unfolds. A common complaint about data-oriented deliverables is that they are not interesting, but we can make them more interesting by understanding the assumptions of the target audience well and looking for opportunities to present results that challenge those assumptions, resulting in interesting new opportunities or ideas for addressing existing problems.

Finally, remember that it can be helpful to collect data about data-driven deliverables themselves. Getting feedback on the deliverables and monitoring how and by whom they are used can provide important insights for making future deliverables even better.

ANALYTICS IN PRACTICE

Showing future energy scenarios

In 2021, New Zealand's Energy Efficiency and Conservation Authority (EECA) collaborated with the BusinessNZ Energy Council (BEC) and Paul Scherrer Institute in Switzerland to develop two scenarios to show how New Zealand's emissions could be expected to evolve depending on whether reducing emissions was prioritised ahead of all other goals or treated more as one of several important priorities. Modelling emissions is complicated, and Kate Kolich, who was then Manager of Evidence, Insights, and Innovation at EECA, and her team had to adapt a data model developed internationally[1] for New Zealand conditions, compile the data inputs, model runs, and analyse the data output.

The team at EECA wanted to make sure that all of that valuable analytical work was not only accessible to climate experts, but also to people working in a variety of sectors and to the general public. As Kate says: *'We did do a 150 page report. I'm still not sure how many people have looked at that. It really explains our methodology. But one of the things that we found to have the most impact was the work that we did to develop our data visualisation tool.'*

(Continued)

[1]Based on the International Energy Agency ETSAP TIMES methodology.

To develop their tool – which you can try for yourself here at www.eeca.govt.nz/insights/data-tools/new-zealand-energy-scenarios-times-nz/ – the team at EECA had to work through many of the considerations discussed in this chapter. They thought about different audiences and how it would be most useful for them to view the data. They thought about the order in which things such as emissions from different fuels should be displayed. And because they had a lot of data to display, they worked with a graphic designer who specialises in data visualisation to develop, test, and refine a detailed colour taxonomy, part of which is shown (though not in full colour) in Figure 5.16, to ensure colours are used in a consistent and intuitive way throughout their visualisation. The team also tested out a number of different ways to present data in interactive charts with a group of users prior to finalising the data visualisations.

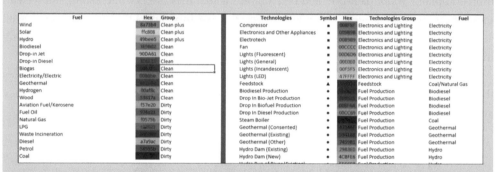

Figure 5.16   Partial example of colour pallet for energy scenario visualisation

The thought and care that the team at ECCA put into their visualisation helped them to achieve their objective of enabling engagement across business, government and communities to be better informed about the relationship between energy use and climate change, demonstrating that a focus on renewable energy across sectors can reduce climate impacts:

> What we've found is that by providing a way for people to explore the data in a way that is really thought through in terms of how a consumer might interact with that data we've actually been able to draw in a lot more engagement in people wanting to understand, in our case, the relationship between energy and climate change.

You can see of video with more of Kate's comments on this project here: https://vimeo.com/702702562/d0bd87db7f

RUNNING CASE STUDY: 4TE, PART 5[2]

Ben had been enjoying his time working on data and analytics for 4tE so much that he had agreed to continue two afternoons a week once his classes started up again. That was now only a week away, and he hadn't even had time to do any analysis of the HR, supplier, or financial data yet. Still, he wanted to spend the last full week he had creating a presentation to go through with Matt and Emily on Friday. It would summarise what he had learned from his analysis so far and provide a good foundation for them to discuss what to focus on next.

Matt had said that he and Emily could set aside an hour on Friday morning to hear Ben summarise his results so far. Ben knew that they both used data in their current and former jobs, but also that it had been at least ten years since either of them had taken a statistics course, and that he needed to take both of those things into account when planning his presentation. He also knew Emily was keen to think about expansion of 4tE, while Matt was a bit more cautious and wondering if it was better to solidify their current position before adding another store, expanding their delivery area, or adding new product lines. Therefore, Ben wanted to be sure to present his results as clearly and objectively as possible so that they could use them to inform their decisions around expansion.

Since Matt and Emily could only spend an hour in the meeting on Friday, Ben's plan was to use visualisations to convey the most important and high-level results and then provide any extra detail that they wanted as follow-ups either in the meeting itself if it was information he already had, or later if not. As he thought about how to structure his presentation, he wondered what types of visualisations to use, and what order to put them in.

EXERCISES

1   The first exercise in Chapter 4 asked you to: 'Check to see if the proportion of men and women in your class is similar to the proportion for your institution as a whole.' Whether or not you did that exercise, draw a sketch showing how you could visualise the results of that analysis assuming that the target audience you want to communicate the results to is the management team for your institution. Make sure to show the type of visualisation you would use and pay attention to ordering, colouring, and labelling.

---

[2]The 4tE case is fictitious.

2   The second exercise in Chapter 4 asked you to: 'Check to see if the proportion of men and women in your institution is similar to the proportion for both genders in the same age bracket in the area where your institution is located.' Whether or not you did that exercise, draw a sketch showing how you could visualise the results of the analysis assuming that the target audience you want to communicate the results to is readers of your local newspaper. Make sure to show the type of visualisation you would use and pay attention to ordering, colouring, and labelling.

3   The third exercise in Chapter 4 asked you to: 'Find house price data for 50 houses that have recently sold in your local area similar to that shown in Chapter 4 for Wellington New Zealand' and then to 'make a histogram to show the distribution of sale prices'. Then use any of the methods described in Chapter 4 to:

i   Calculate the mean selling price.
ii   Calculate the median selling price.
iii Calculate the standard deviation in selling prices.'

Whether or not you did that exercise, draw a sketch showing how you could visualise the results of the analysis assuming that the target audience you want to communicate the results to is customers of a local real estate agent who are in the market for new homes. Make sure to show the type of visualisation you would use and pay attention to ordering, colouring, and labelling.

6
MARKETING ANALYTICS

WHAT WILL YOU LEARN FROM THIS CHAPTER?

- Common ways analytics are used in marketing to:
  - evaluate market opportunities
  - understand customers
  - set prices
  - manage distribution channels
  - design and measure the effectiveness of marketing communications
  - develop new products
  - group customers or other stakeholders.
- Other things to consider when designing and executing marketing analytics for these different purposes.

USING ANALYTICS TO EVALUATE MARKET OPPORTUNITIES

Common Questions

Analytics have become a critical component of virtually every aspect of marketing. That starts with helping inform what market(s) to enter in the first place. Anyone starting a new business or trying to get people to invest in one needs to be confident that enough people will want to buy the thing they hope to sell to make it worth it to sell that product or service. The same applies to existing businesses who are considering offering existing products or services in a new geographical region or offering new products or services in geographical regions where they already have a presence. Even if government and non-profit organisations don't sell products or services, they may want to understand how much demand there would be for a new service they are considering offering to their stakeholders.

Each of those examples is rooted in a 'how many' question, such as:

- How many customers would a doggy daycare in your neighbourhood be likely to attract?
- What's the total addressable market for a new gadget an entrepreneur wants you to invest in?
- How many people in the UK would pay to subscribe to a new online magazine?
- How many people in markets where Disney operates would pay to have access to a Disney-themed virtual reality experience?
- How many people in your city would use EV chargers if local authorities made them available in public locations?

When organisations ask questions like these, they are seldom counting on an answer that's exactly correct. That would be both unrealistic and unnecessary. Instead, they're seeking an estimate that's precise enough to know whether or not it's worth entering the new market or launching the new product or service.

A related question that is often asked in these situations is how quickly the answer to the 'how many' question is changing. For instance, the answer to the question about the number of people in your city who would use EV chargers if local authorities made them available in public locations is probably increasing significantly over time as more people purchase electric vehicles. Understanding the rate of change as well as the current level of demand can be very important in these situations for two reasons. First, if the answer to the 'how many' question is increasing or decreasing rapidly, it may be enough to change an organisation's decision about entering a new market or launching a new product or service, because those things often involve investments intended to pay off over a multi-year time period. Secondly, if the answer to the 'how many' question is very volatile – for example, up one year, down the next two then up again – organisations may require a greater value for the answer to the 'how many' question to decide to go ahead with an investment to compensate for the added uncertainty.

Data Sources

At least initially, organisations often use data collected by others, such as governments, the OECD, the World Bank, consultants, or research organisations to get the data required to evaluate market opportunities. These are often referred to as 'third parties' and their data as **'third party data'**. The reason for that is that the data comes from neither the organisation itself (the first party) nor the potential customer or other stakeholder (the second party). Third party data is useful in a situation like this because data that is fully, or at least partially, adequate for the purpose of evaluating market opportunities has often already been collected by these organisations.

One of the most common forms of third party data used to evaluate market opportunities is census data. In most countries, governments regularly collect data used to count the whole population and describe people according to characteristics such as their age, gender, ethnicity, education, and occupation. That type of data is typically available at a national level and can also be broken down into more granular geographic areas. You can see examples of census data for some English-speaking countries using the following links:

- Australia – www.abs.gov.au/census
- Canada – https://census.gc.ca/census-recensement/index-eng.cfm
- New Zealand – www.stats.govt.nz/topics/census
- United Kingdom – https://census.gov.uk
- United States – www.census.gov

The reason census data can be useful in evaluating market opportunities is that those are often aimed toward specific groups. For instance, government organisations in any of the above countries who were considering offering new services for people who are 65 and older could easily use the links above to find out approximately how many such people there are in their country. Or a company thinking of offering a new product targeting that age group could easily find out how many such people there are in multiple countries and use the answer to inform decisions about which countries to launch in or prioritise. Data from organisations such as the OECD, UN, and the World Bank can be useful in those situations because they aggregate some types of data across their member countries, so you can find it all in one place. You can explore some of the types of data these organisations have using the links below:

- OECD - https://data.oecd.org
- UN – https://data.un.org
- World Bank – https://data.worldbank.org

Other types of data collected by government organisations can also be useful for evaluating market opportunities. For example, through governmental organisations in your area, you could probably access dog registration data to answer the question posed earlier about potential customers for a doggy daycare in your neighbourhood or access vehicle registration and home ownership data for your city to answer the question posed about demand for EV chargers in public places.

Commercial organisations also supply various forms of third party data. For example, some industries have trade associations that aggregate data specific to their sector, and some consulting companies produce reports on particular industries, geographical areas, or trends.

Analysis

Because third party data has already been aggregated to some degree, the analytical work required to evaluate market opportunities typically relates to the selection of the specific data points to use and how to use them. That's because the early stages of evaluating market opportunities typically involve assumptions about who will do what. For example, we may assume that a new app our start-up is considering developing would appeal to university students. If so, we can use third party data sources to estimate the number of university students in different countries and regions to get a sense of the size of the potential market. But we're starting with an assumption about who will find the app most appealing. It's possible that our assumption is wrong and that the app will really be more appealing to high school students than to university students. Or maybe it will appeal to university students, but also to many other people into their 20s and 30s. Even if we're right that the people who will be most interested in it are university students, we would need to make assumptions about what percentage of them might download it. While people don't need multiple copies of apps, in other situations we might need to make assumptions about how frequently people would buy or use something.

Because of the need to make assumptions such as those just described, it can be helpful to test how sensitive our estimates of the size of a market opportunity are to specific assumptions. We could do that by evaluating different possible scenarios: for instance, continuing with the previous example, the potential size of the audience for our app if it appeals primarily to university students only versus everyone between 18 and 30.

Other Considerations

While evaluating marketing opportunities almost always involves making some assumptions, such as those just described, it's important to ground those in careful reasoning and whatever data is available, even if that's limited. That's important for getting answers that are as accurate as possible, but it's also important for avoiding stereotypes. For instance, in the previous example, is there something intrinsic in the proposed app that would make it more appealing to university students than to other people, or are the app developers recently out of university themselves and so that's just the age group they relate to most? Relying on incorrect stereotypes can result in incorrectly estimating the size of a market opportunity or excluding groups of people from products or services that might benefit them.

USING ANALYTICS TO UNDERSTAND CUSTOMERS

Common Questions

Probably the most common application of analytics within marketing is to understand customers. That can take a variety of forms to answer questions such as:

- Which types of people or organisations are most interested in this product category or brand or feature?
- Why do customers select the products and services that they do? What needs or wants does the product or service satisfy?
- How frequently do people or organisations purchase products in this category, and what drives purchase frequency?
- How satisfied are existing customers with products or services they have received or with the organisations that provided them?
- How likely are customers to recommend products or services to other potential customers?

Data Sources

Traditionally, a lot of the data organisations used to understand customers came through surveys. Those would ask customers or potential customers about things such as:

- what products and services they buy
- how satisfied they are with products, services, and organisations
- their values, attitudes, and lifestyles
- their demographics.

Surveys are still a common way to collect data about those things, but app and web analytics have become increasingly important sources of information about customers as more products and services have been sold through digital channels or are digital themselves. Web and app analytics track usage of websites and apps. For example, an online retailer 'knows' not only what other products a customer has purchased in the past, but also what products they have looked at online and not purchased. Some of that same information is available even for offline purchases. The reason many organisations use loyalty cards is that it enables them to connect a given customer's purchases over time to build the same type of picture of their buying patterns that it's possible to develop for online customers. Up until recently, that would not capture the browsing type behaviour in the physical world that is possible to observe through web and app analytics; however Amazon has attempted to change that with its Amazon Go stores that use a large number of cameras and sensors to track what people are doing in physical stores (Walton, 2022).

Other data sources that may be useful for understanding customers include:

- information in organisations' own customer relationship management (CRM) systems and transaction records
- posts or reviews on an organisation's own website or on social sites
- data collected through focus groups and interviews.

Analysis

All of the analytical techniques described in Chapter 4 are frequently used to understand customers. For example, the web and app analytics already mentioned typically provide sums of total users and break them down into percentages based on things such as the country they come from or the operating system they're using. Statistics such as means and standard deviations are used to describe things such as how much money customers spend per transaction or the amount of time they spend on an app or website. Means and proportions can be compared to determine things such as whether certain types of customers tend to spend more than others or are disproportionately likely to buy specific items. Correlations and regression (and more sophisticated machine learning techniques that build on those) can be used to identify whether purchases of one product tend to be related to purchases of others or to customer characteristics, such as age.

Other Considerations

Survey data has two major types of limitations to keep in mind. First, participation in most surveys is voluntary, and those who participate may not be representative of those who don't. For example, the people who answer customer satisfaction surveys tend to be the people who are most and least satisfied as opposed to those who are not particularly happy or unhappy. Second, surveys are very useful for measuring things that can't be measured any other way. Those are often things people are thinking or feeling, such as their attitude toward a brand or their level of satisfaction with a product they have purchased. However, surveys are not particularly accurate ways to measure things such as how important different features are or how often people do things that happen either very often or irregularly.

Answers to survey questions about the importance of different features are often not very good predictors of what people will actually buy. That's in part because people typically buy whole products rather than individual features. In light of that, it's often preferable to infer what features are important analytically by comparing features in products or services people buy to those they don't. If data about how important something is needs to be captured through a survey, a similar process can be used whereby they indicate their preferences among whole products, and then the importance of particular attributes is inferred analytically by comparing the attributes present in the products they preferred more with those they preferred less.

Answers to questions about how frequently people do things or how much time or money they spend on them can be unreliable because they are just difficult for people to estimate. For example, if you were asked how many times in the past week you used one of your favourite apps, you may have trouble coming up with an estimate, and chances are your estimate would not be very accurate. That type of **behavioural data** is more reliable when it comes from things such as app and web analytics where the behaviour is being tracked directly by a computer rather than estimated by a person.

There are also caveats to consider when it comes to web and app analytics though. Those forms of data have become ubiquitous, which is good in many ways but it means that sometimes people rely on them because they are convenient as opposed to being the most useful source of data for questions an organisation has. For example, web and app analytics can be very useful for analysing behaviour related to digital products and services, such as streaming media platforms and social networks, but if an organisation has questions about things that happen offline they can be far less useful.

Even in the digital context, it's important to be aware of the limitations of web and app analytics. For example, the information presented may be based on inferences about things such as a users' gender or race based on the particular content people are accessing. In websites that don't require log-ins, each device visiting a site may be assumed to be a distinct user, but that doesn't account for people sharing devices or having more than one device. Even when users do have to log in, web and app analytics may not be able to account for things such as shared accounts and gift purchases. It's also not always clear how to interpret particular data points. For example, more time spent on a streaming media platform may be interpreted as a good thing, but is the same true of your banking app or could it be an indication that the app is not as easy to use as it could/should be?

Like survey data, data from posts and reviews on an organisation's own website and on social media sites may not be representative of the views of all customers because people can choose to post or not and the people who do post may not be representative of the people who don't. Data collected via interviews and focus groups has the same potential problem of representativeness with the additional challenge that sample sizes for data collected that way can be quite small, which may limit the types of analysis that can be done.

USING ANALYTICS TO DESIGN AND MANAGE MARKETING COMMUNICATIONS

Common Questions

Besides wanting to understand their customers or other stakeholders, organisations need to know how best to communicate with them. This gives rise to a series of questions, including:

- How does the response we get vary based on what messages we use to communicate with customers?
- How does the response we get vary based on what creative executions we use to communicate with customers?
- How does the response we get vary based on what channels (e.g., e-mail, text, phone, Facebook ad, Instagram ad, YouTube ad, etc.) we use to communicate with customers?
- What recommendations should we make to this customer or potential customer to maximise their probability of making a purchase or spending more time on our streaming service?
- To what extent do things such as recommendations from celebrities, friends, or influencers drive sales or use of our product or service?

Data Sources

In digital media, it's possible to generate a lot of experimental data about things such as the number of people who click on an ad or buy a product depending on the message or execution, which can be assigned randomly. Another name for this process is **A/B testing**, where A and B are different alternatives. There could be more than two alternatives, but it's still called A/B testing. So, for example, A could be a version of an ad that focusses more on the people using a product and B could be a version of an ad that focusses more on the product itself. The digital advertising ecosystem is structured in a way that would enable one randomly selected group of people to be shown ad A and the other ad B. The same process could be used if the things being compared were the taglines or music used in an ad or alternative designs for a particular web page.

That type of data from A/B testing or experimentation is sometimes augmented with survey data about attitudes or beliefs people hold about products, services or organisations, or with transaction or usage data collected either through surveys or through other means, such as web, app, or platform analytics. For example, let's say an existing automotive company has produced an electric version of a well-known brand of vehicle, but one that up until now has not offered an all-electric model. Suppose that its advertising agency came up with two alternative digital marketing campaigns, one starting with an emphasis on the existing associations people have with the brand and ending with the information that an electric option is now available, and the other starting with an announcement about a 'new' electric vehicle and ending with the news that it's from a brand people already know. The company or its agency could organise for users of a video streaming service that has advertising to be randomly assigned to be shown one version of the ad or the other. Then, assuming the privacy policy and terms of service of the streaming service permit this, it could work with the streaming service to survey both groups of people to find out whether the proportion who are aware that the car brand now has an electric option differs, or if attitude toward the brand differs between the two groups. The streaming service itself could follow a similar process to test something like whether people who are given recommendations generated by one algorithm cancel their subscriptions at a different rate than people who are given recommendations generated by a different algorithm.

Analysis

Analysing results of A/B testing and other experiments designed to test the effectiveness of different forms of marketing communications is often as simple as comparing means (for numeric variables, such as time spent on a website or average transaction value), or proportions (for nominal or ordinal variables, such as whether someone clicked on a link or mentioned a particular brand attribute) by alternative. For example, did people who saw one version of a website spend more time on it, on average, than people who saw a different version? Or did a greater proportion of people who saw one version of a digital ad click on it compared to those who saw a different version? Since those A/B tests are typically conducted with a sample of users, but the organisation generally wants to be sure results would generalise to all users, they could test for statistically significant differences between means (for numerical variables, such as time-spent) using a t-test or ANOVA or for statistically significant differences in proportions (for nominal variables, such as whether or not people clicked on an ad) using a chi-square test.

Sophisticated versions of predictive models (somewhat like regression, which was discussed in Chapter 4, but more advanced) can be used to inform decisions about what content or ads to recommend to an individual user based on his or her demographics and/ or purchase or viewing history.

Other considerations

The most rigorous experiments are those where people can be randomly assigned to alternative 'treatments' (e.g., view ad A or view ad B). Organisations have that type of control on their own platforms (e.g., Meta showing ads on Instagram or Alphabet showing ads on YouTube); however that can be harder in other situations. For example, it's possible to compare whether a greater percentage of people who view an ad on Instagram click on it compared to YouTube; however, it's not possible for an outside organisation to randomly assign people to view it on either YouTube or Instagram. That means that if the ad performs better on one of those platforms than the other there will be some uncertainty about whether that's because of the nature of the platform or the nature of the people who use the platform.

At a broader level, the types of techniques discussed in this sub-section can be used to test messages about a variety of products, services, organisations, and ideas. There have been concerns about them being used to encourage the sale of products that may not be in people's best interest to consume and to facilitate the spread of mis-information and anti-social messages. For example, these approaches are used to fine-tune ads for unhealthy foods or other products that at least some people may view as socially undesirable.

Platforms such as Facebook use data collected about what people do on it and other platforms, apps, and websites to make (automated) decisions about what content to recommend to individual users. Those decisions can increase user engagement, but they can also have negative consequences. For example, one large US study found that people who used Facebook as a source of news about Covid were less likely than those who don't use Facebook at all to have been vaccinated, and those who used Facebook as their only Covid news source were even less likely to have been vaccinated (Lazer et al., 2021).

USING ANALYTICS TO SET PRICES

Common Questions

How much customers are willing to pay for products and services is a vital question for for-profit companies since it relates directly to their profitability. This question applies when companies are launching products and services for the first time, when they are introducing new products and services or new variations of existing products or services, and if they are trying to find ways to charge different prices to different customers (e.g., business class versus economy on a plane) or at different times (e.g., 'early bird' specials).

Analytics can also inform decisions about pricing promotions. They can be used to answer questions such as:

- If we offer a temporary sale, deal, or discount, to what extent will we attract new customers? Will existing customers buy more? Or will existing customers just change the timing of their purchases to get a better price?
- How big a discount do we need to offer to attract new customers or encourage existing customers to buy more?
- What type(s) of discounts are most effective (e.g., discounted price versus buy-one-get-one-free versus gift with purchase)?

Data Sources

Organisations sometimes use surveys to ask customers and potential customers how much they are willing to pay for products or services, but that has two potential downsides. One is that people may not really know until they are presented with a product or a choice among products and then they either buy or don't. The other is that to the extent that customers really do know how much they would be willing to pay, they may perceive it to be in their interest to state a lower number than what they are truly willing to pay.

One way organisations have tried to address that in the past is using a more specialised type of survey in which customers or potential customers make choices among a series of options in which price and a number of other attributes are varied. That approach presents a more realistic scenario since people are familiar with having to make trade-offs between price and other features they may want. For example it may be important to you to have a phone with all of the latest features and to pay as little as possible for a phone, but when you actually buy a phone you are likely to have to choose which of those things is really more important to you because the phones that have the latest features are unlikely to be the least expensive.

Another approach is to use pricing experiments. In that approach the prices of real products or services are varied. That variation may occur across locations (e.g., stores or restaurants that are part of the same chain in different cities), across time (e.g., products going on sale or on special offer), or across customers (e.g., some customers may be given some kind of special offer). The most effective experiments are those in which the prices customers are exposed to are randomly assigned as opposed to their being able to self-select into groups or employees assigning them to groups. That helps ensure that differences seen are the result of price (in this case) as opposed to some other factor. Pricing experiments were previously expensive and difficult, but digital platforms make them easier. For instance, it's easy to display different prices to different customers on a website and to randomly select who sees which price.

Analysis

If data is collected from a survey just asking customers how much they would be willing to pay, those answers can simply be summarised as an average if people could put in any price they wanted or by showing what percentage gave each answer or group of answers (e.g., between $50 and $100) if they selected from a list of options.

Data in which price is presented as one attribute among many making up different possible offers is typically analysed using a process called **conjoint analysis**. That uses regression or other similar methods to analytically derive the importance of price compared to other attributes and to estimate how a change in price will change demand.

If price is manipulated in a pricing experiment, the results are typically analysed by comparing the proportion of people who choose a product at different price points. Since experiments typically involve samples, those results could be analysed using a chi-square test (because the price point options are an ordinal variable and choice is nominal) to see if any difference in the proportion choosing the product at different price points is statistically significant.

Other Considerations

The types of analysis just described may reveal that some customers are willing to pay more for the same product than others. Even so, organisations need to carefully consider the ethics and potential reputational impacts of charging different customers different amounts for the same thing just because some are willing to pay more than others. Doing so may maximise organisational profits in the short-run, but there is a risk of a longer-term backlash if customers become aware of this practice. For example, Uber's surge pricing, in which prices change depending on how many people are calling for Ubers at a particular time, often elicits complaints – including when some fares surged to over $500 Australian dollars over an event-filled weekend in Melbourne (*New Zealand Herald*, 2022).

USING ANALYTICS TO MANAGE DISTRIBUTION CHANNELS

Common Questions

Many organisations make products and services available through multiple channels. For example, many food products are available through a variety of grocery store chains as well as through convenience stores and mass market retailers. In other cases, retailers may offer things like clothing and housewares in physical stores as well as online. Even within a single channel of distribution, there may be multiple intermediaries, such as wholesalers and retail stores. This gives rise to a series of questions including:

- Which channels and channel partners generate the greatest volume of business, and is that changing over time?
- Which channels and channel partners generate the greatest profit margin, and is that changing over time?
- Which channels and channel partners are favoured by customers overall and by specific groups of customers? Is that changing over time?
- Which channels and channel partners generate the most complaints from customers overall and from specific customer groups? Is that changing over time?
- Is the number of days when a product is unavailable for purchase consistent across channels and channel partners or more common for some than for others?
- Are returns consistent across channels and channel partners or more common for some than for others?

Answers to questions like these can enable organisations to make decisions about things such as adding or dropping channel partners or entire channels of distribution.

Data Sources

An organisation's own internal records are an important source of data for analytics related to distribution channels. Those internal records would show things such as which products were distributed through which channels and at what price. It may also be possible to use internal records to get data related to the cost of serving different channels. That's generally more difficult to get than data related to revenue by channel, but enough information may be available to at least create an estimate based on a combination of direct and indirect costs.

Organisations may also survey customers and potential customers (either directly or indirectly with the help of consultants) to get data related to which channels of distribution they currently use and prefer, and if they would like to be able to get particular products through different channels.

Some organisations also monitor channel partners using mystery shoppers who record information such as how they were treated by staff, which products (if any) were recommended by staff, and if/how a given organisation's products were displayed.

Analysis

If the data is available, analysis of things such as sales volumes, revenue and profitability by channel just requires arithmetic – totalling revenue associated with each channel, dividing revenue by costs, dividing revenue this year by revenue last year, etc. Typically, organisations would be using their own data for this purpose and therefore would have population-level data, so no tests of statistical significance would be needed.

Survey data regarding customer use of and preferences for different channels of distribution can be analysed by calculating the percentage of customers who use or prefer different channels and using chi-square tests to check for statistically significant differences by customer group (since surveys are typically based on samples).

Mystery shopper data could be analysed to see what proportion of channel partners did specific things, such as display a product as directed. One again, if needed chi-square tests could be used to check for differences in those proportions based on characteristics of the channel partner (e.g., what chain they were part of or if they were part of a chain versus independent retail outlets).

Other Considerations

It's often important to analyse data related to distribution channels at a fairly granular level because results may vary by individual product and product category. Even in stores that are part of the same chain, certain products may sell well in one store but not another. For that reason, there are people who specialise in optimising the selection and placement of products within retail stores to try to maximise revenue for the store per square foot of space. That same attention to analytical detail can also benefit the organisations supplying products to those stores.

While analytics can be used to estimate revenue and profit by channel and for individual channel partners, they shouldn't be the only considerations in decisions about adding or dropping channels or channel partners. There may be strategic, ethical, or legal reasons for doing – or not doing – those things too. An organisation might want to operate within a certain channel or maintain a channel partnership for strategic reasons, such as preparing for a future product launch or promotional effort. It may want to operate within a certain channel or maintain a channel partnership for ethical reasons, such as to ensure a traditionally underserved demographic group has access to its products. There can also sometimes be legal reasons for the ways companies organise their distribution channels, such as agreements related to exclusivity for channel partners or avoiding anti-trust concerns.

USING ANALYTICS TO DEVELOP NEW PRODUCTS

Common Questions

Historically new products were often developed in response to a need the person developing the product had or feedback from a relatively small group of people such as friends and family or focus groups. Some new products are still developed that way, but analytics can provide much deeper, more granular, and more generalisable information to guide decisions about new products. Analytics can answer questions such as:

- Are there common complaints that people make about products in this product category that a new product could overcome?
- Are there market trends that create opportunities for new products?

Existing organisations can also use analytics to answer additional questions such as:

- What are the complaints or suggestions for improvement our customers make most often?
- Are people searching for products or product features on our website that we could offer, but don't currently offer?
- Do existing customers have unmet needs that we could address with a new product or a new version of an existing product?

Data Sources

Qualitative data related to both trends and complaints may come from social media or from traditional media.

Existing organisations may also explore ideas for potential new products using data from customer surveys, and data collected through their own apps and websites.

Analysis

Articles in the media and posts in social media can be quantified for analysis using the process described in Chapter 4. That would reveal whether the frequency with which certain topics are mentioned is changing over time or if complaints about particular products, brands, or experiences are changing.

Survey data about complaints, suggestions for improvement, and unmet needs can be summarised by calculating the percentage of respondents who have specific complaints or suggestions. That type of data is often viewed overall as well as using cross-tabs for different groups (e.g., by gender, age, ethnicity, length of time as a customer or frequency of purchases).

Web or app analytics data can be sorted to show the terms that are searched for most frequently as well as behaviour patterns that may provide clues about the need for a new product (e.g., carts/baskets with certain items in them being abandoned more frequently than those with other items in them).

Other Considerations

Since potential new products and services are virtually limitless, choices need to be made about what types of possibilities to explore. Those choices will influence what data is sourced and analysed, but as part of that process it's important to think carefully about whose needs may be being ignored. For example, if an organisation analyses data about its own customers it may be able to identify opportunities for products or services that could meet their needs better, but that analysis would not reveal even more acute needs of people who are not already customers of that organisation.

USING ANALYTICS TO GROUP CUSTOMERS OR POTENTIAL CUSTOMERS

Common Questions

Marketers often want to segment customers or potential customers into groups who have distinct wants and needs, and therefore have different preferences and respond differently to specific marketing tactics. Historically, that was often done by judgement based on demographic variables. For example, it's fairly obvious that children and adults have different wants and needs when it comes to clothes, so it makes sense to treat those as two distinct groups. But those judgements could also be based on stereotypes. For example, traditionally companies who made clothes may have segmented their offerings based on an untested assumption that gender is the most useful differentiator when it comes to clothing preferences. Anecdotally at least, there is reason to question that assumption. For example, some designers are now introducing unisex clothing lines, and many people (e.g., White, 2021) have complained about the absence or inadequacy of pockets in clothing made for women as compared to clothing made for men. Analytics can be used to test assumptions like this.

Data Sources

Two primary sources of data for use in segmentation are surveys and organisations' own transaction data. Surveys tend to include data about things such as attitudes and preferences related to different product attributes, whereas transaction data includes information about which people have purchased which things in the past and at what price. Any of those types of data could be used as the basis for segmentation, and it's often useful to test multiple types of data to see which create segments that are most meaningful for a given organisation. Useful segment structures are those where stakeholders within a segment are all reasonably similar to one another, but different from those in other segments. In those situations, treating the segments differently should result in greater overall satisfaction compared to treating everyone the same way.

Analysis

To continue with the clothing example, at a very basic level, we could do things such as ask people what particular clothing attributes, such as pockets, natural fibres, specific styles, etc. they like and don't like, and see if their preferences vary by gender, and if so, how strongly. We could do that by calculating the percentage of people of each gender who prefer or want to avoid particular attributes, and then use a chi-square test to evaluate whether the difference is statistically significant (since both gender and individual clothing attributes are nominal variables).

We can test other possible bases for grouping customers using other techniques discussed in Chapter 4. For example, we could use correlation or regression to see if spending on particular products is related to age or income (since age, income, and spending are all numeric variables). Since clothing obviously needs to fit people's bodies, we could also use ANOVA or t-tests to see if average body measurements vary more greatly between genders than within them.

There is a more sophisticated way of grouping customers which is called cluster analysis. There are a variety of forms of cluster analysis, and the details of those are beyond the scope of this book, but in general they build on the idea of correlations that is discussed in Chapter 4. The difference though is that instead of focussing on correlations among pairs of variables, cluster analysis is used to group observations based on similarity across a larger set of variables simultaneously. So, for example, we could either survey people about their clothing preferences or go and look in their closets and record the presence or absence of the attributes in each item of clothing. Clustering algorithms could then be used to find the people whose preferences or closet contents are most similar. For example, one cluster might consist of people who tend to prefer more natural fabrics and more classic styles and another might consist of people who gravitate toward brightly coloured fast-fashion type items. Of course, someone who works in clothing or fashion might have their own judgements about segments, but cluster analysis can be used to evaluate how closely those conform to constellations of actual consumer preferences or behaviour.

Other Considerations

In recent years there has been a trend toward individualised recommendations, which allows for even more finely tuned approaches to personalising marketing based on the needs and wants of individual customers than segmentation does. Nonetheless, that level of personalisation is not always feasible from a technical, legal, or privacy perspective so segmentation can strike a happy-medium between treating everyone the same way and personalising to a level where it becomes creepy or illegal. One thing to note however is that everyone may not fit neatly into a segment. There can be people in the gaps between segments or whose preferences span multiple segments, so organisations need to consider how to meet the needs of those outliers and boundary spanners.

SUMMARY

When people think of marketing, it's often the more creative aspects they have in mind, but analytics are used extensively in marketing – including to inform creative decisions, such as which version of a logo or ad to use. That example illustrates how the creative and analytical aspects of marketing complement one another. In some situations, analytics are being used to test alternative creative concepts, and in other situations they are being used to inform and guide creative and strategic processes. For example, rich and detailed personas representing different customer segments can be developed using cluster analysis along with the different analytical techniques described in Chapter 4, and then those personas can provide a starting point and inspiration for developing new products or new promotional campaigns.

Just as small differences in the creative aspects of marketing can make a big difference to the impact of a promotional campaign, small differences in the way analytics are implemented can make a big difference in the amount of impact they have. A subtle difference in what questions are asked or how they are asked in a customer survey can make the difference between identifying a crucial insight and misunderstanding how customers actually feel. Thoughtful use of passively collected data can underpin recommendations that help users discover content they love, but irresponsible use of passively collected data can anger customers and violate laws in many places.

ANALYTICS IN PRACTICE

Beautiful models rely on a good foundation

Rock Zhu joined L'Oréal as Director, Data and Analytics Governance for China & North Asia after extensive experience in data and analytics roles with organisations in China and New Zealand. His new role offered a great opportunity to apply the skills he had developed in the dynamic Chinese market:

In China the pace, the competitiveness, is just so fast. The volume is just huge! And then and there's new things popping up all the time. It will be a new technology. There will be new platforms, where probably people all the sudden like going to TikTok.

The part of L'Oréal Rock works in is responsible for 30 brands, each with many products, in five markets. L'Oréal has an entrepreneurial culture, and employees had already been experimenting with using analytics for things such as designing promotions and targeting ads. The challenge Rock faced was that there was a lot of variation across brands, markets, and distribution channels in things such as what data was stored, how it was named, tagged, and structured:

I'll give you a very simple example: the way how people spell makeup - with a dash, without a dash, with Chinese, with Japanese ... There's no one defining what's the standards, they're all coming through as different files.

Standardising and centralising the data would allow creative ideas for using the data to derive marketing insights to scale across all of the brands and markets and would enable identification of even deeper insights and development of even more sophisticated models for using the data to do things such as target advertising, optimise promotions, and recommend products. It would also mean that in many cases, people who needed to use data to make decisions could access it directly themselves:

For me to be successful is people coming to me for advice not saying: 'I need these reports', 'I need this query'. My success is how many people will be able to do those things by themselves? Which is ten times harder than you doing it ... Because the flexibility comes with agility where business knows the questions.

As that centralisation and standardisation process happened, China adopted the new privacy legislation discussed in Chapter 2. That meant Rock's growing Data and Analytics team needed to delete some data that was no longer compliant with that and rethink the data used in some of their predictive models.

We even have a lot of discussions last week - very senior executives - what we can do, what we cannot do, so a lot of those personalisation ads, which I was talking about, can no longer be done for people without consent ... We actually delete, and then we make hard decisions: we're not going to touch that.

RUNNING CASE STUDY: 4TE, PART 6[1]

Emily and Matt were very impressed with and grateful for Ben's summary of his analysis of 4tE's customer information. The presentation had given them a fairly clear idea of the types of people within their existing customer base. But as they talked about it over the weekend, they realised they still didn't have enough information to make a call on whether or not to expand into new product lines, open another store, or expand their delivery area. As they thought about potentially expanding their delivery area or opening another store, they realised they needed to know if there were many people in Portland who were similar to their existing customers, but were not already shopping at 4tE. And if there were a reasonable number of those people, it would also help to know if they were disproportionately located in certain parts of the city. As Matt and Emily thought about potentially expanding the types of products 4tE carried, they realised they needed more information from their existing customers on what other types of products they might like to buy from 4tE.

When Ben came in to work the first of his two afternoon shifts the following week, Emily explained that she and Matt thought they needed to do two surveys. One survey would focus on determining what proportion of Portland residents fit the profile of 4tE customers, what proportion of them already shop at 4tE, and where those who fit the 4tE profile but don't shop there live. They believed that would help them make the decisions about whether to expand the delivery area or open another store. Emily said that she and Matt also thought they should survey existing customers to gauge their interest in buying various types of products from 4tE that they don't currently offer, but could. Emily asked Ben if he would be willing to take the lead on those two survey projects.

Ben was excited that Emily and Matt had enough confidence in him to ask him to take charge of the survey projects and he readily agreed. One of the first things he thought about was who should be surveyed for each one. The customer survey was easier. 4tE had e-mail addresses for everyone with a loyalty card, and those customers accounted for most of 4tE's business. Inviting all of the customers they had e-mail addresses for to complete an online survey wouldn't cost any more than just surveying a sample of customers and would result in more responses.

The survey of Portland residents was trickier. They obviously couldn't survey all Portland residents, but since the point was to get a sense of what proportion fit the general profile of 4tE customers, the sample needed to be as representative as possible of the broader population. Ben wasn't sure how they could achieve that, so he spent the rest of his 4tE time that week researching options. By the end of that time, he settled on a survey sample provider that had a lot of positive reviews online and could guarantee 500 survey responses from a sample of people that they claimed would be demographically representative of the overall population of Portland.

---

[1]The 4tE case is fictitious.

That left creating the surveys themselves. Ben knew about a few survey platforms from his courses and he spent his two afternoons the following week comparing the features of those and a few other options. He narrowed it down to the one he liked best after signing up for free trials to test what it was like to actually create surveys on what appeared to be the best two platforms. After selecting the platform he wanted to use, Ben worked on a draft of the questions for each of the two surveys. He sent invitations to Matt and Emily so that they could preview the surveys, give him their feedback, and make sure he hadn't missed anything important.

EXERCISES

1. Suppose that an ed-tech start-up has developed a new educational approach for improving learning among 5–15 year olds. As part of making a decision about which country to pilot their service in, they have asked you to find out how many people there are in that age bracket in the US, UK, Canada, Australia and New Zealand. See if you can find the answers using the links provided earlier in this chapter to the census data for those countries.

2. Suppose Tourism New Zealand wanted to attract more international tourists, and that to try to achieve that, they tested two ad campaigns. One campaign highlighted New Zealand's spectacular scenery and the other used cheeky humour to show New Zealand as a fun, friendly, welcoming, place. Ads for each campaign were shown to a random sample of 5000 people in Australia, China, Germany, the UK, and the US on a digital platform that is popular in the relevant country. The number of people who clicked on a link in each ad was then recorded to determine what campaign to feature in each country in digital media, but also in broadcast media and in print. The results for each country are shown in Table 6.1. Using plain language that a Tourism New Zealand marketing manager with no background in statistics could understand, explain which campaign should be used in each country and why.

Table 6.1 Results from ad test

Country	Spectacular scenery ad clicks	Cheeky humour ad clicks
Australia	47	66
China	54	36
Germany	51	43
UK	41	60
USA	59	46

3   Suppose a company in your country that manufactures a food product for sale in supermarkets is facing increasing costs due to inflation, and has asked for your help in determining whether they can increase their prices in the domestic market. The specific question they have asked you to focus on is: 'Will raising our prices 5% or 10% in the domestic market significantly reduce demand for our products in the domestic market?'. Describe how you would go about getting an answer to that specific question, assuming that they have other people focussing on their costs and on international markets, so all you need to focus on is how a price increase could be expected to affect demand in the domestic market.

7
HR/PEOPLE ANALYTICS

WHAT WILL YOU LEARN FROM THIS CHAPTER?

- How data and analytics can be used to:
  - Measure employee performance
  - Monitor diversity, equity, and inclusion (DEI)
  - See what employees are doing
  - Assess the effectiveness of training
  - Evaluate employee satisfaction
  - Identify and recruit future employees.
- Factors that need to be taken into consideration when doing those things.

USING ANALYTICS TO MEASURE EMPLOYEE PERFORMANCE

Common Questions

While the concept of HR analytics dates to the early 2000s (Marler and Boudreau, 2016) and the term people analytics is even newer (Tursunbayeva et al., 2018), managers have probably been trying to measure the performance of their employees for as long as organisations have existed. Performance measurement may still be the most essential part of people analytics because it's important on its own for managing existing employees as well as being an important component of other aspects of people analytics, such as identifying recruitment sources that account for a disproportionate share of employees who perform particularly well or poorly.

Common questions involved in measuring employee performance include:

- How is an individual employee performing, and is that changing over time?
- How does the performance of employees in one location, division, etc. compare to that in others, and is that changing over time?
- What characteristics predict who will perform well in a particular role and who will perform poorly?

Data Sources

While these questions sound straightforward, hidden within them is something that often isn't, and that's what we mean by performance. In some roles, that's fairly obvious. For example, some people who pick fruit are paid based on the volume of fruit they pick that satisfies some minimum quality standard (e.g., it is the correct size or ripeness). In that situation, higher volume means better performance, and if people are working on their own, there's no ambiguity about who is responsible for the performance. In a situation like that where performance equates to a count of some tangible, observable output, it can be measured based on that, usually with passively collected quantitative data of one form or another (e.g., the weight of fruit picked or fish caught).

In most modern workplaces, performance is much more difficult to define let alone measure. Producing something like a car or a computer requires the work of many people, so even though it's easy to count how many cars or computers have been produced, it would be virtually impossible to identify what percentage of that is due to the efforts of the person who put in a battery versus the person who designed the battery versus the person who hired the person who designed the battery versus all of the other people whose work contributed to the creation of the final product.

In situations where it's not possible to measure performance based on some tangible, observable output, such as fruit picked or fish caught, performance is typically measured more subjectively – usually in the form of a rating. That can be done holistically – for example, whether someone's overall performance is rated as meeting, exceeding, or falling short of expectations. It can also be done based on more specific factors that are relevant to a particular role, such as teamwork or client service.

A person's manager is almost always involved in assigning these subjective performance ratings; however, many organisations also use ratings from colleagues, subordinates, business partners, and/or customers or clients for evaluating the performance of individuals in at least some roles. You've probably contributed such ratings yourself – perhaps without realising it – when you've been asked to evaluate the helpfulness of a person who assisted you in a store or when you called a support line. You may again if, when you complete the course you are currently taking, you are asked to evaluate the person who taught it. Those subjective ratings are typically in the form of Likert scales with somewhere between three and eleven points.

Analysis

Analysing the performance of an individual starts with aggregating ratings if they have been given by more than one person. For example, those working in customer or client-facing roles may be rated by many customers or clients, and an average can be taken of those ratings to give a general sense of how customers or clients perceive that employee. Aggregation may be required for more objective performance measures too. For example, in the case of a customer service representative, averaging the number of calls they answer per day or the length of time it takes them to resolve a call.

Whether that type of aggregation is required or performance has just been rated subjectively by a single manager, it tends to be most useful when compared to other people. For example, it may not be particularly useful to know that, on average, it takes a particular customer service representative 12 minutes to resolve a call, that they take 3 calls per hour, and their customer satisfaction rating is 7/10 unless we know that across all customer service representatives, those averages are 10 minutes, 4 calls, and an 8.5 satisfaction rating. Our perception of the performance of that single customer service employee would be very different with those overall averages than if the overall averages were 15 minutes, 2 calls, and a satisfaction rating of 5.

Comparing an individual's performance to an overall average like that is easy in a role, such as customer service, where an organisation may have many people doing the same thing. It's more challenging in situations where there is only one person doing a given type of job. That's part of the reason some organisations measure performance using an overall rating or characteristics such as innovation or professionalism that can be more easily generalised across many roles, and therefore more easily compared.

In situations where it's possible to compare the performance of different employees, organisations can then do analysis to try to identify patterns of variation in performance. For example, they could check to see whether the proportion of employees exceeding or falling short of expectations varies by location or role. They could use a chi-square test to see if any differences found are statistically significant if they are doing that with only a sample of employees rather than with data for all employees. If some aspect of performance had been measured using a ratio-scaled variable, such as sales, or on a Likert scale with a larger number of points, as customer satisfaction often is, and that scale is being treated as interval rather than ordinal, then they could do a similar thing by comparing average ratings for different roles or locations. They could use ANOVA to see if any differences found are statistically significant if they are doing that with only a sample of employees rather than with data for all employees.

Most organisations would love to be able to use analytics to explain and predict performance. While techniques such as regression, as well as more sophisticated machine learning models could be used to do that, they require good measures of both performance and the variables used to predict performance. Some of the challenges associated with measuring performance have already been discussed. Additional challenges are discussed in the next sub-section. Some challenges associated with measuring some potential predictors of performance are discussed later in the chapter.

Other Considerations

As already discussed, performance is often measured using subjective ratings. That introduces the potential for at least two sources of bias or inaccuracy. One possible source is the criteria used to evaluate performance, and the other is how those criteria are applied. People may have different opinions about exactly what constitutes good performance in a particular role, and therefore about what criteria should be used to judge performance in that role. A different set of performance criteria applied to the same role and to the same people could result in a different rank order of performance. And since the criteria themselves are somewhat subjective, their application could be subject to implicit or explicit bias – often in favour of people who share characteristics of the person doing the rating and against those who don't. To the extent that factors such as these mean performance ratings are not a true reflection of actual performance (if there was a way to measure that objectively), associations between performance and other things (e.g., job satisfaction, participation in a particular training programme) may be obscured.

Another thing to be aware of is the potential for tension between the best measure of performance for managing an individual and for use in analytics. Since different jobs vary greatly in terms of their objectives, then someone managing people in a particular role might prefer to use a performance measure that is tailored specifically to that role. On the other hand, it's often not possible to aggregate very specific performance measures across an organisation to be able to compare the performance of individuals across roles or to compare the performance of different parts of an organisation to one another. Therefore, more generalisable measures of performance tend to be preferable for use in analytics.

USING ANALYTICS TO MONITOR DIVERSITY, EQUITY, AND INCLUSION (DEI)

A growing trend over the past few years has been for organisations to use data to quantify their diversity, equity, and inclusion (DEI). Many organisations now publish a report on their progress toward improved diversity, equity, and inclusion in their workforce. You can find examples by searching for 'DEI report' followed by the name of an organisation, industry, or country.

Common Questions

- Do the demographics of our workforce match those of the surrounding area, or are some types of people over- or under-represented? Are any differences identified more acute in particular types of roles, at particular levels, or in particular locations?

- Does employee compensation vary by non-work related factors, such as race, gender, age, or sexual orientation, and if so, how much of that variation can be explained by work-related factors, such as role, experience, or education?

Data Sources

Organisations already hold most of the data required to monitor diversity, equity, and inclusion (DEI) within their own internal systems. That includes information related to various aspects of identity (e.g., race, gender, sexual orientation, disability status) that are either required or supplied voluntarily during the hiring process, as well as compensation data, which is held within HR information systems. The main outside data source that's required is census or similar data that provides information on the demographics of the surrounding area that can then be used as a benchmark to compare against the demographics of the organisation's workforce.

Analysis

To see if the composition of an organisation's workforce mirrors the composition of the population in the area in which it's located, the proportion of employees in certain groups can be compared to the proportion in the surrounding area. For example, if 15% of people in the area where an organisation is located are Asian, are about 15% of employees also Asian? Similar comparisons can be done for other races and other aspects of identity. If the data for the surrounding area comes from census data and data for the organisation comes from its own records, then there is no need to do a chi-square test because both of those are population-level data sources. What may be useful though is to see if similar patterns hold across different levels, roles, etc. For example, many organisations find that their workforce mirrors the demographics of the surrounding area fairly well at lower levels of seniority, but becomes more skewed in various ways at more senior levels of management.

Looking for differences in compensation by gender, race, or any other aspect of identity can start with comparing average or median compensation across groups (with no test of statistical significance needed if that's done for the entire workforce). However, if people in certain identity groups are disproportionately likely or unlikely to be in particular roles or at particular levels, that needs to be taken into account in doing that analysis. That can be done by doing the analysis role-by-role or level-by level if there are enough people from the different identity groups at different roles and levels. Doing that analysis both overall and for specific roles or levels would reveal whether any gap in pay by gender, race, or any other identity-related characteristic is a function of people in different groups being in different roles/levels or people having different compensation even when they are in similar roles at similar levels. That distinction is important in making future decisions related to staff recruitment, development, and compensation.

Other Considerations

As discussed in Chapter 2, when collecting data about a group of people it's important that representatives of that group are involved in the design of the data collection process to make sure it is done as effectively as possible and does not unintentionally cause offence or create other problems. That's especially true with data related to diversity, equity, and inclusion because the whole point is to try to improve representation of traditionally under-represented groups, and the fact that they are under-represented suggests that the organisation has traditionally not been particularly effective in connecting with them. Including a diverse range of people in the design of the process to collect DEI data can help ensure the response options available for different variables are fully inclusive (i.e., there is not a variable for which no option seems suitable for a particular person). It can also help ensure that the questions and response options are unlikely to be perceived as offensive to or by anyone. That approach also helps ensure that data are collected in a way that will make it possible to produce useful and accurate analysis. For example, since people can identify with more than one race or ethnicity, it's important for that to be a 'select all' rather than a 'choose one' type question on a form.

One issue that has arisen in the quest for more useful DEI insights is disaggregation of data to show intersectional results: for example, not just showing results for race or gender, but also the intersection of the two. That may reveal patterns of under-representation or pay inequity that are obscured when examining results at a higher level of aggregation. While that's very useful, if results are reported in situations in which any of the disaggregated groups are very small, it risks breaching the privacy of the individuals in them and means that the results for those small groups could be strongly influenced by individual observations.

USING ANALYTICS TO SEE WHAT EMPLOYEES ARE DOING

Common Questions

- How long are employees working?
- Where are employees going?
- To what extent do employees interact with one another?
- How much of something did a given person produce in a given time period?

Data Sources

Employees have been clocking in and out of workplaces for decades, so that one source of passively collected quantitative data about what employees are doing has been available for a long time even if the specific technologies used to clock in and out have changed. More recently the **Internet of Things** – or devices communicating with other devices via the Internet – has created many more potential sources of data about what employees are doing. Many employees need to be logged in to software such as Slack or Teams to do their jobs and that creates another source of data about what employees are doing.

Even without anyone formally clocking in or out of their job, GPS sensors in devices make it possible for employers to know if an employee is in their place of work. That same data can be used to see what routes people such as couriers or Uber drivers are taking. Within buildings, many employers require employees to badge in and out of different locations or use cameras to monitor who is where. Even if employees are sitting at their desks, software such as Microsoft's Viva can keep track of how much time employees are spending in meetings and who is meeting with who. There is even software that tracks individual keystrokes and who is using what software when. According to *The New York Times*, as of 2022, 8 out of 10 of the top US employers were using software to track what at least some employees were doing some of the time (Kantor and Sundaram, 2022).

Analysis

Analysing data about the time spent working first requires subtracting the start time from the end time to create a new duration variable, and data from that can then be summed to calculate the total hours worked for a given employee over a specified time period. That, in turn, can be summed or averaged for a relevant set of employees, such as everyone working in a particular factory.

The quantity of data available from the Internet of Things' data sources can be enormous since it typically consists of sensors monitoring things on an ongoing basis. Consequently, even the way that data is captured and stored may be a function of planned analysis by an organisation. For example, for something like a bus, Uber, or courier, only the location and time of stops may be recorded. Those could then be summed over some time period, for example, to enable managers to see how many stops drivers make in an average day or hour or what route between two places is most efficient. Comparisons could be made to see if, for example, the average number of stops varies according to things such as the type of vehicle being driven or the time of day. More complex forms of analysis than those covered in this book can be used to do things such as determine which routes are most efficient for drivers to take and which employees tend to interact with people outside of their immediate teams most often.

Analysing data about how much of something an employee produced in a given time period typically simply requires summing readings recorded by a sensor over some period.

The things being summed could be steps taken by a warehouse worker, keystrokes made by someone doing transcriptions, or calls taken by a help desk worker.

The types of analyses just described are normally done with population level data, so in those situations there is no need to test for things such as statistically significant differences.

Other Considerations

An obvious consideration that emerges from the examples just described is the extent to which employees feel uncomfortable about the different forms of data collection just described being used to monitor their work. For example, some of the software used to monitor productivity takes photos at random intervals (Kantor and Sundaram, 2022), which many people are likely to perceive as overly intrusive. Laws and employment contracts give employers the right to monitor employees in a variety of ways; however even when that's the case it's worth considering whether the benefits of doing that in a particular situation are sufficient to outweigh employees' concerns. That includes both current employees and potential employees whose choice about whether or not to work for the organisation may be influenced by use of particular types of HR analytics by the employer.

Some recent research (Thiel et al., 2022) also suggests that employees who are monitored may be more likely to cheat on the task on which they are being monitored than those who are not. That's not only not the outcome that employers want, but it also produces data that is inaccurate and could therefore produce erroneous results if used in analytics.

A related concern is whether the things being measured are the things that are really most important to the organisation. While certain things, such as keystrokes or where a given employee is at a given time, are fairly easy to measure, in many cases those things are being used as proxies for something else that is much harder to measure, such as how hard someone is working. For example, while we can measure keystrokes, it's much harder to tell whether those are generating masterful code or prose or unnecessarily long outputs riddled with errors. Similarly, we can know where an employee is or whether their mouse is moving, but not whether they're thinking about work or what to have for dinner. Measuring the wrong things can lead to employees trying to game the system and to managers making poor decisions.

From a more technical standpoint, data from sensors accumulates very quickly and is likely to require special technical expertise to collect, store, and analyse or else use of software as a service solution that does those things. And any of those options can only analyse the data that they have, so may miss work-related activity that occurs offline or on non-work devices.

USING ANALYTICS TO ASSESS THE EFFECTIVENESS OF TRAINING

Common Questions

- Were participants satisfied with a particular training programme or initiative?
- Did a given training programme or initiative achieve its objectives?
- Do people who have participated in a particular type of training perform better than those who have not?

Data Sources

The most common source of data related to the effectiveness of various types of training are surveys at the end to find out if participants felt that the training was beneficial, how it could be improved, and so forth. Surveys like that typically include a combination of Likert scales, on which people rate things such as their overall satisfaction with the training, and open-ended questions where participants can provide feedback on what they liked best or thought could be improved.

In addition to getting that type of input directly from participants, in some situations data might be captured that relates to knowledge of the topic or performance of the skills that were the topic of the training. For example, people who participated in health and safety training might be given some sort of test at the end to see if they know the things they were supposed to learn in the training. The data that would result from that could just be whether each individual person passed or failed, or their score on the test. Sometimes both a pre-test and a post-test are given and the change between those is measured as a way of isolating learning that is directly attributable to the training from what a participant already knew at the start of the training. Another possible source of data related to the effectiveness of training is real-world data related to the area of the training. Continuing with the health and safety example, that might be the number of accidents per month experienced in a particular workplace.

Analysis

One way to analyse survey questions asking people to rate their overall satisfaction with a training programme (or similar things, such as whether they would recommend it to a friend or believe it will be useful in their work) is to calculate the percentage who give each response; however, this is one of those situations in which many analysts choose to treat a Likert scale as an interval scale and calculate averages. Whether overall satisfaction ratings are summarised as a percentage or an average, it can also be useful to compare percentages or averages across groups. For example, some types of training might be more or less successful for people of different ages or with different prior exposure to the subject.

If participants in a training programme have been given some sort of test at the end, then those results could be summarised with a mean, a median, or the percentage who scored above a certain threshold. Similar things could be done with rates of improvement if both pre-and post-tests were given.

If data is available on some real outcome that is believed to be affected by the training – for example, accidents in the example used previously, then we could count the number of accidents experienced by people who did the training and compare the rate of accidents among them (e.g., 1 accident per 100 employees per month) to that for people who did not do the training. Or we could compare the incidence of the outcome before and after the training for the group of people who did the training.

Other Considerations

Typically, if a survey is used to measure the effectiveness of a training programme, everyone who participated in the training will be given an opportunity to respond to the survey, but not everyone will take that opportunity. In situations like these, it's often the most and least satisfied people who take the opportunity to provide feedback. We need to bear this in mind in analysing the data. We only have responses from a subset of people, and yet that is not the result of a sampling plan that we implemented, but instead the result of individual choices to respond or not. So while we can do things such as calculate averages and proportions, we need to keep in mind that those are averages and proportions of the people who chose to respond. It's not appropriate to treat that as a sample and use statistical techniques to see if the results from the sample generalise to the population as a whole because individual employees were essentially making their own choices about whether to be included in the sample or not. What we can do however is report on the number of people who participated in the training and the number who provided feedback. The greater proportion of participants who provided feedback, the more confident we can be that the results are representative of the group as a whole.

It's also important to note that people's perceptions about the benefits of a training programme may not match objective measures. For example, research has shown that while students perceive themselves to have learned more when taught using passive learning methods (i.e., traditional lectures), they do better on objective measures of learning when taught using active methods of learning, such as group activities (Deslauriers et. al 2019).

If we are trying to evaluate the effectiveness of training by measuring the performance of employees who participated in the training, but we did not measure that prior to the training, we also need to consider the possibility that some employees may have had more exposure to the topic prior to the training and the effect of that on their post-training performance might be as great or greater than the training itself.

USING ANALYTICS TO EVALUATE EMPLOYEE SATISFACTION

Common Questions

- Are our employees satisfied with their jobs overall and with specific aspects of them?
- Do employees feel comfortable and empowered at work, or do they believe they are subject to bullying, harassment, or other negative forms of behaviour?
- Has employee satisfaction been changing over time?
- What percentage of our employees leave within a given time period? Is that percentage changing? What are our employees saying to others about our organisation in social media?
- Are our employees recommending us as an employer?
- Is there an association between employee performance and satisfaction?
- Do answers to any of the previous questions vary based on work-related factors, such as role, level, or location, or by non-work related factors, such as race, gender, age, or sexual orientation?

Data Sources

Many organisations survey their employees to measure their satisfaction and engagement with their work. As with the surveys described in the previous sub-section on training, those typically include a combination of Likert scales, on which people rate things such as their overall satisfaction with their jobs, and open-ended questions where people can provide feedback on their role or the organisation.

Social media has created another way of monitoring employee satisfaction. While some organisations use contractual provisions to restrict what employees can say about them publicly, including in social media, many do not. In those cases, comments made in social media can be used as a data source for assessing employee sentiment. Sites such as Glassdoor also aggregate anonymous reviews from employees about their organisations.

Other data sources that may be used as proxies for employee satisfaction are the rates of attrition and recommendations. If the percentage of employees who leave the organisation within a given time period (attrition) is reducing, it suggests that employees may be more satisfied with the organisation compared to if the rate of attrition is increasing. Similarly, if the percentage of job applicants who report hearing about the job they are applying for through an existing employee is increasing, that could be an indication of improving employee satisfaction.

Analysis

Employee surveys typically contain questions that use Likert scales to measure things such as satisfaction and engagement overall and with specific aspects of the organisation or an individual's job. If those are being treated as interval rather than ordinal, averages can be calculated and compared across aspects of the organisation or job as well as across time and across groups (e.g., role or level within the organisation). Results for a specific organisation can also be compared to benchmarks for an industry. If the scale is being treated as ordinal, the same can be done with comparisons of proportions – for example, the proportion of employees who rate a particular aspect of their jobs as being above or below a certain threshold.

Sentiment analysis can be used to analyse social media posts from employees. That requires humans or machines classifying posts as expressing positive, negative or neutral sentiment and then calculating the number or percentage of posts in each of those categories. Posts can also be classified according to topic and then the number and percentage of posts can also be calculated, as can the combination of sentiment and topic (e.g., what percentage of posts about organisational culture are positive, negative, and neutral?).

Rates of attrition and recommendation from existing employees can be aggregated as counts and then expressed as percentages. Expressing them as percentages adjusts for the fact that a change in the number of employees leaving or candidates applying as a result of employee recommendations could be a function of the total size of the workforce or applicant pool changing as well as being a reflection of changing employee satisfaction.

Other Considerations

While many organisations use satisfaction or engagement surveys, many employees may be sceptical of them. Even if the surveys are described as anonymous, employees may be suspicious that their responses may be viewed by their manager or others within the company and they will be able to be identified even if their name isn't explicitly attached. This may be a particular concern among employees who have been bullied at work or groups that have been marginalised. Others may question whether any action will be taken as a result of the survey and choose not to participate because they don't believe it will make any difference (Conboye and Smith, 2022).

By definition, employees who choose not to participate are different from those who choose to participate in terms of their views about the organisation, so we cannot assume that the results for people who do participate will generalise to those who don't, or use a statistical test to infer whether that's the case. For that reason, it's likely to be more useful to focus on the trends in survey results over time than on precise values at a given point in time. As with surveys related to training, it's also useful to note the total number of employees and the number of those who participated in the survey. Once again, the greater the proportion of employees who participate, the safer it is to treat the results as representative of the whole workforce.

This desire to get responses from all or most employees creates the temptation to incentivise or mandate participation, but that creates its own problems. If participation is incentivised or mandated employees might just put in minimal effort to comply or give answers that they believe are safe to give rather than providing answers that are a full and accurate reflection of what they really think.

While rates of attrition and recommendation may be related to job satisfaction, each is likely to be related to other things too. For example, during periods of high unemployment or recession, people may be less likely to leave their jobs even if they are dissatisfied with them. Or the percentage of candidates for jobs who heard about them from employees may increase, even if existing employees are not particularly satisfied with their jobs, if an organisation is offering incentives for such recommendations or is offering benefits that some applicants may find attractive, even if existing employees are not particularly satisfied with their own roles for reasons other than the benefits offered.

USING ANALYTICS TO IDENTIFY AND RECRUIT EMPLOYEES (TALENT ACQUISITION)

Common Questions

- What percentage of applicants for particular roles learned about the role through different sources (e.g., LinkedIn, other online platforms, advertisements in publications, contacts who work at the organisation, etc.)?
- Do employees who were recruited via a particular source perform better than those recruited through other sources?
- Do employees who were recruited via a particular source stay with the organisation longer than those recruited through other sources?
- Which candidate(s) have the highest probability of being successful in a particular role?
- Do answers to any of the previous questions vary by work-related factors, such as role, level, or location, or by non-work related factors, such as race, gender, age, or sexual orientation?

Data Sources

Organisations very frequently know how a particular applicant heard about a particular role. They may have applied through a third-party site, such as LinkedIn, so the source is known in that case, and many job applications also ask how people heard about the role for which they are applying. Most job applications also ask for basic demographic information so that is also available. If an employee is ultimately hired, the organisation would also hold information about their performance, the day they started, and their last day if they are no longer with the organisation.

As part of the hiring process, some organisations also use psychometric testing. This is a way of trying to understand if people's personality or skills are likely to be a good fit for a particular role. It's done by having people answer a series of questions about things such as their preferences or how they would respond in various hypothetical situations. If job candidates have participated in psychometric testing, that data may also be available to the organisation which is considering hiring them.

Analysis

Identifying the recruitment sources that generate the greatest number or highest percentage of applicants is simply a matter of doing a count. That process can be repeated for different job and personal characteristics to see if the recruitment sources that generate the most candidates vary by job type or demographic group. The same process can be used for seeing which recruitment sources produce the greatest number of people who are actually hired, and if that is consistent across different types of jobs and people. Comparisons can also be done to see if the sources that generate the greatest number or percentage of total applicants also generate the greatest number or percentage of successful applicants. Once successful applicants have been on the job long enough to have had their performance measured, that can be compared across recruitment channels to see if certain channels produce a disproportionate share of above or below average performing employees.

The process of psychometric testing itself typically relies on forms of analysis that are more complex than those described in Chapter 4, but it ultimately generates scores for individual candidates on specific traits such as detail-orientation or creativity. Initially managers may have just made assumptions about what traits are most important for a given role, but eventually the scores for the different traits can be analysed in conjunction with performance data for existing employees to confirm whether scores on the different traits identified do predict actual job performance. That can be done using regression when performance is measured using a numeric variable or by comparing the average scores on the different traits for those with different performance ratings if performance has been measured on an ordinal scale.

Other Considerations

Analysis of recruitment sources can only measure those that have actually been used. It's possible that a different source would produce even better results, but that can't be known without testing it. There may also be linkages between recruitment sources and diversity, equity, and inclusion considerations. For example, some organisations have traditionally recruited at specific colleges and universities, but if those colleges and universities have different demographics from the overall population, people recruited from that college or university may be unrepresentative of the community where an organisation is located or the customers it serves.

Many academics are critical of the use of some of the most well-known personality-based psychometric tests, such as Myers Briggs, in corporate settings (see Pittenger, 2005). As discussed in the Analytics in Practice section in this chapter, there can also be situations in which the people who have the functional skills that are best suited for a particular role are not the best fit from a psychometric perspective or vice-versa. In those situations, organisations would need to choose which is most important in that particular situation.

SUMMARY

Of the four major application areas of analytics within organisations, HR analytics are probably the most challenging and least well-developed. As discussed in the Analytics in Practice example in this chapter, people are varied and they also have concerns about their privacy and both of those can make implementing analytics related to employees more difficult than implementing analytics related to things such as revenue or inventory. And while marketing analytics also involves data about people, privacy legislation controls data about customers, but often not data about employees, so those involved in HR analytics have to make more of their own decisions about when the organisational benefits of collecting and using data are sufficient to justify what their employees may perceive as overly intrusive monitoring.

Nonetheless, analytics hold great promise for improving HR decision-making. Often when people think about that they worry about threats to human privacy, autonomy, and creativity. Those threats are real; however so is a history of judgement-based hiring decisions made more on the basis of who people are or who they know than what they can do. Already, simply calculating and publishing data about the demographic composition of organisations' workforces has resulted in many organisations making different decisions about recruitment, hiring, and promotion. Analytics offers the potential for more objectively measuring performance and the characteristics associated with success in different roles as well as identifying candidates most likely to have those characteristics or the potential to develop them.

ANALYTICS IN PRACTICE

The perils and potential of people analytics

During the more than ten years that Varun Chaudhary has worked in HR, he has seen organisations slowly and carefully incorporate analytics into their HR decision-making. Varun is currently an Organisational Design consultant based in Montreal, but his experience as an HR professional working within an organisation initially and now consulting, spans Canada, the United States, and India.

Varun explains that peoples' attitudes toward data about them being used for work-related purposes is different than in the rest of their lives:

> The thing with HR – the challenge with HR – is you've got to be mindful of employee privacy. It's funny, the same employee out in the real world gives all their data to Netflix and Amazon, and that's fine, but the minute they feel like: 'my employer is watching me' it's not okay.

In part because of that, he explains that organisations have adopted HR analytics gradually, with technology companies and other large employers leading the way. According to him, some of the first areas of HR analytics that organisations adopt tend to be talent acquisition and talent management – or analytics focussed on recruiting employees and retaining those who are most valuable to the organisation. Part of the reason talent acquisition analytics are adopted by many organisations before other forms of HR analytics is that it applies to people who are not yet employees, and therefore is less likely to elicit the type of reaction described in the quote above.

According to Varun, many organisations are in the process of building analytics into their DEI (diversity, equity, and inclusion) programmes. While many organisations are now using analytics to quantify the representativeness of the demographics of their workforce, he says that technology companies and larger, legacy, organisations are disaggregating all types of employee data to identify differences based on demographics.

> Think of all the analytics of all the surveys and programmes that HR runs for all of the employees, and they end up putting a DEI lens specifically on those programmes so they can see what's the discrepancy between the average and the minorities or the marginalised communities and how are we treating them. But again, this is happening in a lot more detail, and a lot more fleshed out manner, in the tech companies or legacy companies which have already robust analytics system. The rest of the companies, they are implementing it, but it's more basic.

Another area Varun describes as having grown in use during his career relates to the use of analytics to help predict HR outcomes, such as the likelihood an employee will leave, as opposed to simply quantifying outcomes that have already happened. Varun has also worked with clients who are using analytics to measure productivity and performance, but he notes that this is an area where particular care is required to make sure the things being measured are truly reflective of performance and take individual differences into account.

With all type of HR analytics, Varun stresses the importance of HR analytics drawing on expertise from both HR and analytics.

> *When you approach it from a data scientist mentality, you look at data very differently than suppose someone who's like let's say a talent management specialist. Their expertise is different. They might have dabbled a bit in data, but their mind is not open to the purest possible cuts. Conversely, the data scientist would be all about the data, but they might do some analysis that makes absolutely no sense, so we always recommend to our clients if you're having an in house HR analytics team, have a blend of the HR expertise as well as the pure data scientists and put them together with teams, so then you get some really powerful quantitative analysis coming out, which will be tempered by the HR professional to understand and bring in the nuance that people are human beings and that this will work, but this may not work.*

You can hear more about Varun's experience applying analytics to HR in this video: https://vimeo.com/741714478/98564730d7

RUNNING CASE STUDY: 4TE, PART 7[1]

Like most small business owners, Matt and Emily each pitched in to get things done as needed at 4tE. In general Matt focussed more on the financial and operational side of the business, while Emily focussed more on marketing and HR. Now, between inflation, workers being in short supply, and pandemic assistance feeling like a distant memory, both Matt and Emily were concerned about their overall wage bill.

Having seen Ben's presentation, they both felt that they now had a better handle on their customer base. They thought they could use the time Ben would have to wait to get the survey responses back to have him do some analysis of their labour costs. Specifically, they wanted him to use their accounting system to calculate total expenses for salaries and wages by year and investigate how those related to revenue and the number of employees for each year.

(Continued)

---

[1]The 4tE case is fictitious.

As Emily was briefing Ben about that, she also mentioned that she would welcome his input on how they should be measuring employee performance. Given how crazy things had been up to this point, they hadn't really done formal performance reviews. Emily and Matt were good at praising employees for hard work or when they really went above and beyond the call of duty for a customer. They were also proud to be paying a living wage and of raising everyone's wages based on the rate of inflation. But they did that for everyone and now wanted to be able to better differentiate the really great workers from the not so great and reward them accordingly. Emily also asked Ben if he thought that having formal performance metrics might be useful for other forms of analytics that could help them run 4tE more efficiently and more fairly.

EXERCISES

1   Use a site such as LinkedIn to find an advertisement for a job you might be interested in. Consider how performance could be measured for that job, and how the organisation might use that measurement as part of its HR analytics.

2   Search for 'DEI report' along with the name of an organisation. If you don't get a result for the first organisation you try, keep trying until you do (if you're having trouble finding one, try a technology or consulting company). Once you find a report, look through the results and identify at least one decision you believe the HR managers at the organisation might make based on the results.

3   Suppose that your local hospital has a large number of nursing vacancies, and has asked for your help in using analytics to determine the best ways of recruiting new nursing staff. What would you advise them to do?

8
OPERATIONAL ANALYTICS

WHAT WILL YOU LEARN FROM THIS CHAPTER?

- How organisations use analytics to:
  - manage supply chains
  - operate more sustainably
  - predict when equipment will require maintenance
  - detect fraudulent activity
  - manage organisation-specific operations.
- Things organisations need to be mindful of when doing those things.

USING ANALYTICS TO MANAGE SUPPLY CHAINS

Complex products, such as cars or computers, require coordination of hundreds or even thousands of suppliers. To be able to sell finished products, all of those components need to come together, sequenced in a way that ensures everything is in the right place at the right time. As many of us learned through the Covid pandemic, that can be very challenging. Many supply chains experienced major problems during the pandemic. For example, production of some models of cars was cut back because the manufacturers were unable to get an adequate supply of computer chips used to run some of the systems in the cars (Boudette, 2021).

Common Questions

To be able to anticipate potential problems like that, or to mitigate their impact if and when they occur, organisations need to be able to answer questions such as:

- How much of particular parts or supplies do we have on hand, and when do we expect more?

- Are certain suppliers disproportionately likely to have their products arrive late or with quality problems?
- Are our current levels of inventory sufficient to satisfy expected upcoming demand, and does that vary across products, regions, distribution partners, etc.?
- Do we have too much inventory of certain products and does that vary across products, regions, distribution partners, etc.?

Data Sources

Data related to supply chains is typically captured passively through things such as purchase orders, invoices, and statements documenting the receipt of goods. That's now often complemented by technology that enables individual shipments of supplies to be tracked as they make their way around the world, using things such as tracking numbers, bar codes, and QR codes, in the same way that many of us track packages coming to our homes.

Analysis

Counts can be done of the quantity of different supplies in stock and those can be compared to upcoming production requirements. This can be a precarious balance because organisations want to ensure they have enough components to produce the finished goods needed to satisfy demand, while also not having so many sitting around that they become obsolete or spoiled or just redundant. Even just having parts sit around a long time before they are needed may harm an organisation's financial position, but on the other hand so can having to curtail production because of the inability to get critical parts. Therefore, organisations may want to analyse the difference between the amount of a particular supply they have on hand in relation not just to estimated demand, but also the variability in demand. All other things being equal, an organisation might want to have more backstock of all of its supplies on hand if demand for its own products is more variable than if it's more predictable.

Suppliers may vary in things such as their quality and reliability, so tracking the proportion of shipments that arrive on time and the rate of defective products by supplier allows an organisation to monitor which suppliers tend to deliver high quality products on time and which tend to run late or deliver products with flaws or defects. With that information, they can shift more of their business to the suppliers that tend to deliver on time and with minimal defects, or, if that isn't possible, then account for delays and defects in their own planning (i.e., by keeping more of the item that supplier provides on hand). Since all of that analysis is typically done with population-level data, tests for statistical significance are usually not required.

Other Considerations

One thing that became very clear during the pandemic is that external events can be very disruptive to supply chains. Up to that point, many organisations had developed very efficient supply chains with many components arriving just in time for when they were needed. But the fairly stable historical patterns that enabled all of that efficiency were upended during the pandemic as consumer demand swung first toward more home-oriented products and then back again and Covid ravaged the workforces of individual companies. All of that made it harder to predict how much of an organisation's products would be sold and if the components required to make those products would be available according to originally agreed timelines. It seems likely that one consequence of the pandemic will be that more organisations will allow for more cushion in their supply chains to be able to better withstand similar shocks in the future as opposed to optimising purely for efficiency under normal operating conditions.

USING ANALYTICS TO OPERATE MORE SUSTAINABLY

Common Questions

Many organisations are attempting to operate more sustainably, whether that's to satisfy investors, customers, or employees, or to be a good corporate citizen. As part of that, they need answers to questions such as:

- What volume of greenhouse gas emissions are generated by our organisations' operations, and what are our biggest sources of greenhouse gas emissions?
- What volume of water is used in our operations, and what aspects of our operations use the most water?
- What volume of waste is generated by our operations, and what aspects of our operations generate the greatest amount of waste?

Data Sources

Most of the data needed to answer those questions comes in the form of passively collected quantitative data. In the case of things such as water, waste, and electricity, those things are likely to be measured directly by water or electricity meters or the weight of the waste the organisation disposes of. Some organisations also measure some emissions directly – for example, organisations engaged in some types of manufacturing might use sensors to measure the amount of CO_2 being generated through their production processes. Often however at least part of measuring CO_2 emissions and total greenhouse gas emissions involves making estimates based on things such as the amount of gas, oil, or electricity used. That's because the CO_2 involved in many of the things an organisation does may be difficult to measure directly. For example, an employee flying to a conference is contributing to CO_2 emissions, but while the total CO_2 emissions of the plane could conceivably be measured, the share attributable to that one employee would need to be calculated. Similarly, agriculture generates a large volume of greenhouse gases, but those are estimated based on things such as the amount of feed and fertiliser used rather than by detailed measurements from every cow and tractor.

Analysis

Before doing any analysis of emissions, estimates need to be derived for anything, such as CO_2 emissions, that is not being measured directly. That can be fairly complicated because it may depend on things such as how electricity or agricultural products were produced, so organisations often get help from consultants who specialise in doing those estimates.

   Once direct measurements or estimates are available, analysis typically involves calculating or visualising the rate of change over time and the percentage of emissions, waste, water use, etc. that are attributable to different parts of the organisation. For example, Apple's sustainability report for 2022 (available at: www.apple.com/environment/pdf/Apple_Environmental_Progress_Report_2022.pdf) shows how Apple's total emissions have reduced since peaking in 2015, and breaks down emissions from different sources, including product manufacturing, product use, product transport, and business travel. You can see similar examples from other organisations by searching for 'corporate environmental report', 'sustainability report', 'greenhouse gas inventory' or ESG (which stands for environmental, social, governance) followed by the name of an organisation, industry, or country.

Other Considerations

While the analysis of sustainability data can be fairly straightforward, knowing what data to include in such analysis can be more complicated – especially when it comes to greenhouse gas emissions. The data for all greenhouse gas emissions is often expressed as CO_2 equivalents, but converting things such as business trips or hot water usage into CO_2 equivalents can be complicated. For example, the CO_2 emissions from a direct flight are likely to be different from a non-direct flight to and from the same places, someone sitting in business class takes up more space on the plane than someone in economy so therefore should be allocated more of the emissions, and there are more passengers to share the emissions across on a full flight than a half empty one.

Further complicating the situation are the facts that emissions are often discussed in terms of gross versus net and scope 1, 2, or 3. The gross versus net part refers to whether or not offsets, from things such as planting trees, are deducted from total emissions. In net emissions they are, whereas in gross emissions they are not.

Scope 1 emissions are those the organisation itself is directly responsible for, scope 2 are the emissions created generating the energy used by the organisation, and scope 3 are emissions that result from the activities of the organisation – including suppliers creating and transporting things to the organisation and the organisations' customers or clients using the products or services it produces. For instance, in the Apple example described previously, Apple's corporate operations are scope 1, electricity usage is scope 2, and business travel and product manufacturing, transporting products to stores and customers, and product use by customers are scope 3. The reason manufacturing and transporting products are scope 3 rather than 1 is that Apple generally contracts with other companies to do those things. These categories are the product of international agreements; however, many people are not aware of these distinctions. That makes it very important to clearly state what is and is not included when communicating emissions-related data to audiences without detailed knowledge of what is and is not included in the different scopes and for what purposes the different scopes are used. Failing to do that could lead to misunderstanding the data and that in turn could lead to poor decision-making.

USING ANALYTICS FOR PREDICTIVE MAINTENANCE

The growing presence of sensors on a variety of types of equipment has given rise to the use of analytics for predictive maintenance.

The goal is to predict when a given piece of equipment or machinery will need maintenance, so that can be done before it fails, but not before it's necessary. The idea is to reduce both the cost and downtime associated with maintenance, but also the cost and downtime associated with unexpected failures.

Common Questions

- When should we service a particular piece of equipment?
- When are we likely to have to replace particular equipment?

Data Sources

Some of the data for doing this type of analysis typically comes from the equipment itself. For example, many modern cars generate data about things such as usage of specific parts of the car, such as how often and how hard the brakes have been applied. Other data may also be used to make the predictions. For example, for something like a car, aspects of the places it was driven may be relevant. In that example, those might include things such as the types of roads, the weather, and the elevation.

Similar things apply to other types of equipment. For example, an organisation operating a data centre would know the age of each computer in it, and could know things such as how often each computer is in use and whether the tasks being performed are pushing things like memory to their maximum capacity or not.

Analysis

Predictive models would be used to predict the likelihood of failure for each piece of equipment. That could be done with regression, but often the types of predictive models used in situations like this might be more complex machine learning models that could take into account even more factors and be updated more frequently. That also allows greater scope for identifying factors that influence how frequently particular machines will need maintenance that human analysts would not have thought of.

Other Considerations

As with any predictive model, predictions may be less accurate if made from data that is different from that on which the model was developed. For example, a model made to predict when brakes will fail developed from cars driven on mainly flat terrain is unlikely to make good predictions for cars driven on very hilly terrain. Or a model made to predict when computers in a data centre need to be replaced developed in a data centre with a very constant cool temperature is unlikely to make good predictions for computers in a data centre that has no temperature control and therefore more varied temperatures and a higher average temperature.

USING ANALYTICS TO DETECT FRAUDULENT ACTIVITY

A surprising number of organisations may be vulnerable to various forms of fraud. These could include external threats, such as fraud related to credit cards, gift cards, ad clicks, phishing, taxes, and insurance. And nearly all organisations are potentially vulnerable to fraud by employees, including things such as falsification of expenses or invoices.

Common Questions

Questions related to fraudulent activity are different than many other applications of analytics in that they tend to involve very large volumes of small questions as opposed to smaller volumes of larger questions. Many of these questions are asked and answered by automated systems, with only particular answers leading to additional investigation by human decision-makers. These types of questions include:

- Is this e-mail likely to be spam?
- Is this transaction likely to be fraudulent?
- Should this insurance or expense claim be approved automatically or flagged for further investigation?
- Is this tax return likely to be an accurate reflection of the true situation of the person or organisation who filed it?

Data Sources

Most of the data needed to answer the questions just described is internal to the organisation; however, it may be supplemented by other sources of data. For example, data reported on a tax return may be cross-checked against other sources of data such as property ownership records. The specific internal and external data sources used would vary depending on the nature of the fraud the organisation is attempting to detect. For example, variables such as sender e-mail address and IP address for detecting spam, and the amount, merchant, and merchant location of a transaction for detecting credit card fraud.

Analysis

While forms of fraud vary significantly, the analytical approach for detecting fraud is fairly similar. That is to identify normal patterns so that anomalies can be detected and investigated by humans. So, for example, if you have ever had a call from a bank to investigate a transaction that they think may be fraudulent it will be because it appears to be outside your normal pattern of spending. That may be due to where the transaction happened — for example if you had a transaction in a restaurant in Sydney this morning, but then one in London two hours later. It also could be something about the category or amount of the transaction.

This type of analysis relies on very large datasets to identify sometimes subtle characteristics that differentiate fraudulent behaviour from normal behaviour. It also requires constantly checking and updating models because once a characteristic becomes known to be associated with fraudulent activity, those engaged in the fraud may change their behaviour to attempt to avoid detection.

Other Considerations

Organisations using analytics to detect fraud need to walk a fine line. On one hand, they would like to catch every attempt at fraud; however, the more zealously they strive for that, the greater the risk of mistaking some legitimate transactions for fraudulent ones. For example, a bank's fraud detection systems might identify a particular transaction as being potentially fraudulent because it is so much larger than the transactions an account holder typically makes. But there are many legitimate reasons a person may make a single transaction that is much larger than usual. Similarly, we have all probably had the experience of finding a legitimate e-mail in our spam folder. There is often inconvenience associated with situations like these. Perhaps the credit card charge for the vacation you've been dreaming of doesn't go through or an e-mail checking your interest in applying for what would be your dream job goes unread in your spam folder.

The essence of this application of analytics is to assign a probability that a particular instance of something is fraudulent. That generally leads to a rule for classifying things over or under a certain threshold as likely to be fraudulent or not likely to be fraudulent. The lower the threshold for classifying something as fraud, the more likely it is you'll accidentally classify something as fraudulent that really isn't and the higher you set it, the more likely it is that some people will get away with fraud.

USING ANALYTICS TO MANAGE ORGANISATION-SPECIFIC OPERATIONS

Beyond the more general uses of analytics, the specific types of operations different organisations engage in vary a lot from organisation to organisation and so there may be additional applications of operational analytics that are relevant to specific organisations. The day-to-day operations of a manufacturer are different from those of a government department, and those are different again from a service business. So the analytics used to monitor and manage those operations often need to be different too.

Common Questions

For example, teaching is a key part of the operations of colleges, universities, and other educational institutions, and a growing number of them are adopting learning analytics, which focus on things such as the extent to which specific forms of engagement in a course are associated with outcomes such as passing, earning a particular grade, or completing a degree.

In contrast, the operations of many government departments are focussed on policy development, so they might be focussed on analytics related to things such as how long it takes to develop policy advice, how many people and organisations make submissions as part of policy consultation, what proportion of that advice is taken up by the government, and if policies that are implemented achieve the intended policy outcomes.

Or consider a hospital. Their operations focus on healthcare delivery, so their analytics may focus on things such as waiting times and the rates of readmissions or adverse events.

Other organisations may use analytics to inform operational decisions around things such as scheduling (e.g., flights for an airline), quality control (e.g., for a manufacturer), or managing capacity or equipment (e.g., for a data centre). As you can see from these examples, the specific types of questions organisations use analytics to address probably vary more greatly for operations than for marketing or HR, and the same is true for finance.

Data Sources

Because these applications of analytics focus on an organisation's operations, the organisation itself generally has all or most of the data needed, and it's generally population level data. There may however be instances when an organisation would still use a sample even if it had population-level data. For example, part of the operations of many food and pharmaceutical companies would be testing a sample of their products to ensure it matches specifications for things such as nutrients and active ingredients. That's done with a sample because it's a situation in which measuring something involves damaging or destroying it. In digital contexts a sample may be used because the computational power required to investigate something for the whole population makes doing that unfeasible, and probably unnecessary because it would be very unlikely to achieve a different result.

Analysis

All of the techniques discussed in Chapter 4 are applied as part of organisation-specific operational analytics in some situations, but, because the specific applications are so varied, the analytical approaches used are too.

Other Considerations

Since these organisation-specific applications of operational analytics are so varied, the additional considerations are too. One thing to keep in mind, however, is that as always, the insights from the analytics can only be as good as the data upon which they're applied. The things being measured as part of organisational analytics are often things rather than people, and there's a tendency to think that means there is less potential for error and problems. But that's really not the case. The potential sources of error and problems may be different, but they exist when we're collecting any kind of data. For example, when we're using data generated by machines, it's very important to ensure that the machines are correctly and consistently calibrated, and that we understand exactly what they're measuring and how they are measuring it.

SUMMARY

Analytics can help the vast majority of organisations run their operations more efficiently and effectively, but because the specific details of organisations' operations are so varied, the details of those analytics and the data upon which they draw are equally varied. A growing number of organisations are applying analytics to measure and manage the sustainability of their operations. Fraud detection and predictive maintenance are two other increasingly common use cases for analytics within the broader umbrella of operational analytics. Analytics have been applied to the measurement and management of supply chains of organisations for a long time; however, supply chain problems during the pandemic highlighted both the importance of that and the challenges associated with it.

RUNNING CASE STUDY: 4TE, PART 8[1]

Matt's background in supply chain management had been extremely helpful in setting up arrangements with 4tE's suppliers. Stores that sell grocery items tend to sell a lot of different products. Even though 4tE's selection was much more limited than large supermarkets, they still carried hundreds of different products, which they purchased from many different suppliers. Some of those suppliers were negatively impacted by supply chain problems of their own during the pandemic, and some had been late with orders during the pandemic due to sickness among their own workforce.

---

[1]The 4tE case is fictitious.

Given that most of 4tE's suppliers were supplying food products that are vulnerable to things such as bad weather, never having orders arrive late or undamaged was probably unrealistic, but Matt wanted to understand if certain suppliers were responsible for a disproportionate share of late orders or damaged products. Once he knew if that was the case he could consider whether those differences were likely to be the result of something unique to their circumstances. For example, some orders for products made from berries had gone unfulfilled one year due to a heat wave causing great damage to the crop that year.

When Matt talked with Ben about the analysis he wanted, Ben also suggested doing the analysis not just by supplier, but also by product category. That would allow them to test Matt's assumptions about some product categories being inherently more prone to delayed and damaged orders than others. Matt thought that was a great idea. Fortunately, Ben was already familiar with Matt's order spreadsheet from his initial data inventory and clean-up, so he could start right in on that analysis of late and damaged orders by supplier and by category.

EXERCISES

1   Search for 'environmental report', 'sustainability report', 'greenhouse gas inventory' or 'ESG report' along with the name of an organisation. If you don't get a result for the first organisation you try, keep trying with different organisations and/or different versions of the name of the report until you do. Once you find a report, look through the results and identify at least one decision you believe managers at the organisation might make based on sustainability-related results in the report.

2   Suppose you are the operations manager of a supermarket, and you have a dashboard that, among other things, calculates how much of each SKU (stock keeping unit) sold each day divided by how much stock was on hand at the start of the day. So a value of 1 would mean that by the end of the day, the supermarket sold everything it had on hand at the start of the day, a value below 1 would mean it sold less, and a value greater than 1 would mean it sold more (which would mean it received a delivery during the day and sold at least some of what was in the delivery as well as what they had on hand at the start of the day). Further suppose that the dashboard allowed you to see the average and standard deviation for that value for any time period you chose. Think of four items that you personally buy in the supermarket, and describe if/how you think the means and standard deviations for the value for 2020 would compare to 2019, and why.

3   Have a look at the spam or junk folder in your e-mail application and compare that to what's in your inbox. Based on what's in that, try to identify some variables you think your e-mail application is using to predict whether a particular e-mail is spam or not.

9
FINANCIAL ANALYTICS

WHAT WILL YOU LEARN FROM THIS CHAPTER?

This chapter discusses how data and analytics can be used to understand the financial consequences of marketing, HR, and operational decisions as well as to evaluate the overall financial position of an organisation or the expected financial consequences associated with particular risks faced by the organisation. It also discusses things to keep in mind when executing financial analytics. For example, forecasts are not good at anticipating significant changes that break previous patterns or in situations in which historical data is very limited, and financial analysis may provide an incomplete picture of what's happening in an organisation.

USING ANALYTICS TO UNDERSTAND THE FINANCIAL CONSEQUENCES OF MARKETING DECISIONS

Most marketing activities cost money to execute, and many are intended to generate revenue for an organisation. Analytics can be used to quantify those financial effects or expected results from marketing decisions.

Common Questions

- How much revenue are we likely to generate over an upcoming time period?
- Does our profitability vary by product or other factors such as by store or region? If so, which are the most and least profitable?
- Are some of our customers more profitable than others to serve? If so, what types of customers are high and low value?

Data Sources

Data related to revenue and costs overall can be obtained via accounting records from nearly any organisation. Those are compiled from transaction records, which may make it possible to attribute revenue to individual products, locations, customers, and so forth in at least some cases. Accounting data is also likely to be the primary source for data needed for forecasting purposes.

Analysis

Regression analysis can be used to generate forecasts to predict sales in future periods, whether that's at an overall organisational level or for a specific product or region. The dependent variable would be sales and the independent variables would probably include sales in previous periods, since past sales tend to be good predictors of future sales. Other predictors would be likely to include internal factors, such as marketing spending for the period, and may also include external factors, such as consumer confidence or interest rates.

Profitability is calculated by taking the difference between revenue and costs and expressing that as a percentage of revenue, so that can almost always be done for an organisation as a whole. It can also be tracked over time to get a general sense of whether financial performance overall is improving or deteriorating. Any changes in profitability can then be evaluated in the context of marketing initiatives that might have been undertaken to increase revenue and the cost of marketing programmes.

Calculating profitability for individual products, parts of an organisation, or customers can be even more helpful. That's because some products, stores, customers, etc. may be much more profitable than others. The catch is that to be able to calculate profitability by product, region, customer, etc., the accounting data has to record revenue and costs at that level. For revenue, that's often, but not always, the case. Costs are generally harder to attribute in that way, but may be able to be estimated based on other internal records such as the number of calls to customer service, whether customers tend to buy in stores or online, and so forth.

Once profitability has been calculated for different products, regions or other parts of an organisation, comparisons can be done to see if the results suggest it would be wise to change what products are offered, how they are delivered, or anything else. For example, products that are not profitable could be dropped, have their prices raised, or be reformulated to reduce costs and therefore make a previously unprofitable product profitable. For example, inflation was higher in 2022 than it had been for a long time, and there were many reports (e.g., Reiley, 2022) of companies responding to that by reducing the size of food products while keeping prices the same or even increasing them.

Once profitability has been calculated for individual customers, they are often grouped into segments and then the resulting groups are profiled based on their spending patterns and demographics to see if any patterns emerge. For instance, in many situations a relatively small proportion of customers may generate a much greater proportion of an organisation's profits. Such analysis can also reveal that certain types of customers may be unprofitable for organisations to serve.

Other Considerations

If any organisation does the type of analysis just described and discovers that some of its customers cost more to serve than they generate in revenue its options include raising prices or lowering costs. Either of those could have negative consequences for the customers involved, who may be parts of groups that are already disadvantaged in other ways. That creates ethical issues the organisation would need to work through. The organisation would also need to think through potential strategic reasons for continuing to serve unprofitable customers. For example, they may believe that a customer who is unprofitable now may become a profitable one in the future. That could apply to people, such as students, or to organisations, such as start-ups.

This is also one of many situations in which it's important to be mindful that predictions, including forecasts, are generated based on historical data. That means they are likely to be reasonably accurate as long as the thing being forecast, the variables used to make the prediction, and the relationship between them are fairly constant. But we know that over time, things change. For example, changes to media habits changed the relationship between various forms of advertising and sales for many organisations. That means that it's important to validate forecasts and other predictive models regularly to make sure they are still predicting as well as they did originally.

USING ANALYTICS TO UNDERSTAND THE FINANCIAL CONSEQUENCES OF HR DECISIONS

Employee wages, salaries, and benefits, and HR activities such as training and recruitment cost organisations money that they expect to be recovered through the revenue generated through the labour of those people. Analytics can be used to quantify those financial effects or expected results from HR decisions.

Common Questions

- Is there an association between performance and compensation at our organisation, and if so, is it as strong as we would like it to be?
- How does the rate of growth in total compensation compare to the rate of inflation?

- How does compensation for particular roles compare to advertised rates for similar roles in other organisations?

Data Sources

Most of the data needed to answer the types of questions just described would be available through human resource information systems, which many organisations use, though often through a vendor providing it on software as a service basis. This software would include information such as employees' start date, salary, role, information supplied during the application process, and end-date, when that's relevant. It would also be likely to include information from performance reviews, and potentially things such as certifications or trainings completed.

Another data source that could be useful for the types of analysis described is salary data for similar roles at other organisations. That could be collected through job advertisements or through sites such as GlassDoor.

Analysis

If performance has been measured with a numeric variable, regression or correlation could be used to check for a relationship between salary and performance. If performance has been measured using an ordinal variable, then average salaries could be compared by performance levels to see if people in the higher performing categories are earning more than people in the lower performing categories. Depending on the nature of the workforce, those things could be done by role, seniority, etc. since those things are also likely to influence salaries.

Year-to-year differences in mean or median salaries could be calculated as a percentage growth rate, which could then be compared both to inflation and across different roles, seniority levels, etc. to see if, overall, salaries are keeping pace with inflation and if any difference is greater for some types of employees than others. Mean or median salaries for different roles could also be compared to similar roles at other organisations to see if an organisation is under- or over-paying compared to other organisations, and if any difference is greater for some types of employees than others.

Other Considerations

This type of analysis is fairly simple to execute, but may be misleading if not combined with good domain knowledge. For example, a comparison of the average salary an organisation is paying to people in a given role to that being offered to people with the same title at another organisation may reveal a big discrepancy, but understanding whether something needs to be done about that requires knowing whether or not the actual work undertaken by people with that same title in the different organisations is at least roughly comparable. In some cases, people with the same titles at different organisations have very different levels of responsibilities, requiring different levels and combinations of skills.

Another way in which subject matter expertise can help to make sure this type of analysis is meaningful is understanding how well, and how comprehensively performance is being measured. If performance has been measured very well, then you would expect that, on average, people who perform better than others in a similar role would be paid more. But if performance has been measured fairly narrowly, then there may be circumstances in which the relationship between salary and performance is less strong because salaries are reflecting dimensions of performance that are not being captured in formal performance metrics.

USING ANALYTICS TO UNDERSTAND THE FINANCIAL CONSEQUENCES OF OPERATIONAL DECISIONS

Analytics can also be used to answer a variety of questions about the financial consequences of operational decisions, such as those listed below.

Common Questions

- Which suppliers are most cost-effective?
- How much do we expect our production costs to be over a given time period?
- Could we save money by offshoring or outsourcing some of our operations?

Data Sources

Much of the data needed to answer questions such as those listed above should be available within an organisation's internal systems. That includes things like the accounting and procurement systems, which would document prices paid for products from different suppliers, as well as potentially things like tenders revealing prices offered by different suppliers. Internal systems would also be likely to have information on things such as the rate of defective products from different suppliers. Organisations producing manufactured products would be likely to have information on things such as the total costs associated with manufacturing particular products, including the inputs, labour, and cost of running equipment and so forth.

Analysis

Historical data about purchases and defects, or other measures of quality, could be combined to calculate the average cost of particular components by supplier so comparisons could be made to identify the least expensive supplier after controlling for quality.

Total production costs could be estimated based on volume and other variables that might influence production costs, such as seasonality. Similar analysis could be done for different locations by including variables such as prevailing rates for costs that vary across locations such as wage rates and electricity costs.

Other Considerations

Quantifying the quality provided by different suppliers may prove challenging. For example, a component provided by one supplier may cost less, but take longer for an organisation's employees to process for some reason, such as the way it's packaged. Therefore, this is another situation where subject matter experts may be able to identify reasons why care needs to be taken in the interpretation of a particular result. That is especially true when it comes to things such as location. For example, it may appear that total production costs will be lower in one location than another, but if there is a greater risk of disruption of supply from that location that might change a decision about whether to move production to the lowest cost location.

USING ANALYTICS TO PRICE RISK

One particular form of financial analytics relates to the quantifying of the expected cost of different forms of risk an organisation might face. As the questions below show, that's of interest to the organisation itself, as well as to any other organisation providing it with insurance.

Common Questions

- (For organisations such as insurance companies) How likely is this person or organisation to experience an event we're insuring them for, and how much is it likely to cost if they do?

- How likely is it that our operations will be disrupted by an event, such as a natural disaster, and how much is it likely to cost if they are?
- Is our organisation's risk of experiencing a particular type of event such as a natural disaster likely to affect our insurance premiums or financial ratings?

Data Sources

The types of risks that organisations are trying to price tend to fall into two broad categories: risks to people and risks to property. Data on the overall number of people who experience certain types of injuries or illnesses or death by particular causes is generally available through public health records, typically maintained by governmental organisations such as the CDC in the USA or Ministries of Health or National Health Services in other places. Data related to variables that might help predict the likelihood that any individual person might contract a particular illness or die of a certain cause within a given time period would typically come from their health records, which are increasingly available in electronic health record systems, though sometimes are still in paper files.

Data about adverse events that have affected property in the past come at least partially from external passively collected data, such as weather data and geotechnical data in the case of earthquakes. Those quantify the number of times different things have happened in a given location, such as winds over a certain speed or earthquakes over a given magnitude. The other type of data that's important for this type of analytics is data about the costs associated with different adverse events, such as the average cost of damage from a tornado or earthquake of a particular size happening in a particular type of place, such as a densely populated city or rural farmland.

Analysis

As discussed in the Analytics in Practice section of this chapter, there is a whole profession focussed on this form of analytics. The people who practise that profession are called **actuaries**, and they have developed specific, standardised ways of pricing and documenting different types of risks. While the details of those are beyond the scope of this book, they generally involve building models to predict the likelihood of particular events happening to particular people or pieces of property, and also to predict the financial costs associated with those events if they should occur. Multiplying the likelihood of an event occurring by the expected cost if it does gives them an estimate of how much that event is likely to cost them, and that information can then be aggregated by individual or organisation to estimate things such as the expected costs of covering an organisation's or individual person's insurance claims for the next year.

Other Considerations

Predictive models rely on historical data, so the relevant data needs to exist to develop a model, and that may not be the case for all types of risks that someone might want to predict. Furthermore, if conditions are changing from what they were during the time covered by the historical data then the models may lose accuracy. As discussed in the Analytics in Practice section, the Covid pandemic changed everything from how people lived to how often they went to the doctor and that changed their patterns of health-related insurance claims. Similarly, climate change could cause predictions about natural disasters based on historical climate data to become less accurate.

USING ANALYTICS TO UNDERSTAND THE FINANCIAL POSITION OF AN ORGANISATION OVERALL (INCLUDING COMPETITORS)

One of the oldest applications of analytics within organisations is to understand the financial position of the organisation itself or that of its competitors. This type of analysis can also inform decisions about whether to buy or sell stock/shares in a given company.

Common Questions

- Is our organisation (or another organisation) in a solid financial position, and likely to remain so?
- Do we need to borrow money or raise capital?
- Do we need to protect ourselves against potential currency fluctuations?
- What can we learn about our competitors from their financial statements?

Data Sources

Organisations' internal accounting systems include data on income, expenses, liabilities and assets. That information can be used for internal analysis of an organisation's own financial position.

Every public company is required to file financial information, including their income statement and balance sheet. Analysis of data in the financial documents competitors are required to disclose can reveal a lot of important information, including their revenue, costs, and growth rate.

Analysis

A lot of the analysis of this type of data focusses on changes from previous periods. For example: are revenue or expenses increasing or decreasing? In organisations such as retailers, who are strongly affected by seasonality, those comparisons are often made between the current quarter and the same quarter in previous years.

Comparisons can also be made between a particular organisation and its competitors to see things such as whether an organisation's competitors' revenue or expenses are increasing or decreasing more or less quickly than their own. That can help managers understand whether any change in their own position is due primarily to losing or gaining ground on their competitors versus overall trends affecting a whole industry. It can also be used to identify which competitors pose the greatest threats due to growth in their market share, margins, etc. relative to the organisation itself.

Financial analysts also calculate and analyse various ratios to evaluate the health of a company. The details of those are beyond the scope of this book, but examples include things such as earnings per share and return on assets.

Other Considerations

This type of analytics draws from a variety of internal data sources. Those may be kept in different information systems, creating the potential for inconsistencies and challenges creating one integrated dataset for the whole organisation (Deloitte, n.d.), whether that's being done for internal purposes only or to create the types of documents that public companies need to disclose. Another thing to keep in mind is that the financial position of an organisation at any given moment may or may not be a good predictor of its position in the future. The types of data described in this sub-section are backward looking, so may not take into account the future effects of new trends, up-and-coming competitors, changing demographics, and so forth.

SUMMARY

Financial analytics give organisations a high-level view of their overall financial position as well as quantifying the financial consequences of decisions made in the other functional areas of the organisation. Those things are important for making future financial decisions, such as whether to raise additional capital through debt or equity, make new investments, or embark on a cost-cutting programme. Another thing that informs those future decisions is the level of uncertainty associated with particular potential outcomes, including adverse events that could affect the organisation or its employees. Analytics can also be used to predict the likelihood of events like that, and their expected cost if they do occur.

ANALYTICS IN PRACTICE

Predicting the price of perils

As should be clear by now, business and organisational analytics encompass a range of different applications, and grew out of a range of different disciplines. One of the older applications of analytical techniques within organisations is to quantify risk. The specialised professionals who do that are actuaries. While many of the techniques they use are similar to those used in other applications of analytics, actuaries have developed specific ways of quantifying risk and documenting their process for doing so.

Risks to people

One group of actuaries focusses primarily on risks to people. Their employers or clients are typically insurance companies, and they help them decide on what premiums to charge by estimating the likelihood of a person with particular characteristics (age, gender, etc.) dying or developing certain health problems, and the expected cost to their insurer if they do.

Joe Salz works as a health actuary for Deloitte Consulting. Many of the clients he works with are governmental organisations responsible for covering the cost of healthcare services, such as through the Medicaid Programmes in different US states. Joe and his colleagues generate estimates of the expected cost of insurance benefits for the population covered by their clients. As he explains:

> That one number is a very complex process of all of the benefits that would be incorporated... That number is important because they need to book what their Medicaid spending is going to be for the next year, so they look to us for what that's going to cost for the average person, multiply that by their entire expected Medicaid population. And that is a budget number that can change the policy agenda.

> If we booked their Medicaid spending at a certain level that they weren't anticipating, they may need to create some budget actions or change benefits or create some sort of like global spending cap and so it can have a lot of downstream political or budgetary impacts for sure.

That complex process was made even more so following the early part of the Covid pandemic. The estimates that Joe and his colleagues create are based on predictive modelling that uses historical healthcare data about things such as the number of hospital visits for various forms of illness and injury as an input. The way people in the USA lived their lives and accessed medical care in 2020 was very different from previous years, which created questions about what to do about the data from that year when predicting the cost of medical care in subsequent years:

> We're not going to use a pandemic affected dataset to project a non-pandemic future year because that's just not a good representation.
>
> So, one thing we've done is we've either modified our base data, we've used a different source or a different time period, or we've applied adjustments on that data, and have documented those...
>
> Typically, what we've done is we've just skipped 2020. We've stayed in 2019 and then you know now that we're projecting ... 2023 costs, now we're using 2021 data so now we've just skipped 2020 altogether.
>
> We saw 2021 actually rebound pretty well, so when we calculated 2021 rates off of 2019 that was actually a pretty appropriate approach to just skip over 2020 because 2021 bounced back so quickly.

Risks to property

While some actuaries, such as Joe, focus primarily on risks to people, others focus primarily on risks to property. One company that specialises in those types of risk is bms.re (BMS). They are a reinsurance company, or an insurer of insurers. Reinsurance means that insurance companies themselves don't have to bear the full brunt of the cost of a major catastrophic event, such as a hurricane, tornado, or earthquake because they share the cost with a secondary insurer.

As explained by Scott Christian, the Executive Vice President of Catastrophe Analytics for BMS, they use different tools to build a model to estimate the overall expected cost of providing an insurance company with reinsurance against specific types of risks, including accounting for correlations among those risks and across different properties covered by the insurer:

> We have in the model what we call primary and secondary uncertainty. So the primary is whether the event occurs, and then the secondary is the probability of loss; what's the distribution of loss? And in that vulnerability, or in that in that distribution of loss, there is a correlation. So what's the correlation of a home that has been subjected to wind speeds from a tornado that has maybe a 50% damage ratio, and what's the correlation to the risk next to it? It's probably pretty correlated.

(Continued)

As Scott points out, some of these risks are very difficult to model:

Tornado risk is an extremely difficult peril to model because they'll touch down, they'll come up, they'll touch down..., so it's very selective in what risk it hits.

Data availability also creates challenges. One aspect of that is the data BMS gets from its clients about the properties being insured. As Scott explained:

No client is the same as another in terms of what columns they collect, what data attributes they collect, so every client has a unique dataset.

Getting historical data about the types of perils BMS models can also be challenging, as Scott's colleague, Andrew Siffert, Senior Vice President for Meteorology at BMS explains:

There's written records right that go back maybe 130 years 140 years, and maybe there's some even longer historical records of volcanic eruptions and these sorts of things, but when you look at the true data that we need in the insurance industry to help start the price catastrophe risk, and the details that are involved in that, it's a pretty short period of record...

Because when it comes to an extreme event, what is an extreme event? It's something that's defined by the word extreme. It's something that doesn't happen very often. So naturally you need a longer period of record for those extremes to show up.

The combination of the events being modelled being relatively rare and the historical record being relatively short means that new data can result in big changes to predictions, as Andrew notes:

So a classic example is: you might hear the one in 1000 year rain event. Well, that's likely because the rainfall record we have to encompass the one in 1000 year event is probably in the order of 100 years to 75 years. And there might be one record in there that's really extreme in that 75 year period, right? But if all of a sudden you get a new rainfall event that is very similar in magnitude, that one in 1000 year event drops to 1 in 500 or one in 250. So, automatically with one new event in your dataset, you're drastically changing the return period.

The facts that the events are relatively rare and the record is relatively short makes it hard to determine whether particular types of events are becoming more or less frequent as a result of climate change. Further complicating the already challenging task of doing this type of modelling is the fact that the way people live has changed over time, and that could change the costs associated with an adverse event because the amount of damage caused could be greater even if the frequency of the event isn't. That could be because people are living in places where they didn't previously live or because the nature of the built environment in a particular area exacerbates damage caused by different types of weather events and natural disasters rather than mitigating them.

As awareness of these issues and concerns about property damage resulting from climate change has grown, so has interest in catastrophe modelling. As Andrew noted, the ratings company Moody's recently purchased one of the companies that makes the software BMS uses for catastrophe modelling:

> So they're going to be applying these models to a company's financial risk to climate, right, and to climate change. And that's gonna potentially influence like OK, well are you gonna go and build a group of hotels along the coastline? Well, what are you doing to mitigate that risk for a future climate? And that's going to ultimately influence your rating. So we're seeing definitely a big move into this area of basically the financial and the true financial industry of banking, of lending – so it's not just insurance.

You can hear more from Joe, Scott, and Andrew and their work trying to estimate the cost of different types of risks here: https://vimeo.com/751492104/c55fb2d437.

RUNNING CASE STUDY: 4TE, PART 9[1]

All of the work Ben had been doing had been giving Matt and Emily a much clearer picture of where things stood with 4tE, but Matt thought that one additional piece of information that would be useful to have would be an analysis of the profitability of their different existing product lines. 4tE sold 209 different vegan and vegetarian products that they grouped into eight categories: baking, chilled, condiments, drinks, pantry, snacks, spices and supplies (these were mainly their reusable packages that could be purchased filled or unfilled and could be returned for commercial cleaning and re-use, in which case the customer would receive a credit).

Knowing which product categories were most or least profitable would be helpful in deciding whether to add products to the existing categories or whether to raise prices in some categories – especially to accommodate recent inflation in the prices being charged by some suppliers. It could also help inform the broader decision about whether to expand beyond these categories. For example, Emily was very excited about the

(Continued)

---

[1]The 4tE case is fictitious.

possibility of leasing the space next to their existing store and turning it into a fresh produce market, and they had also thought about offering frozen foods.

Matt asked Ben to calculate revenue, cost of goods, and profitability by category. This was a somewhat complicated task since it involved pulling sales data from the POS and combining that with cost data pulled from the accounting system, but by this point Ben was becoming increasingly confident with and knowledgeable about 4tE's data. Still, Ben did wonder how he should deal with packaging for the purpose of this analysis. Since people received credits when they returned packaging for commercial cleaning and re-use, the supplies category might appear to be unprofitable; however the original cost of the packaging was included in the prices of products in other product categories since those all incorporated the price of both the packaging and the food in them.

EXERCISES

1   Select a publicly traded company that has been in business for at least ten years and search online for their annual reports for the past ten years (this can typically be done by searching for the name of the company combined with 'annual report' or investors). Create a visualisation or visualisations showing the organisation's income, expenses, assets and liabilities for the past ten years. What can you infer from your visualisation(s) about the financial health of the company? Can you explain any patterns revealed in the visualisation based on what you know about the organisation?

2   Suppose that the institution where you are taking this course asked you to forecast total enrolments next year in the programme you are currently part of. What technique(s) and variable(s) would you use to generate your prediction? Describe the process you would use to generate your prediction in as much detail as possible, then consider how accurate you would expect it to be and why.

3   Suppose that you and some friends were discussing the effect the Covid pandemic had on university students and got the idea of providing insurance coverage against a similar event happening in the future. The idea would be to charge students a premium that would then entitle them to have their university costs (tuition, fees, accommodation, etc.) reimbursed if their studies were significantly disrupted as a result of a pandemic or some other large-scale event, such as a natural disaster or war. You and your friends like the idea, but one friend is questioning whether you would be able to come up with an accurate model to predict the likelihood of such events and the cost if such an event were to occur. Those things would be important to your potential business because you would need them to determine how much you should charge for your study disruption insurance. Could you develop an accurate model? If so, how?

10
THE FUTURE OF
DATA AND ANALYTICS

WHAT WILL YOU LEARN FROM THIS CHAPTER?

- How advances in technologies such as the Internet of Things, augmented reality and virtual reality, artificial intelligence, and edge computing may influence how data and analytics are used in the future.
- What opportunities there are for building analytics into your career.

TECHNOLOGIES THAT HAVE IMPLICATIONS FOR THE FUTURE OF BUSINESS ANALYTICS

Historically, new generations of technology have often given rise to new or updated forms of analytics. For example, the web created the need for web analytics, and also made collection of survey data easier. Social networks increased interest in network analysis, mobile devices enabled the collection of geolocation data, with apps came a need for app analytics, and wearables made it much easier to gather health-related data at scale. Given that history, it's worth considering currently emerging technologies and their potential implications for analytics.

Internet of Things

The term the **Internet of Things (IoT)** refers to all of the machines connected via the Internet, including 'smart home' devices, such as speakers, lights, doorbells, and locks you can control via apps. There are also industrial IoT applications, such as the Predix platform operated by GE Digital, that enables companies to remotely monitor equipment via sensors to predict when maintenance is needed and to pinpoint the source of problems.

The IoT has been around for a while, but is gradually transitioning from novel to normal. As that happens, the things that are connected to the Internet are generating more and more data. That, in turn, creates opportunities for organisations to leverage that data in various ways. There are many potential operational analytics applications. In addition to predictive maintenance, those include tracking products and components as they move through supply chains and distribution channels to ensure things are where they are supposed to be and even to monitor their condition as they travel – for example to ensure things are kept at a particular temperature or free from impacts over a certain force. Data generated for the IoT also has great potential for analytics related to capacity utilisation because it makes it easy to identify not only how much equipment and facilities are being used, but also patterns of over- and under-utilisation.

The IoT also offers potential HR and marketing analytics applications. For example, there are theories about what types of interactions among employees lead to the greatest productivity and innovation, and IoT devices would enable those to be tested. They could also be used to monitor the health of employees in real time. IoT devices could also produce data that could be analysed to understand patterns of consumer behaviour at a much more granular level than is possible using data from things such as interviews and focus groups.

Obviously the HR and marketing applications of the IoT just described don't only involve things; they also involve people, and potentially very sensitive data about them. For example, many people now wear devices that have sensors on them monitoring various aspects of health. That data can be analysed to provide personalised medical care or to identify unsafe work practices, but it's potentially very sensitive data. Therefore, great care needs to be taken in any IoT application involving people to ensure the planned collection, analysis, and use of data is ethical and appropriate given the organisational and cultural context and relevant privacy policies and legislation.

Augmented and Virtual Reality

Augmented and virtual reality are other technologies that have been talked about for a long time, but appear to be gaining traction at the time of writing. **Augmented reality** overlays real world content with digital content. **Virtual reality** immerses the viewer's field of vision in a virtual environment. The company formerly known as Facebook changed its name to Meta, in part to signal its commitment to the metaverse – the broader virtual context for virtual reality. Other technology companies, such as Microsoft and Snap, are actively involved in creation of augmented reality hardware and software.

New waves of technology, such as the web, apps, and social media, have all given rise to new sources of data for analytics, new questions that can be addressed through analytics, and new analytical techniques, and it seems likely that widespread adoption of virtual or augmented reality could change analytics too. This is particularly true for augmented reality since it could involve simultaneous collection of data about where a user is in the physical world, what they are seeing in the physical world, and what digital content is being overlayed over that. Each of those types of data is already used in other types of analytics, but the combination of the three offers the potential to answer new questions. For example, does providing augmented reality content related to things like directions and obstacles help drivers drive more safely, and is that true on all types of roads and driving conditions? An enormous amount of data could be collected through augmented and virtual reality and would need to be analysed to answer questions like these, and that could also give rise to new analytical techniques that are able to cope with, and take advantage of, extremely large datasets. The Analytics in Practice section of this chapter provides additional insights about potential analytical implications of augmented reality.

Artificial Intelligence

There are entire books, courses, and degrees about **artificial intelligence (AI)**, but one way of thinking about it for our purposes is as highly automated versions of the types of analytical techniques described in this book. Instead of an individual analyst considering what variables to include in something like a regression model, AI can churn through a virtually infinite set of possibilities in a relatively short time to come up with the very best model. And it can do that not only with the variables, but also with the type of model or models to use to make a given prediction.

This level of automation is appealing because it enables much more data to be analysed much more quickly than is possible with more manual methods, and it also makes it possible to identify patterns within data that humans would never think to look for. This could leave you thinking that AI will replace humans working in business analytics, but that's very unlikely to be true. It may, however, change the nature of their jobs. It's likely to mean that people working in analytics will need to spend less of their time executing and implementing analytical techniques and more of it thinking and exercising judgement about the most useful questions to ask and what data to use to answer those questions. That's because at least for the foreseeable future, AI models can only work with the data and questions they are given, and both of those require human judgement. People working in analytical careers are also likely to spend more time scrutinising results being produced by AI for transparency, fairness, and usefulness.

Edge Computing

One mechanism for getting the benefits of AI and the IoT while retaining privacy is to keep the data that is collected through the IoT and analysed using AI on the device through which it's collected rather than sending it to the cloud for centralised storage and analysis. That's often referred to as **edge computing** because the computing is happening out on the edge of a network on end user's own devices rather than in a central data centre.

You may not be aware of it, but that type of thing is probably already happening on your phone when you use features such as facial recognition. While that has significant benefits in terms of privacy and security, one downside is that it may limit availability of data for more ad hoc and aggregated analysis – for example, comparing usage patterns among different groups of users.

BUSINESS ANALYTICS AND YOU

I hope that this book has inspired you to think about how you want analytics to fit into your own career. There are options for people with any type of interest in analytics. As shown in Figure 10.1, I think of them on two dimensions: expertise with tools and techniques versus domain, or subjective matter expertise. Ideally, we'd all like to have both, but time is limited, and so we all have to make choices about how we spend our time.

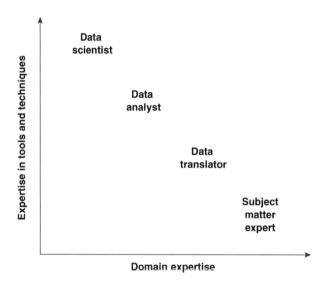

Figure 10.1   Analytics-related career options

People who work as data analysts tend to divide their time between both of the dimensions. They typically have more expertise with tools like Excel, and often other tools such as PowerBI and SQL, than colleagues who are not in data science. They may have some exposure to programming languages used for data science, such as R and Python, but they are typically less expert in them and in computer science than full-time data scientists are. But compared to data scientists, people working as data analysts typically have more domain expertise, and therefore have a better understanding of the questions the data is being used to answer. There are many other titles for the type of job just described, including research analysts and quantitative analysts.

Another type of role that lies between the extremes of pure data scientists and subject matter experts is data translation. Again, exact titles vary, but this type of job often involves less direct analysis of data and more interpretation of analysis that has been done by others and explanation of it to decision-makers, and sometimes to the general public. This includes people who visualise data to make it more intuitive and easier for people without statistical backgrounds to understand.

Those who love the statistical or computing aspects of working with data and really want to focus on the tools and techniques may want to consider a career in data science where that's the focus. And data has become so ubiquitous that there are opportunities for subject matter experts who understand analytics well in virtually every field.

FINAL THOUGHTS

Analytics can already help organisations do a lot of things more efficiently and effectively, and the developments described in this chapter are likely to enable new and deeper insights as well as opportunities to gain the benefits of analytics while mitigating the risks to privacy.

Organisations that use analytics are likely to be more efficient and effective than those that don't, and that's important in any competitive environment. It's even important for public sector organisations and non-profits since they need to use taxpayer and donor funds as carefully as possible to achieve their goals.

Implementing analytics takes time and often money too, so even well-resourced organisations need to make choices about which specific type of analytics to implement. I hope this book has helped you understand how to think about those choices given the broader circumstances and priorities of an organisation.

I hope the book has also made you more aware that many applications of analytics raise ethical questions, and it's important to ask those questions before implementing any type of analytics. In some cases they raise legal questions too, so it's also important to consider the legality of any planned use of analytics.

Another thing that I hope you've learned is that while we talk about analytics as a single thing, it's actually a broad container for an almost infinite amount of variety. The specific data we need in a given situation and the way we analyse it has to be driven by the nature of the question we are trying to answer with the data or the problem we are trying to solve. That, in turn, is a function of the needs of our target audience.

Different organisations, and different people within organisations, have different questions and problems. In the case of organisations, that may be because of the nature of what they do, their competitive position, and so forth. In the case of the individuals, it's likely to be a function of their roles and responsibilities. Therefore, the same data may be used to answer different questions to meet the needs of different people or organisations. And in other situations, different data may be used to answer the same question just based on what's available to a particular organisation. The types of new technologies described in this chapter are likely to give rise to new types of questions that can be answered with analytics – for example, about how people behave when experiencing virtual and augmented reality.

As we've seen, different analytical methods are appropriate for different combinations of questions and data, so we need to be thinking about both of those things in considering which forms of analysis to apply. As I hope you've learned as you've worked through the book, even quite simple analytical methods can produce useful insights when deployed on the right combination of data and question. I also hope you've discovered that often answering one question with one set of data and one analytical approach gives rise to additional questions which we might then answer with the same or different data and analytical techniques.

While I hope the book has given a sense of the benefits that can be derived from careful application of analytics, I also hope that it has made you aware of the limitations inherent in most applications of analytics. Real world data can be big, messy, inconsistent and incomplete, and variables may not be defined as clearly or conveniently as we would like. That's why it has become common to say that about 80% of time spent working with data is spent preparing and structuring it. Hopefully that will improve as organisations get better at structuring, collecting, and storing data. For example, data coming from sources like the Internet of Things is likely to be in better shape than data collected by humans because it starts out more structured and comes in via an automated process. Nonetheless, the work required to prepare data for analysis is unlikely to go away completely in the foreseeable future, and it remains essential to generating useful, reliable results.

The final point I would like to leave you with is that details really matter when it comes to analytics. For analytics to enable more efficient and effective actions and decisions we need to engage good judgement about:

- what questions to ask of the data
- what data to use to answer the questions
- how to process and analyse the data
- how to interpret the results
- how to communicate the results as clearly as possible given the target audience and objectives.

ANALYTICS IN PRACTICE

Evolving analytics for augmented reality

As discussed earlier in this chapter, in the past, changes in technology have resulted in changes in the questions people within organisations ask, the data available to answer those questions, and the analytical techniques applied to the data to answer the questions. Takeshi Tawarada, who is Ads Research and Insights Lead for Augmented Reality for Snap believes that any changes to marketing analytics resulting from augmented reality (AR) will be evolutionary rather than revolutionary. He believes many existing marketing analytics metrics developed for the web and subsequently social media and apps will remain relevant to the measurement of experiences involving augmented reality:

> We're in a transition phase with augmented reality - similar to when we were moving from desktop to mobile when it comes to analytics. We still have the relics of that past ... things like impressions, and click throughs, and view rates ... for augmented reality, saves and shares I think are very important, in addition to the time that you engaged with the augmented reality experience.

However Takeshi also notes that there are questions about how to measure engagement that cut across older and newer digital technologies.

> I think the measurement industry, in general, is trying to use that notion of time, and evolve it into something around attention.

The idea is that, while up to this point time may have been the main available proxy for engagement, it may not be a particularly good one. For example, someone may be doing something else while a video ad is playing on their device and not watching the ad at all. Or they could be spending a lot of time on a website, but perhaps that's because they are having trouble finding what they're looking for or doing what they're trying to do and not because they find it particularly interesting.

Measuring time spent has always been tricky - for example - how long does an app have to be open to count as having been opened deliberately rather than accidentally? Takeshi described similar questions that are arising when trying to use other measures of attention or engagement in AR. For example, AR can be used to let people virtually 'try on' things such as clothing, glasses, new hair styles, and beauty products. Arguably, actively trying something on - even virtually - is a stronger indictor of attention or engagement than just passively watching something online, but:

(Continued)

We're currently trying to investigate what that attention means and when we can consider a try-on a try-on. If an experience just renders on your face and is on for one second, and you didn't really pay attention to it, and skip over to the next one, does that really count as a try-on?

In addition to inheriting metrics from previous generations of technology, Takeshi stressed the importance of those involved in generating metrics from and about AR carrying forward privacy-related lessons from the past:

I hope that technology companies have learned their lesson when it comes to their privacy policies and the ways user data is handled.

He noted this attention to privacy is especially important in the context of AR due to its potential to be perceived as creepy or intrusive if not managed carefully. Those wanting to collect and analyse AR-related data also need to do that in an environment in which privacy regulation and access to data via platforms and partners have also evolved to be more restrictive.

RUNNING CASE STUDY: 4TE, PART 10[1]

On a warm spring afternoon the day after Ben finished his final university exam, he, Matt, and Emily met one last time before he finished at 4tE. Ben was going to take some time off before starting his new full-time job as a data analyst with a consulting firm that he had secured, in part, on the strength of the work he had done for 4tE. One of the reasons Ben was excited about that job was that during the interview process he heard a lot about the firm's plans to develop an AI consulting practice.

Those conversations were on Ben's mind when Matt and Emily asked whether he thought there was any further analysis they should do now before finalising their business plan for 4tE for 2023–2024 (their financial year ended at the end of June) or that they should build into that plan. Ben suggested that they could consider using AI to make personalised product recommendations based on customers' past purchases. Emily was excited by the idea, but Matt wondered both about who would implement that and if their customers would find it creepy. For example, he did find it creepy when he looked something up on the Internet and then all of a sudden started seeing ads for that product or for similar products. He also pointed out that they had great staff, and argued that staff members talking with customers would be able to provide better recommendations than AI could.

---

[1]The 4tE case is fictitious.

After realising that was not a discussion they were likely to resolve that afternoon, Matt and Emily thanked Ben for all of his hard work and wished him well in his new job. When he left, they got to work finalising the parts of 4tE's business plan for the following year that they did agree on.

EXERCISES

1   Find a dataset that is of interest to you or one that you have used as part of doing the course you are currently taking and open it in Excel. Click the 'analyse data' icon and see what comes up under 'Discover Insights'. Are they the most useful insights that could be derived from the dataset? Those insights are generated using artificial intelligence. What does that one example suggest about whether that particular form of artificial intelligence can replace more manual forms of analytics?

2   Choose one of the virtual reality apps listed here: https://robots.net/ai/best-augmented-reality-apps-to-try/. Consider what question(s) could be answered using data generated by the app. What type(s) of analysis would you need to do using the data to answer the question(s)? How could you ensure that using the data in the way you've described would be both legal and ethical?

3   'Smart Cities' is a way of describing the collection and analysis of data – typically at a reasonably large scale – to make cities function more effectively. The Internet of Things is frequently a primary means of gathering data for Smart City initiatives. Identify one way that your city or local area could make use of the Internet of Things to do something more efficiently or effectively, and what data and analytics would be involved in implementing that process.

GLOSSARY

A/B testing   experiments in which alternative versions of something are compared. Examples of things that are subject to A/B testing include specific elements of advertising campaigns, promotional offers, prices, and specific elements of websites and pages.

Actively collected data   data that is collected for a specific purpose and with the explicit knowledge of the party providing it.

Actuaries   people who estimate the likelihood of different types of risks to people and property and the estimated cost if the particular type of peril occurs. This is typically, though not always, done so insurance companies can determine how much premium to charge to insure against those risks.

App analytics   aggregated statistics about app users, including how many of them there are, what countries they come from, how much time they spend using the app, and what device they use to access it.

Artificial intelligence   highly automated analytical processes used to identify and act on patterns in data.

Augmented reality   real world content is overlaid with digital content.

Behavioural data   data related to observable things people do, such as opening an app, visiting a website, or making a purchase.

Big Data   data that has high volume, variety, and velocity. Volume refers to the total quantity of data, variety relates to the form the data takes (i.e., how predictable it is), and velocity relates to how rapidly it is being changed or added to.

Binary variables   variables that can only have the value of 0 or 1, usually 1 if a particular characteristic is present and 0 if it is not.

Bubble chart   chart with data points plotted in the x and y axes, and the size of the marker at each data point used to represent a third dimension.

Cases   individual units of investigation. Normally represented as rows within a dataset.

Conjoint analysis   analytical method used to infer the relative importance of attributes such as price and quality as well as to see how changing the level of those attributes may affect the probability of people choosing that particular option.

Correlation   formal way of describing a statistical association (generally between numeric variables).

Cross-tab   stands for cross tabulation, and is used to show the joint distribution of two or more nominal variables.

Dataset   table in which rows represent different observations and columns represent different variables.

Disaggregation   breaking data down so that it can be analysed by sub-group (e.g., by gender, ethnicity, age, or a combination of those).

Double y axis chart   visualisation with vertical (y) axes on both the left and right of a chart.

Dummy variables   binary variables used in regression analysis.

Edge computing   analysis is performed on the device used to collect data rather than being transferred to a central repository for analysis.

Frequency distribution   table showing how many observations correspond to a particular value (or group of values) of a variable.

Grouped column and bar charts   charts that show data for one group in a vertical column or horizontal bar. May include multiple bars or columns representing multiple groups.

Granularity level of specificity   More granular analysis focuses on more narrowly defined sub-groups whereas less granular analysis focuses on an entire population or sample or broadly defined groups.

Heat map   use of colour, shading, texture or pattern to show varying levels of one or more variables on a table, map or other type of image.

Histogram   graphical representation showing how many observations correspond to a particular value (or group of values) of a variable.

Internet of Things (IoT)   all of the machines connected via the Internet (e.g., connected speakers, doorbells, lights, etc.).

Interval variable   numeric variable with equal intervals, but an arbitrary origin point.

Legend   the part of a chart, graph or table that shows which symbols, colours, patterns, etc. are used to represent different data series. Also sometimes referred to as a key.

Likert scales   the types of scales, often used in surveys, where people are asked to evaluate things such as their agreement with a statement or satisfaction with something by selecting one of a relatively small number (usually 11 or less) of possibilities along a continuum such as strongly disagree to strongly agree or very dissatisfied to very satisfied.

Line charts   show data series as lines connecting points plotted on two axes.

Mean   another word for average. Add all values for a specific variable across all observations, and then divide by the total number of observations.

Median   the value of a frequency distribution that an equal number of observations are above and below.

Metadata   data about data (e.g., the timestamp documenting when the data was recorded or the geolocation of where it was recorded).

Metrics   particular measures derived from analytics, such as average revenue per user or sales per square foot. This term is usually used to refer to measures that are tracked over time.

Mode   the most common value for a variable.

Nominal variables   numbers are arbitrarily assigned to different groups or responses for convenience.

Numeric variable   variables expressed as non-arbitrary numbers, with equal intervals between them.

Ordinal variables   variables in which the numbers reflect an ordering, but the intervals between the numbers may not be uniform.

Outliers   values that are accurate, but unusual.

Passively collected data   data collected in the background without any active participation by the person the data is about.

Pie charts   round charts split into pizza or pie type slices showing the proportion of observations that fall into different categories.

Population   all items, elements, or entities to which the thing being investigated applies.

Qualitative data   things such as text, images, video, and audio that don't start out as numbers, but can be converted into numbers for analysis.

Quantitative data   anything that starts as a number or can easily be converted to a number, such as the answer to a particular closed-ended survey question.

Ratio-scaled variable   numeric variable with an absolute zero point reflecting a total absence of the thing being measured.

Sample   a sub-set of all items, elements, or entities to which the thing being investigated applies. Often used to make inferences about the population as a whole.

Scatter plot   chart with data points plotted in the x and y axes and equally sized markers for each data point.

Segment   A group of customers or stakeholders who have similar characteristics, preferences, or behaviours.

Stacked column and bar charts   charts in which columns or bars are divided into slices representing the number or proportion of observations with different values on the same variable. May include multiple bars or columns representing multiple groups, time-periods, or variables.

Standard deviation   the square root of the average squared distance between individual observations of a variable and the mean for that variable.

Straight-lining   an individual giving identical survey responses to a series of questions where responses would be expected to be more varied. This and other unusual patterns of responses may be an indication the person responding did not provide accurate answers to the questions being asked.

String variable   variable expressed as text rather than a number (e.g., a name).

Tables   data or other information presented in rows and columns, such as in a spreadsheet.

Third party data   data that comes from an organisation such as a government statistical agency, trade association or consulting company rather than an organisation or its customers or other stakeholders.

Variables   characteristics of the cases being investigated. Normally represented as columns within a dataset.

Variance   the average squared distance between individual observations of a variable and the mean for that variable.

Virtual reality   viewers' entire field of vision is immersed in a virtual environment.

Web analytics   aggregated statistics about website users, including how many of them there are, what countries they come from, how much time they spend using the site, and what device they use to access it.

REFERENCES

BBC (2021). Three Years of the GDPR: The Biggest Fines So Far. Available from: www.bbc. com/news/technology-57011639 (accessed 20 November 2021).

Boudette, N. E. (2021). Want to Buy a Car? You Might Have to Get on a Plane to Claim it. Available from: www.nytimes.com/2021/12/22/business/economy/car-chip-shortage-pandemic.html (accessed 31 August 2022).

Burgess, M. (2021). Ignore China's New Data Privacy Law at your Peril. Available from: www. wired.com/story/china-personal-data-law-pipl (accessed 22 November 2021).

Carroll, S., Garba, I., Figueroa-Rodríguez, O., Holbrook, J., Lovett, R., Materechera, S., Parsons, M., Raseroka, K., Rodriguez-Lonebear, D., Rowe, R., Sara, R., Walker, J., Anderson, J., and Hudson, M. (2020). The CARE Principles for Indigenous Data Governance. *Data Science Journal*, *19*(1), 43.

Conboye, J., and Smith, S. (2022). The Real Reason Employees Don't Fill Out Surveys. Available from: www.ft.com/content/7a98515c-9a00-4b25-9131-c19c99d3a190 (accessed 18 August 2022).

Davis, M. S. (1971). That's Interesting!: Towards a Phenomenology of Sociology and a Sociology of Phenomenology. *Philosophy of the Social Sciences*, *1*(2), 309–344.

Deloitte (n.d.). Finance Analytics. Available from: www2.deloitte.com/content/dam/Deloitte/ca/Documents/Analytics/ca-en-analytics-finance-analytics.pdf (accessed 13 September 2022).

Deslauriers, L., McCarty, L. S., Miller, K., Callaghan, K., & Kestin, G. (2019). Measuring actual learning versus feeling of learning in response to being actively engaged in the classroom. *Proceedings of the National Academy of Sciences*, *116*(39), 19251-19257.

Kantor, J., & Sundaram, A. (2022). The Rise of the Worker Productivity Score. *The New York Times*, August 14.

Lambrecht, A., and Tucker, C. (2019). Algorithmic Bias? An Empirical Study of Apparent Gender-Based Discrimination in the Display of STEM Career Ads. *Management Science*, *65*(7), 2966–2981.

Lazer, D., Green, J., Ognyanova, K., Baum, M.A., Lin, J., Druckman, J.N., Perlis, R.H., Santillana, M., & Uslu, A. (2021). The COVID States Project #57: Social media news consumption and COVID-19 vaccination rates. Available from: https://osf.io/uvqbs/ (accessed 24 March 2023).

Mahajan, J. (1992). The Overconfidence Effect in Marketing Management Predictions. *Journal of Marketing Research*, *29*(3), 329–342.

Maōri Data Sovereignty Network (2018). *Principles of Maōri Data Sovereignty*. Available from: https://static1.squarespace.com/static/58e9b10f9de4bb8d1fb5ebbc/t/5bda208b4ae237cd8 9ee16e9/1541021836126/TMR+M%C4%81ori+Data+Sovereignty+Principles+ Oct+2018.pdf (accessed 26 November 2021).

Marler, J., and Boudreau, J. (2016). An Evidence-Based Review of HR Analytics. *The International Journal of Human Resource Management*, *28*(1), 3–26.

New Zealand Herald (2022). Melbourne Uber Prices Soar During Grand Prix Weekend. Available from: www.nzherald.co.nz/travel/melbourne-uber-prices-soar-during-grand-prix-weekend/U2BZ4LGSVH3FCTK7EXHMQNIRSM/ (accessed 1 July 2022).

Office of the Privacy Commissioner (2021a). Compliance Notice Issued to Reserve Bank of New Zealand Following Cyber Attack. Available from: www.privacy.org.nz/publications/statements-media-releases/compliance-notice-issued-to-reserve-bank-of-new-zealand-following-cyber-attack/ (accessed 20 November 2021).

Office of the Privacy Commissioner (2021b). Privacy Commissioner: Facebook Must Comply with NZ Privacy Act. Available from: https://privacy.org.nz/publications/statements-media-releases/privacy-commissioner-facebook-must-comply-with-nz-privacy-act/ (accessed 20 November 2021).

Pittenger, D. J. (2005). Cautionary Comments Regarding the Myers-Briggs Type Indicator. *Consulting Psychology Journal: Practice and Research*, *57*(3), 210–221.

Ransbotham, S., and Kiron, D. (2018). Using Analytics to Improve Customer Engagement. *MIT Sloan Management Review*, *59*(3), 1–20.

Reiley, L. (2022). It's Not a Trick: Your Halloween Treats are Getting Smaller. *The Washington Post*. Available from: www.msn.com/en-us/money/companies/it-e2-80-99s-not-a-trick-your-halloween-treats-are-getting-smaller/ar-AA13gpn6 (accessed 24 October 2022).

Stokes, P. (2017). The 'Five Safes' – Data Privacy at ONS. Available from: https://blog.ons.gov.uk/2017/01/27/the-five-safes-data-privacy-at-ons/ (accessed 30 November 2021).

Thiel, C., Bonner, J. M., Bush, J., Welsh, D., and Garud, N. (2022). Monitoring Employees Makes Them More Likely to Break Rules. Available from: https://hbr.org/2022/06/monitoring-employees-makes-them-more-likely-to-break-rules (accessed 22 August 2022).

Tursunbayeva, A., Di Lauro, S., and Pagliari, C. (2018). People Analytics – A Scoping Review of Conceptual Boundaries and Value Propositions. *International Journal of Information Management*, *43*, 224–247.

Walton, C. (2022). 5 Reasons Why Amazon Go is Already the Greatest Retail Innovation of the Next 30 Years. Available from: www.forbes.com/sites/christopherwalton/2022/03/01/5-reasons-why-amazon-go-is-already-the-greatest-retail-innovation-of-the-next-30-years/?sh=5096c9021abc (accessed 17 June 2022).

White, S. (2021). Of All the Ways Clothing is Gendered, Pockets are the Most Ridiculous. Available from: www.instyle.com/fashion/clothing/womens-clothing-with-pockets (accessed 1 July 2022).

Zaric, G. S., Maclean, K., and Mann, J. (2021). *Ethical Implications of Artificial Intelligence, Machine Learning, and Big Data*. Canada: Ivey Publishing.

INDEX

Page numbers in *italics* refer to figures; page numbers in **bold** refer to tables.